"MAKE IT A GIRL, GRACIE"

With love to Carol,
Sally Flynn

"Make It A Girl, Gracie"

A Memoir of My First Twenty-One
Years as Sally Hamlin Gilbert

Sally Flynn

Copyright © 2015 Sally Flynn
All rights reserved.

ISBN: 1517626374
ISBN 13: 9781517626372

"Make It a Girl, Gracie."

The title is a direct quote from my grandfather to my mother as she was being wheeled down the hallway at the Hartford Hospital to give birth to me.

This memoir is dedicated to my four wonderful children for bringing such pleasure to my life, Andrew, Julia, Molly and Jennifer; my talented, brilliant granddaughter Grace; and my eight fantastic, fabulous grandsons, Brian, Alex, James, Jack, Henry, Matthew, Charlie and Danny. I also thank my children for enriching our family with such a good choice of spouses, Margaret, Roger, Matthew and Bill.

Special appreciation goes to three men who helped me put this together. My husband Ted patiently read and edited each chapter and responded to my frequent cries for assistance regarding grammar and punctuation. My brother Bill was a fountain of information and facts regarding our relatives and helped me make some memories even more vivid with his recollections. My son-in-law, Bill Sparrow, was my digital connection to the publisher and without his assistance I would have floundered trying to put it all together.

Those of us born in the thirties were called "Depression Babies," and when we matured, we were called "The Silent Generation."

We were born during our nation's worst depression and grew up during the Second World War. As youths we witnessed our nation growing into a world power and then humbled by the horrors of the Vietnam War and the knowledge that we weren't that powerful after all.

We grew up without television or travel by airplane and in our middle age saw the world shrink in size by the omnipresence of television news. Being able to reach anyone, anytime with our cell phones and learn about everything, anytime with the internet both thrilled and overwhelmed us. We are the last generation introduced to computers after our formal education was completed. In our old age we have witnessed the tragedy of world terrorism and the fear of global warming.

But if you were to ask, most of us would say, we were lucky to grow up when we did.

Cedar Grove & Upper Montclair, New Jersey, 1941-'46

In the summer before I entered first grade in 1941, our family moved to 52 Overlook Road in Cedar Grove, New Jersey. My brother, Billy, was four years younger. I loved my neighborhood. The streets curved around and intertwined into a cozy network of safety. All the kids played outside in decent weather. When we had snow we would coast on our sleds down the one street that went steeply downhill. One of the moms on that street would sometimes invite us inside for cocoa. When we hauled our sleds back up the hill we usually talked about our chances of being invited in that day.

Winter was fun, but warm weather was the best. All the dogs roamed freely around the neighborhood. Lease laws did not exist then. We had a sable collie named Peggy who looked just like Lassie. She had all the herding genes of that breed. She insisted on being on the outside of the sidewalk and constantly pushed me in away from the street with her body whenever we went walking anywhere together. It was really a nuisance because she pushed hard. Our favorite game was Hide and Seek. Peggy always "hid" with me and usually she would be quiet as I waited. I always hoped I would be the last one found.

To call us home, my mother rang a large bell. Most parents had a distinctive "come home" signal – different sounding bells, whistles, shrieks of "David, you come right home right now!" My bell always seemed to ring when I was in a wonderful hiding place or doing something else extra fun like roller skating and wanted to postpone going home for just a little while. Not Peggy. The minute she heard that bell she raced home. So my mother took to taping messages on her collar like, "Sally, I want you home right now." She'd then tell Peggy to go find me which Peggy did with deliberate speed. It sounds really cute and amazing now (especially since I have had 5 dogs since and I can't imagine any of them being that obedient or smart.) But at the time I didn't find it the slightest bit funny or cute.

My best friend was Toby Rowe who lived across the street. Her father was in the service and her grandmother, Mrs.

Zabrieski, lived with them. She had difficulty walking and spent most of her time in her first floor bedroom, usually in bed, listening to the symphony or the opera on her radio. We couldn't understand anyone wanting to do that.

Toby had an older brother and when I was in fourth grade he got pneumonia for the second time. Toby told me the doctor said if he got it one more time it could kill him. From then on I always looked at him with great apprehension, thinking he must be frightened all the time.

Parental attendance at PTA meetings was very competitive. I don't remember what prize the winning class received, but we all wanted our class to come in first. Toby's mom was allowed to raise two hands at the head count because her husband was in the Army. To us this was an exceptional bonus and we all wanted Toby to be in our classroom.

On Tuesdays we brought in our money to buy war-stamps that we pasted into long rectangular books. We were told these stamps would help the war effort and in ten years we could cash in our stamp books which were like bonds and get $25.00. The stamps cost either ten cents or twenty-five cents. Most of us bought the ten cent ones because we felt they filled up our books much faster than the twenty-five cents ones. They also took a lot longer to lick which gave them a more valuable feeling.

Our house in Cedar Grove was rented from a young man who had joined the Army months before Pearl Harbor. My father and mother were 29 at the time and like many of that age and that era couldn't afford to buy a house. In the middle of 1944 our soldier landlord asked my father if he'd like to buy the house. My parents hired an architect to see what could be done. The house was on a corner with no backyard and a huge side yard, giving no privacy. It had three bedrooms, one bathroom upstairs and the typical living room on the left and the dining room and kitchen on the right. There was a screened porch off the living room and a half- basement walk-out where I had a mini school room set up with two desks and a blackboard where I practiced teaching school to my younger brother Billy. I loved to stand at the blackboard with chalk in my hand and ask him questions in a very authoritative voice. My mother called it my teacher voice. I always insisted he raise his hand before answering, even though he was the only student in my class. He was very cooperative and always had an answer even at age three. At age seventy-five he still always has an answer.

My sister Pamela was born May 7th, 1944. She was christened in the Unitarian Church as my brother and I had been. Now my parents really wanted four bedrooms. After long discussions which I remember well, they decided not to buy, too many problems, a fatal flaw of no backyard and only three bedrooms. I loved my neighborhood. I loved my school. I didn't want anything to change. I was in third grade and relished my popularity.

For Valentine's Day we all decorated shoe boxes at school with a slit on the top so our classmates could easily deliver their valentines to each other. This was the era when you didn't have to give to everyone and it was very competitive. That year I got twice as many valentines as Toby and I remember being happy over my fat card count, but sorry for Toby who received half as many cards as I until she made a few disparaging remarks about me. I don't recall the remarks, but I remember being very hurt at what she said, but still secretly pleased that I got all those valentines.

Right after Pearl Harbor, in fervor of patriotism, my father successfully talked his two best friends into going with him to the Induction Center to enlist. They were accepted, but he was rejected because of his age, 29, his myopic eyes and probably the fact that he had two children. So my father became a neighborhood warden. When they blew the sirens, which luckily were always practice warnings, but very frequent, he had to rush out with his special warden's helmet and extra strong flashlight to be sure no light of any sort was coming from anyone's house. My brother had severe asthma and my parents were often up in the middle of the night with him and needed light. All the upstairs windows had black out shades, but we had a central entrance stairway and light traveled down to the lower windows. So my grandmother, a good seamstress, created an enormous green velvet curtain that hung from the top of the staircase to the bottom. Like a curtain it had two sides and my parents pulled it together before they went to bed every night. My father, like most adults, smoked all the time. There was no concept that smoking might be harmful to a child with severe asthma!

My mother was always home when I got home from school. We only had one car and gas rationing was very strict. My father was issued an AA gas ration book which was the best one to have because he had a half hour commute to Newark for work. I don't remember any of the families having two cars. Few of the moms went anywhere and none of the kids I knew did any organized sports after school. You were really embedded in your neighborhood.

We had a milkman, a vegetable man and an Italian meat market that delivered. My father paid top prices for our meat. He willingly did so because the owner, Mr. Aliano, was very liberal about the number of ration coupons he would require for our order. The amount of meat you could buy was determined by how many ration coupons you received which was based on the size of your family. The same restrictions applied to butter and sugar.

Our Borden's milkman delivered milk in a horse drawn milk wagon. I always thought that's what milkmen prefer to a truck because the horses knew exactly where to stop for each delivery. My mother told me years later that it was really an advertising gimmick by Borden's to emphasize that they were the most patriotic milk company because they didn't use a drop of gasoline delivering their milk.

"Make It a Girl, Gracie"

The event that became a treasured neighborhood story involved the Sheeley's who lived next door to the Rowe's. Their house was built on a slight hill which rose in the back so that one edge of the roof of the garage was only four feet off the ground. Their teenage daughter's bedroom was in the room above the garage. But, first a story about Mrs. Sheeley. My mother told me Mrs. Sheeley couldn't bear to have any clutter, dust or dirt in her house. She was neurotic about always having everything in perfect order so she rarely entertained. Finally it was her turn to host the neighborhood pot luck group and one of the male guests slipped on the sleek, waxed floors and emptied his entire plate on the floor. My mother said there was an audible gasp from the guests, but he immediately plopped down, pulled out his fork, started eating and said,

"Marge's floor is cleaner than most plates and this is delicious."

The real story is about their daughter. She was sitting at her dressing table combing her hair when she saw in her mirror a reflection of a man's face looking in at her through her bedroom window. She did not panic, but continued to brush her hair, casually walked out of the room for a minute and called the police to tell them she had a peeping Tom. She returned to her dressing table, put on some powder, looked at her different lipsticks, just stalled until she heard the police car. And they caught him! She was eighteen years old, which seemed old and wise to me at the time, but my mother said that showed remarkable bravery and poise in a girl that young.

My mother, who grew up in Hartford, had no regional accent. She spoke what is known as "broadcaster English." She was horrified that my brother and I were getting a New Jersey accent so she decided to give us weekly elocution lessons. We had, which my father was very proud of, hand hooked area rugs designed with big flowers all over them. Billy and I had to stand on a certain rose and recite whatever my mother said. The phrase I remember best is, "How now brown cow." We said the same words as my mother, but our "ow" sound was the same sound Henry Higgins successfully removed from Eliza Doolittle's speech. Mother finally succeeded. My brother and I still speak broadcaster English even though I lived in Boston two years and he lived in Maine a few years. The inhabitants of those two regions think the letter "r" is silent.

All my friends collected what we called "trading cards." These were not like the baseball cards the boys collected and traded, but cards from different real decks of playing cards. We didn't care about the numbers on the cards, we were only interested in the pictures on the back of the numbers. We all bound our cards with a rubber band and kept them in our pocket so when we had free time, at recess or after school, we could pull them out and check the other person's deck to see if there was anything we wanted. Most of us had a specialty that directed our trading. Mine was sunsets, rainbows and dogs. So whenever I saw a card with one of my specialties in a friend's pack, I tried to trade. It was also important to collect cards other people really wanted even though you didn't so you had desirable cards to trade when you ran across a rainbow or dog that you really wanted. Some of the boys participated, but it was mostly a female hobby.

We visited my grandparents a lot. It was a four hour drive to Hartford. Until they started going to Florida in November, we always went for Thanksgiving, sometimes Christmas, school vacations and long periods in the summer. In the car my parents would often break up the monotony by singing and harmonizing together. My dad carried the tune and my mother sang the alto, harmonizing part. My favorite song of theirs was "Molly Malone." I loved hearing them sing and my brother and I often joined in, but it never sounded as good as when just the two of them sang.

Genetically I was short changed. My brother Bill was a tenor in the Yale Glee Club and the Yale Russian Chorus and now accompanies his guitar, singing lovely, melodic solos all the time. He has also taught students how to play the harmonica. My sister, Cynthia, who sounds like Joan Baez, sang at Wellesley in an a cappello group and now sings with a Junior League group in Summit, New Jersey called "The Larks." I appear to carry a tune if I'm standing in church next to a strong, loud soprano. Often when a comedy series on TV needs to get a laugh, they have someone with no ability attempt to sing. My heart breaks out of empathy for that embarrassed, untalented soul. To make this unkind genetic cut even worse, none of my children have a singing voice likely to take center stage.

I have an especially vivid memory of getting off the school bus, starting up the hill to my house and seeing a woman I didn't know, rush out of her house, come right up to me with tears all over her face, and shout, "Roosevelt is dead!" Her anguish was so intense that I ran the rest of the way home to tell my mother who already knew from the radio. She said Roosevelt had been President for as long as she had been old enough to vote. My feelings were ambiguous. I adored my grandfather, but he was always lambasting Roosevelt who he said was ruining the country by making everyone feel the government owed them a living. He especially disliked Eleanor Roosevelt and would imitate her voice in a very nasty way.

When I was in fifth grade, the war ended. Our landlord was coming home from the war and he wanted to live in his house. I cried and cried over the thought of leaving our neighborhood and my school. I prayed another house would be for sale close by, but it didn't happen so my parents started looking elsewhere. They definitely wanted to buy so they would never again have to go through the trauma of suddenly being forced out of their home. With all the soldiers returning from the war, houses and apartments were in high demand and there wasn't enough supply. Nothing had been built during the war. Nobody wanted to move out of their house because there was no place to move to.

My father's younger brother was in the Navy and when he came home he got a job in New York City and bought a tiny new house near Hempstead, Long Island in one of our nation's first planned subdivisions. All of the houses were to be built in one year. The builder, Abraham Levitt, allowed the buyer to choose one of three plans. He named the area Levittown. The building site was a former potato field with no trees in sight. This town was the first truly mass-produced suburb and was considered a model for postwar suburbs throughout the country. When I visited my uncle thirty years later the trees were now tall and impressive and almost every house had put on an addition.

My mother finally found a house she loved. It was built at the turn of the century with high ceilings, an elegant staircase going all the way up to the third floor, four bedrooms, two bathrooms, a huge living and dining room, no den, no family room and no yard. The yard was there, but there was no grass. The house had been rented previously to a bachelor Episcopal bishop who had no housekeeping or house repairing skills. A Congregational church was right across the street. The house was at 167 Cooper Avenue in Upper Montclair, New Jersey.

The house needed everything, but especially critical was the necessity for new plumbing and a new electrical system. My father, with little money to support these aspirations, always felt you should go first class on any endeavor. The house cost $10,000 in 1946 and he spent close to $10,000 that same year putting in all new copper pipes, the best electrical system money could buy and carpeting upstairs that was mothproof, fireproof, green and scratchy to walk on. The bathrooms, kitchen and painting were to be put off until another year.

My brother, who was seven, was intrigued with the idea that the carpeting was considered fireproof. He had a scientific bend to his personality even at that young age and decided to find out. I don't know where he got the matches or how much of a flame or smoldering occurred, but it did alarm him to the extent that he hastily grabbed the nearest thing he could find that would smother the fire – the coverlet on the bed in Pamela's room embroidered with a field of flowers by our great grandmother. Now according to my father, all would have been forgiven if he had not lied. Our dad had tunnel vision when it came to lying. He considered lying the ultimate sin. My brother said it was a mystery to him why that black, flaking smudge was on the carpet and the coverlet was stuffed in a waste basket. The punishment was a spanking with a hairbrush. To my knowledge that was the first and only time corporal punishment was used in our family.

For the first time I could walk to my new school whose name I cannot remember. I now know it is commonplace for cliques to start forming in sixth grade, but at the time I was devastated at not being invited to birthday parties and just generally being ignored. I was the new girl and the only person who was friendly to me was Jean Mortimer and she was a Mormon. Being a Mormon encompassed her life. I was in awe mixed with awful about all the restrictions in her life plus all the time she had to spend at religious gatherings. She invited me to a few which were interesting and different, but I mostly just enjoyed having at least one friend.

My parents didn't belong to a church then, but when I was much younger I remember going to a Unitarian Church a few times and singing Onward Christian Soldiers as we exited. I loved marching out singing that song. My mother had been raised a Unitarian and my father, an Episcopalian. I don't think my parents ever attended the Congregational Church across the street, but after a few weeks I started going there to Sunday school. I thought for years that the King James version of the bible I still have with my name and date inscribed inside the front cover was from that church, but I just reread the front dedication and it was given to me by a Presbyterian Church on June 26, 1944 when I was in third grade and living in Cedar Grove. I have no recollection whatsoever of that church.

In that first year in Upper Montclair my second sister, Cynthia, was born on December seventh, one day before my birthday. I felt such relief that I didn't have to share my birthday. My brother's birthday is November 30th and he had the same anxiety. My mother had a hard time with the delivery and her recovery was slow so my dad hired a maid who came every day. She told us there was a rule that a full time maid must have a place in the kitchen to rest when she gets tired. So my parents put an outdoor chaise lounge in the kitchen. I guess it was a good resting place, but even at age eleven I knew it looked weird.

Then another rule hit our family. All the soldiers returning from the war were causing an extreme housing shortage, so the government decided that anyone who spent a certain percentage or a certain amount updating their house had to rent out a bedroom or a small portion of that house. We were the perfect candidates – bought the house for $10,000 and spent $10,000 fixing it up. We had to rent out a room. Luckily we had a huge third floor divided into two rooms plus a storage area. My parents had to add a bathroom, paint the walls, buy curtains, but adding a kitchen was not required. The staircase was wide and elegant as befit that era, but anyone using it to get to the third floor walked right through the middle of our second floor.

Harold and Ellen Storrs were our renters. They were both bookkeepers and were gone all day. They were older than my parents and very quiet and unassuming. When Harold came home he would go up the stairs whistling loudly, I guess to alert us of his presence. They agreed to the rent my father proposed and then came another financial shock. A representative of some new government agency came to inspect their rooming arrangements to see if the rent charged was appropriate. I was the only one home when they came. I let them in, traipsed up three flights with them to the very sunny, large living room, big bedroom and new bathroom and we saw together that they had a hot plate and a limited amount of food in one section of the room. The inspector asked if they had a refrigerator and I replied that they owned a gas refrigerator, but since there was no gas on the third floor and they didn't want to buy a new one, they put their refrigerator in the basement. We then both descended to the second floor, the first floor and finally the basement. I could sense his dissatisfaction over our renters having to descend three staircases before they reached a bottle of milk. I'm sure we both wondered why they didn't just buy another refrigerator.

My parents were very apprehensive when I relayed what had happened. Our house had had nothing but problems from the government. Two weeks later a letter came saying the rent charged was too high for the accommodations and it was to be reduced by such and such an amount, retroactive to when the Storrs first rented. It was obvious to the Storrs as they climbed through our house every day that we did not have much extra money. They accepted the lowered rent, but did not ask my father to pay them back for the months they had already lived there.

The exterior of the house was an eyesore with no grass and badly flaking paint. My father decided to paint it that spring. My mother always dreamed of having a yellow house. The painter applied a small patch in the shade of yellow my mother chose to see if it met her approval. It didn't. He had to "brighten" up the yellow three times before my mother was satisfied. Perhaps she stopped paying attention after that or maybe he painted really fast. The next thing we knew our very tall house gave the impression of a yellow, flashing neon sign without the lettering. It hurt to look at it like it hurts to look at the sun. The neighbors pointedly avoided making any comments as though they hadn't even noticed we had painted the house. I thought they were being kind because they liked my mother and silently forgave her for making such a grievous mistake. The painter assured my mother that it would fade in time.

Just before the start of the war, my father inherited a 1935 airflow DeSoto from my grandfather who upgraded to a spacious green Lincoln Zephyr that I loved to ride in. The DeSota was the color of cocoa or mud, depending on your mood. It had a sloping rear with two tiny windows and an extra wheel in a protective covering attached to the back. I think that wheel was meant to be decorative. It certainly was never removed in the ten years we had the car.

My mother decided it would be wise for her to know how to drive and even wiser to take driving lessons from a professional teacher instead of my father. She passed her exam and got her license. She didn't get the chance to practice very often because we only had one car and it went to work with my dad. Billy and I were often her passengers and she had trouble smoothly transitioning from one gear to another as she let up on the clutch. When she tried to go forward after stopping for a red light, the car would lurch forward in a leaping kind of motion for a few feet, followed by some more lurches. Finally she would get it under control. There were beeps and nasty yells from the cars behind us. No one had air-conditioning then so with car windows always down except in the winter, we heard a lot of verbal road rage. Instead of being supportive and encouraging to our mother, we both hid on the floor out of embarrassment.

As soon as the first production of cars came off the line after the war, my father bought a 1947 maroon Studebaker Starlight Coupe with a seat in the back, but only two doors. It had a new trunk design that allowed wrap around rear windows. We gathered crowds wherever we went exclaiming, "You can't tell the front from the back!" My father loved that car and as soon as the next larger model came out, the Land Cruiser, he bought that one. It was green. My brother who inherited it as his first car in 1955 corrected me. It was "Highland Mist" and had flecks of gold mixed in with the green.

Five months later my father decided to switch from being in life insurance sales to going into management. The Connecticut General was revamping the way its branch offices were organized, especially in relating to the managers who were now being trained extensively in estate planning. It was a new program and involved undergoing training in their Philadelphia office for two and a half years. We left our yellow house with no grass, original bathrooms, original kitchen, but state of the art electrical and plumbing systems after just one year.

2

Whitemarsh, Pennsylvania, 1947 - 1949

When I was eleven I went to Girl Scout camp for the month of July with Lucy Ringrose, a friend I'd known since I was three. She lived one house away from my grandparents in Wethersfield, Connecticut. Lucy had gone to this Girl Scout Camp the year before and loved it and continued to love it the summer we were both there. I was miserably homesick and hated camp. The things I remember are living in a tent, having to walk a block to the outhouses which terrified me at night and being afraid of the water, even though

I could sort of swim. My only real enjoyment was picking the wild blueberries. I gave a big bucket to my parents on visiting day, but that didn't stop my picking. I picked my way to an even bigger bucket that I brought home at the end of camp. I don't understand this obsession. I'm not even that fond of blueberries. I think I felt the need to be doing something productive. If they had offered a pottery class or interesting arts and crafts or any of the phenomenal choices my children and grandchildren had at camp I might have enjoyed it.

My grandmother took me to the beauty parlor just before camp to get a permanent so I wouldn't have to fuss with my hair. They rolled my hair in metal rollers that they plugged into some electrical contraption and then I think they just forgot about me. I had tight, kinky curls and couldn't bear to look in the mirror. I couldn't even get a comb through those curls. I have never had a permanent since except Toni's given by my mother at the height of their popularity.

During my absence in July my parents found a house to rent in the Philadelphia area for two years. The housing shortage was still acute in 1947 and my father felt lucky to hear about Harold Proctor who owned a company that made fancy wood cabinets to house television sets. Mr. Proctor was also known as a "gentleman farmer." He owned three stone houses built in the early eighteen hundreds, one for him and one for each of his two daughters. One of the daughter's husbands had been transferred abroad for two years so it was a perfect fit for both families. They were the only houses on that mile and a half of road and were surrounded with acres and acres of farmland and undeveloped land. Mr. Proctor walked around in a tweed jacket and a cane which we were told had a secret panel where he kept medicine to take immediately if a bee ever stung him because a bee sting would kill him. Whenever my brother and I saw him we would concentrate on the space around his body. If either of us hoped to see a bee sweeping in, we did not share this thought with each other.

Ralph was the real farmer. He had worked for Mr. Proctor for years. He was in charge of everything on the farm. At the end of our yard was a large cantaloupe bed. Ralph said we had picking rights and if a cantaloupe wasn't perfect we could just toss it out. Across the driveway was a huge barn and Ralph told us with great conviction that it was a known fact that Lafayette's horse slept in that barn. I told everyone that bit of news and they seemed quite impressed. I believed it. My brother just informed me that "our" barn was built long after 1777 and the barn where Lafayette's horse slept that Ralph referred to was further back on the property and all that was left when we were living there were some stone walls forming the framework, but no roof.

The farm had a bunch of chickens, a pen full of pigs and raised corn for the steer. The strawberry bed was almost the size of a football field and we learned there is nothing more tasty than a fresh picked strawberry. The steer were Black Angus and brown and white Herefords. The steer lived right across our driveway behind a split rail fence with an electrical wire on top. There were dozens of them. At least two times we got off the school bus to see all of them roaming around our front yard and Ralph yelling,

"Git along there, git out of there, you, hey, go, go!" and running and poking at them with a long rod.

On the first floor, the house had lots of small rooms and one huge dining room with a door to the outside that we always used. The kitchen had been modernized and probably added on to the house as there was a new, small apartment above the kitchen with four tiny rooms, a living room, a bedroom, a kitchen and a bathroom. There were five fireplaces, three upstairs and one in the living room and in the front hall. The hall was a square shape like the living room and both were small with the fireplaces almost taking up an entire wall. We had an artesian well in an underground cut out cave in the front yard. I kept begging my father to let me see the inside and he finally did. It was a disappointment, very small, very cold and nothing there but pumps.

The public school was Barren Hill Consolidated School which ran from kindergarten through eighth grade. My parents wanted me to go to Chestnut Hill School for Girls. The girls had to wear a uniform with long black stockings and I would have to take remedial French to catch up as they all had taken French since first grade. I argued and cried and pouted and won. I went to Barren Hill School with my brother who was entering second grade. The bus ride was 40 minutes long. The oldest girl in my seventh grade class was sixteen and the whispered rumor was that she had already had a hysterectomy. The students came from families living in absolute poverty, families in the lower middle class, middle class and on up to upper middle class. Diane Hill was from the latter. She lived in a huge house and had her own horse. She fell off that horse in a jumping competition in eighth grade and broke her neck. She appeared to recover, but I heard later that she died in tenth grade from complications from that fall.

The next bus stop from mine, a mile down the road, was Judy Sucro's house. They had five or six children in a house that on the outside didn't look habitable. On the huge front porch, instead of inviting wicker chairs, they had boxes and old looking bikes and all the stuff you normally put in a garage which they didn't have. I was never asked inside. Judy was terribly overweight and always wore to school what we used to call a housedress. She could draw anything you told her and it would look like a photograph. Her specialty was horses and she drew them in all different sizes and poses on our long bus rides.

One day that I will never forget, all of the girls were all in the cloakroom which ran the length of the classroom, but was separated by a wall with two glass topped doors at each end. The boys started pushing against one door trying to hold the girls in who were pushing back when suddenly the glass broke and fell in towards the girls. Judy screamed, "My arm, my arm." I looked and on the inside of her wrist I saw all the arteries and veins and bones exposed. The principal and eighth grade teacher, Mr. Parnell, came running in, pulled off his necktie and made a tourniquet around Judy's arm. We were all ushered back into our classroom and Judy was taken to the hospital. She was out of school for over two weeks and when she finally rode on the bus with me again she said she was so relieved it wasn't her drawing arm.

The other dramatic event was a girl in the class above me. One day after school she was on her bike holding on to the back of a truck to get a free ride. When she decided to let go, her ring got caught on some metal on the side of the truck and her finger was instantly amputated. We were all given a lecture by Mr. Parnell about the dangers of hiking a ride on a truck. When she came back to school we all tried to casually catch a glimpse of her hand, but she always keep it closed in a fist. She must have finally become fed up with our constant sneaky attempts to see that vacant space and thrust her hand up into the air with her fingers extended wide and shouted,

"There, have you seen enough now!"

One of my friends, Jeanette Savareese, invited me to spend the night. They had a small house, meticulously maintained. We were not allowed in the living room with our shoes on. We ate dinner with her parents at five o'clock at a table in the kitchen so tiny we rubbed elbows when we ate. Dinner was black bean soup and I had never had black beans. That was the entire dinner. I hated those beans, but managed to swallow them by constantly drinking water until Mr. Savareese said,

"Don't you like our bean soup? You keep drinking water after every spoonful. This soup is Mrs. Savareese's specialty."

So I had to finish emptying that bowl unassisted by any water to help ease those horrid beans down my throat. The image of those beans backing up in my throat stayed with me for decades. It is only this year that I have discovered black beans are very tasty in a salad. A soup I still could not do. That night when we were in bed and talking about school, Jeanette told me in very serious tones about her own five year plan;

"When I'm a junior in high school, my mother is going to let me spend much more money on my clothes, 'cause in those last two years it's real important to look good."

I thought this was interesting advice and I had better remember it, but I didn't until my oldest daughter was a freshman in college and preparing to go through sorority rush.

"Mom, I have to have an increase in my clothing allowance. When I go through Rush this fall I've got to have more clothes. It's really important to look good."

Our eighth grade graduation trip was a day at the Hershey Chocolate Plant in Hershey, Pennsylvania. It was not the huge park it is now that my grandsons in New York City love to visit. We were to tour the plant, get free chocolate and swim in the large pool. I sat next to Leroy on the bus, the only black student in our class. He was outgoing and vivacious and one of the most popular kids. He kidded me and others the whole bus trip that he would duck us in the water, show us how to dive, swim faster than all of us. He was in a wonderful mood.

We got there, toured the plant and then were told to wait before we put on our bathing suits. The wait lasted a really long time and then Mr. Parnell came out and told us Leroy would not be allowed to go swimming in the pool, but Leroy didn't want us to just go home as Mr. Parnell suggested. He wanted us to go swimming. And we did. If it crossed anyone's mind to object vocally to a Hershey worker, it wasn't voiced. The forties was not an era of activism for thirteen year olds. You were told and you obeyed. And we had all looked forward to that swim. The bus ride home was somber and seemed to take forever. Leroy kept to himself and we all talked about Hershey and what a horrid thing to do and vowed to never buy a Hershey bar again. I still have negative feelings about that company to this day.

In eighth grade I was president of our class. We had sixty students. The president and vice president's job was to write the Class Prophecy which we read at the graduation ceremony. I just found it in a scrapbook tucked away in an old toy chest the dog sits on to look out the window. It predicted I would become an auditor. Why would I have picked that occupation? I could have written anything – famous author, renowned scientist. I obviously lacked imagination. Auditor? - I don't even like math.

At our graduation the girls wore long white gowns and the boys wore a wide variety of outfits. We all sat in chairs up on the stage. The principal and the English teacher called your name to come up to the front of the stage to accept individual academic awards. I won four of the ten awards. I heard someone behind me mumble, "All she does is go up there and grab another prize." I felt guilty and uncomfortable and embarrassed, but kind of thrilled inside. The worst part was my blushing which didn't stop until I was in my seventies. As I walked across that stage to accept each prize my face would get redder and redder and feel hotter and hotter. I could always feel the start of a blush. It would start at my neck and slowly inch itself up my face. I would always fervently pray, "Please dear God, make it stop." But it never did. It was humiliating to know that everyone knew you were embarrassed, probably insecure and definitely not cool.

I have put off telling the saddest memory of Whitemarsh and the story that changed our family forever. When I left camp at the end of July and saw our house in Whitemarsh for the first time, my three year old sister wasn't there. My parents told me Pamela was in Children's Hospital in Philadelphia. They said she was suffering from anemia. It was obvious my mother was distraught and my father unusually quiet. Every evening he walked alone up to the top of the hill behind our house. When I asked him what he was doing, he said he was praying for Pamela's recovery. I still believed that Pamela was ill with anemia and would soon get better. My brother and I were only told by my parents at Pamela's death that she had leukemia. She stayed in the hospital week after week, transfusion after transfusion, losing weight every day.

After six weeks my parents were told there was nothing more the doctors or the hospital could do and to bring their daughter home. My mother was raised Unitarian and my father, Episcopalian, but they wanted to try anything that offered hope. They hired a Christian Science lay reader who sat in a chair by Pamela's bed all day. My brother and I would tiptoe by the room and stare in at this old lady in the frumpy dress who sat there hour after hour with a thick book in her hand that didn't really look like a bible. Neither of us had any idea Pamela had a fatal disease. We muttered to each other how could she possibly make Pamela better by just sitting there reading. I am sure we didn't voice these thoughts within ear shot, but our parents told us this lay reader sensed doubt within the house which would hurt her chances of helping Pamela get better. We both felt very badly and decided to stay clear of Pamela's room.

One week later we were woken up at 6am and asked to come into our parent's room. It was September 29, 1947. They told us that Pamela had died during the night. We both started crying. My brother stopped after a few minutes, but I, being older and knowing more what death meant, couldn't stop crying for most of the morning. It was not just the shock of Pam's death, it was the shock that I had no idea she was that sick and was going to die. I would have prayed much harder, was all I could think.

The funeral was at our house with only my grandparents and a friend of my parent's who had driven down from New Jersey. She also had lost a daughter. My parents knew nobody in the area except the men in the office with my father. We had no neighbors. We had no support group of relatives or friends nearby. My father was able to cope with the loss much better than my mother. He had been an acolyte in the Episcopal Church when he was young and he told us his faith had helped him accept Pamela's death. He wanted our family to join St Thomas Episcopal Church at the end of our street. The cemetery surrounding the church had been established in the 1800's and my parents bought three plots, one for Pamela, and two for them. They were thirty-five years old.

My brother and I started going to Sunday school and I was confirmed in that church. We had to be re-baptised as the Episcopal Church did not accept a Unitarian christening as a legitimate baptism. My father went to church once in awhile and my mother even less. She told me years later that the minister told her God acts in ways we can't always understand, and maybe God felt it necessary to take this child to bring my mother back into a faith that believed Jesus was the son of God. It's hard to believe he would have used those words, but that is the thought my mother felt was conveyed to her.

My mother was alone with nine month old Cynthia every day, isolated on a farm in a huge house. There was nobody nearby to drop in and cheer her up, chat for awhile or even go out for lunch. She couldn't even take Cynthia for a walk as there were no sidewalks and the road was narrow. My parents had always sat down to relax and talk and have a cocktail before dinner. My father often had two, but rarely my mother. We never saw her drinking other than at cocktail hour, but it became obvious that she was drinking during the day. My father, who had been athletic throughout his life, joined a country club called The Manufacturers Golf Club. He loved playing golf and it helped him relieve stress from work and stress from the sorrow he felt over Pam's death. My mother had no such outlet. She was not an athlete. She had never even ridden a bicycle as a child. But my father's golfing which he needed emotionally and physically meant he was away at least part of most week-ends leaving my mother alone even more. Her consolation was going to the grave daily and secretly drinking.

Pamela was a planned pregnancy as my brother and I were and she was to be their last child and she was doted on as a last child is. She had golden blond ringlets and huge blue eyes. She was a beautiful, sweet, endearing child and she loved playing with my brother and me.

Pamela, May 1947

Cynthia had been unplanned and instead of being thankful for this unexpected child, my mother could only think of the child she had lost and resented God for taking Pamela, this most precious child of hers. This feeling didn't last, but it was intense right after Pam's death and my father realized he had to hire someone right away to help take care of Cynthia and help with the housework.

I don't remember if he used an agency or how he found Gladys, but she came and moved into the small apartment above the kitchen. She served our meals, did the housekeeping and helped take care of Cynthia. When I came home from school those first weeks after Pam's death, some days my mother was dressed and greeted my brother and me warmly and other days she would be up in her bedroom with the shades pulled down. I sometimes quietly knocked on the door and when I went in she'd tell me over and over how much she loved me and that she didn't know how it was possible to feel as sad as she felt. We would hug each other and cry together and I'd tell her over and over that she still had three children who loved her so much and we wanted her to get better.

One time Gladys knocked on mother's bedroom door when we were both in there crying together and asked if we wanted anything or some such phrase. I think she was worried and didn't know what to do or if she should be doing something. I was sad and scared because I also didn't know what to do or if I should be doing something. After a few weeks my mother was much better. She no longer was in bed when we got home from school and asked us to tell her all about our classes and activities. She cooked dinner every night and she became Cynthia's primary caretaker.

After Gladys had been there about two months, my mother asked her to take me into Philadelphia for my orthodontist appointment. We boarded the train at the tiny station a half mile down the street. The Pennsylvania train tracks ran 100 feet behind our house. When a freight train went past, you had to stop talking if you were on the patio. Intersecting these tracks a mile back were the Reading tracks which ran the commuter trains. Their station was a six foot platform with a crank you pulled down if you wanted the train to stop. The engineer got to know my father and as the train approached our tiny station, he looked out to see if my father's Studebaker was speeding down the road and if it was, he would stop the train and wait for my father. The train only had two cars. Gladys and I got on and then transferred to a bus once we were in Philadelphia. I was looking out the window when the bus started to slow down and Gladys suddenly jumped up and rushed forward to the door. I leapt up and quickly followed her, yelling,

"Wait up, wait up."

She turned abruptly, stared at me and then said, "Oh, I forgot you were with me."

That was the start of the end of Gladys. The next week she served dinner and then sat in the kitchen at the counter with her head in her hands staring straight ahead for over an hour. My father kept sending my brother and me in to check on her. We didn't know what to do. Finally she stood up and did the dishes. After a couple more similar incidents, Gladys was asked to leave. We later discovered that she had walked away from a home for emotionally disturbed people in Illinois years before.

Now my father decided that since that apartment above the kitchen was newer and had a bedroom and a living room, perhaps we could hire a couple and the man could go to his job during the week, but mow the lawn on the week-ends which my father hated doing and the wife would do the housework and help with the baby. They put an ad in the paper, interviewed a few couples and chose the McGarys. I don't remember what he did for a job, but I do remember she wore a white dress with a frilly apron that made her look like a servant from a forties movie. She had not been told to wear a uniform, but I guess she thought she looked cute in it and she did. She was tiny with blonde curls and lots of energy. This was a second marriage.

We later learned that they and another couple had actually traded partners. His son by his first wife used to visit sometimes and he and my brother had fun playing together. One day when Mr. McGary was mowing the lawn, Mrs. McGary went to the doorway and screamed and screamed at him with many swear words thrown in for emphasis. She was finishing off an argument they had started earlier. She could be clearly heard over the lawnmower. My parents had commented on a few other negatives before this outburst, but this last one convinced them that this was not the kind of family they wanted taking care of their one year old daughter. The McGarys were asked to leave.

It was decided that the problem was the difference in social classes and what we needed was a couple from our own social class. My father put an ad in a few medical school newspapers and Bob Decker replied. After getting back from the war he had entered Optometrist School and had two more years to go. Betty, his wife, was a secretary in Philadelphia and hated it. They saw the ad and thought it was the perfect fit for them. The first night they ate in the kitchen as Gladys and the McGarys had. The second night they ate at the dining room table with us and quickly became an important part of our family. That friendship continued through all their lives.

Cynthia, age one and a half

After my sister died, my father decided we should get a dog. It would be a collie, of course. Our wonderful collie, Peggy, had died from a kidney problem years before. We named our new dog, also a sable collie like Peggy and the famous

Lassie, Baron Scarlett of Whitemarsh. He was too big to sleep on the bed with me as my adorable Havanese does now every night, but ten years after Baron entered our life, I wanted him to sleep beside me the last night before my wedding. He had been my confidant and my wailing wall for a decade.

My English teacher in seventh grade had a single copy of a play she had saved from high school that she loved and she wanted our class to put it on. I was given one of the leads and took the play home to copy my part. There were no copy machines then. I left it on the coffee table for a few minutes and when I returned Baron had the remains of it in his mouth. I was horrified. I didn't want to go back to school. I tried to think of any lie that wouldn't make me look bad. My father liked to give advice and most of it was good.

"Sally, there are times when you just have to own up to something, bite the bullet and get it over with. You were careless and you have to apologize."

I apologized the next day at school, she was furious and very emotional, but I recovered.

One Saturday afternoon when my brother and I were playing outside, a car pulled into our driveway and a nice looking couple with two children got out and walked over to us. They said they could no longer keep their bunny who had been their pet since she was born. Her name was Flopsy and they wanted to find a good home for her. They had seen us outside before and came back to ask if we might like to take over the care of Flopsy. My brother was very excited and ran inside to get permission from my parents. I don't remember any details, but he obviously got the okay because the dad immediately went back to their car, pulled out the cage with Flopsy inside and brought it over to us.

Flopsy was sitting up on her all white haunches and wiggling her whiskers and looked adorable. We kept the cage on one side of the house, the side furthest away from where the cats and kittens always congregated. I have no recollection of where we put Flopsy in the winter. But I remember well the ending. The next year the couple and the two children came back to visit their bunny. Over that year of ownership, Flopsy had disappeared. I'm guessing her cage was not fully locked one night. None of us had any idea what had happened to Flopsy, but my brother had a good imagination. He replied to Flopsy's former family in the somber tones of a eight year old,

"The foxes got her."

I gave him the evil eye, but he refused to look at me. I professed over and over that we didn't really know. She was just missing from her cage one morning and there was no blood or sign of aggression. The two children looked crestfallen and they all were anxious to get back in their car and drive off. They did not want the cage back. After they left, I growled at my brother and said he shouldn't have said that because it made those children so sad. He just repeated,

"I'm pretty sure it was a fox."

Ralph kept cats in the huge barn to help control any mice or rat problem. He paid for a gallon of milk to be delivered to our house once a week.

"Now don't you go feeding those cats nothin' else. I know you don't want rats running around everywhere."

We didn't want rats running around, but still we ignored that advice and bought and fed them cat food. They were always ravenous and most of them were kittens. You can't expect a kitten to catch a rat. We gave them all names. They weren't house broken so lived at night in the barn and around our house in the daytime. They loved Baron and I took dozens of pictures of Baron sleeping curled on his side with six or seven kittens snuggling up in his fur. We had an enormous turnover of cats. We think it might have been the proximity of the train tracks. The females were prolific. We were always having to come up with new names for the kittens that arrived on a regular basis.

Rural Pennsylvania is an area full of ticks. This was before Lyme disease was ever heard of, but Rocky Mountain Spotted Fever was something you got from ticks and it could be fatal so we all got the series of three shots to protect us. Dogs didn't get the shots, but they got the ticks. Every night someone, usually me, had to sit down with Baron and carefully go through his fur and use tweezers to pull out the ticks, usually at least a dozen. If you missed one it would be the size of a fat blueberry by the next day.

The real scare our entire childhood was polio. We would see pictures of young children lying in an iron lung with only their head protruding. It was terrifying. Every time I got a sore throat or a stiff or pulled muscle I was sure it was polio. We were not allowed to go to any public pools, but we could swim in the pool at the golf club where we belonged. My mother said that unlike a public pool if someone came down with polio the club would inform us. I never understood then and still don't, how knowing a club member caught it, would help us not get it.

Movie theaters were also out of bounds in the summer as the polio cases seemed to rise in the warm weather. The movies in the forties were always double features, the movie you came to see and a second B movie, as they were called. It was usually a western and my father loved them. A newsreel was also part of the movie experience. It was our only medium that showed the news in live action. We'd be shown a hospital with dozens of children lined up in those iron lungs. Sometimes they even interviewed those children as they lay there. They also showed war action clips and a lot of propaganda shorts against the Germans and the Japanese to rive up our patriotic zeal. And, there almost always was a short cartoon. My favorite was the Road Runner.

Ralph liked to showoff his farming acumen and gave my brother some information he had not requested, but which he remembers to this day although he's never felt the need to use it. It's regarding shooting rats at the farm dump or what we would call the recycling area today.

"First you gotta tape a flashlight onto your .22 barrel gun in the place where the siting scope fits and when that flashlight hits those rat's eyes it makes them glow real good and the minute you see that glow you pull that trigger fast."

My brother needed allergy shots every day and my father got very good at giving them. Just before April Fools Day he said it would be fun to inject some of the leftover Valentine candy with vinegar. I could bring those chocolates into school as a treat and after a few people had bitten into them, yell, "April Fools Day!" I was all over that idea. I carefully placed the injected chocolates on top of my radio in their little white, crinkled holders so the dog wouldn't get them and went to sleep thinking what a fabulous April Fool's joke I had. When I woke up in the morning the heat from the radio, even though it was not turned on, had melted them all.

My brother wanted a train set for Christmas. My father who never did anything half way, bought three or five Lionel train sets plus all the accessories that go with them. He had log drops and bridges and tunnels and water towers and houses and people and lights. Those lights made the train room a magical place at night. There were little smoke pellets you dropped down the train chimney and smoke spouted out. The huge electrical panel to control everything tested my brother's engineering skills, but he mastered it. My father and Bob Decker spent hours setting it all up and even more hours playing with it.

The second year we were in the house my father thought why not just put the dead Christmas tree in the 8 foot fireplace in the living room instead of hauling it outside. He carefully placed the tree in the fireplace, lit one match and with a huge crackle the entire tree burst into flames and gave off this intense heat. My brother and I raced upstairs to his bedroom above the living room to see flames licking up out of the fireplace, but just for a few seconds. I know we didn't call the fire department. I don't remember what we did. It was over so quickly we never got much soot which I later learned in my own house can be an unpleasant aftermath of an out of control fire in your fireplace.

There was a graduation dance at our school near the end of eighth grade and one of the boys asked me to be his date. His sister was going to drive us and they would pick me up at 7pm. About ten after seven a car pulled up in the driveway next to the side door and tooted. I could see a girl driver and my date so I started to go out. My father yelled,

"STOP, no daughter of mine is going out until that boy comes up and rings the bell like a gentleman and introduces himself."

I pleaded with him to just let me go. My father was adamant. The sister tooted one more time, a long five minutes passed in which I was dying of nervousness and embarrassment, until finally my date walked up to the door. That is the only thing I recall about the entire evening.

In eighth grade in 1948 in that part of Pennsylvania spinning the bottle was what you did at birthday parties. I don't remember the decorations or the cake or the presents, or the guests, but I do remember we spun a coke bottle on our living room floor over and over and the two winners then exited to the hall and kissed. My mother told me later that she and Betty Decker spent the evening peeking through a keyhole to see what was happening.

In July of 1948 our lease was up, but my father still had until December to finish his training. My parents didn't want to move us in the middle of a school year so it was decided we would live with my grandparents in their house in

Wethersfield and go to school there for a year. My father would get an apartment in Philadelphia and come up every week-end. So we put our furniture in storage and moved to Connecticut.

3

Wethersfield, Connecticut, 1949-1950

My grandparent's home at 624 Ridge Road was more "home" to me than anywhere else I had lived. We spent Thanksgivings there before they went to Florida in November. We spent week-ends and sometimes weeks there in the summer. I had lived there an entire school year when I was in kindergarten. It had a comforting familiarity that was a constant in my life. There were four bedrooms, but my grandmother couldn't sleep in the same room as my Grandfather because of his snoring. I understood this. A few years before when my uncle was also visiting with his family and we were short on bedrooms, my grandmother had me sleep on a cot in their bedroom.

"Sally, if your grandpa or I snore, just whistle. It won't wake us up, but it will stop us from snoring."

Both of them snored in different rhythms and I felt like I never slept at all, but I was too timid to whistle as I was sure it would wake them up and I didn't want to be mean.

To accommodate our family of five, my grandmother put a twin bed in a back corner of the room we called the library. She slept there, but went upstairs to the master bedroom for dressing and bathing. The library was very spacious. It was my favorite room. My grandfather had a huge desk angled kitty corner with bookcases lining the walls all around him and the walls on the other side of the room. I would sit for hours poring over all those books, many of them over fifty years old, pulling one out to look at it, then picking another one and finally deciding on which book to read.

My favorite series was about very young girls living in different states during the Revolutionary War era. They all did brave and marvelous things to help defeat the English. On the front cover there was always a picture of a young girl in Revolutionary period clothing, sometimes with her mother, sometimes with a soldier and always in a dramatic pose. Those books rode in our moving vans six different times. They have criss-crossed the country with me. They're now in a bookcase in the playroom in the basement. I went downstairs and examined them again. I have four, all by Alice Turner Curtis, published between 1916 and 1920. I googled her and discovered she wrote nineteen books in the "Little Maid" series. I saved these books because I enjoyed them so and wanted any daughters I might have to enjoy them as well. I have three daughters. Not one showed the slightest interest. Not one would even open the front cover. I think the prim little girl in eighteenth century clothing turned them off. The next in line to cherish these stories, I thought, might be my granddaughter. She smiled sweetly and said maybe on the next visit she'd take a look. I never had another granddaughter. Perhaps I'll save them for my great granddaughters. Not promising – my granddaughter and twin grandson, my oldest, are only 18 and Grace hopes to become a veterinarian ophthalmologist with ten years of formal education ahead of her and I am seventy-nine.

My parents and my three year old sister, Cynthia, slept in the large four poster twin bedroom. We always called it the four poster bedroom. Bob and Betty Decker later inherited those four poster twin beds. My brother Bill was in the smallest room which had been our Nanny's room when she lived with my grandparents. Nanny was my grandma's mother. When I was born this great grandmother was sixty-one years old, the same age I was when I had my first grandchild. I had the back bedroom with a door to a sundeck built over the porch which I was not permitted to go on. My brother and I called this bedroom the zebra room because it was filled with furniture my grandmother's father and my nanny's husband, Percy Hamlin, had built as a hobby at the turn of the century. The furniture has one inch strips of one inch thick veneer of chestnut, now extinct, burled maple and another dark wood. There are six pieces plus a Jenny Lind three-quarter bed. When my father moved out of their house I was given this furniture and my brother was given a roomful of marble topped mahogany furniture that had been in the family a hundred years. My sister, being too young to have her own home, didn't get any furniture. She does remember this!

My brother started fourth grade in Chester Elementary school, a block across the street from my grandparent's house. I had gone to kindergarten there when my parents lived with my grandparents after an earlier job change. In Connecticut you must be five by January first. I made the cut-off with a December eighth birthday. In New Jersey you must be five by December first so I had to have a special waver to start first grade and not repeat kindergarten. This made me usually the youngest child in my grade at every school I went to.

I enrolled at Wethersfield High School as a freshman. My friend Lucy Ringrose, Jane Lowe and Patricia Alonso lived on the same street so I wasn't starting school not knowing anyone as I had in my previous schools. My brother had the same anxiety as I on the first day of school, but his always manifested itself physically. He never made that first day as he would inevitably have a bad asthma attack.

The big high school was overwhelming, but also exciting. I was really pleased when Jerry Fain, the boy who sat in front of me in class, invited me to a school dance. He was tall with curly hair and quite shy. I was nervous, but thrilled to be going to my first dance in high school.

I was very self conscious about having braces and wearing glasses. My first pair of glasses was in fifth grade and as is typical of children with myopia my eyes got worse every year. It was very scary as there weren't contact lenses or lasik or anything other than eyeglasses and mine kept getting thicker and thicker. Glasses were not considered a stylish adornment in the fifties. The jingle that always rang in the head of a bespectacled female was, "Boys don't make passes at girls with glasses." And, worst of all, I was almost flat chested. This worried me more than anything else. My mother kept saying she couldn't understand it. She was embarrassed when she was young about being too busty. Those words were not comforting, especially as the years progressed and my bosom did not. I did have two good things going for me. I was thin and I didn't have pimples. However, a thin build was not the hint of perfection it is today. A Marilyn Monroe body was the ideal. If padded bras had been as commonplace and acceptable then as they are now, I would have had a more self-confident adolescence.

I started to remove my glasses for social events, like the dance. This voluntary removal of my ability to see anything clearly continued through college. I can remember coming downstairs from my dorm room to meet my date in the living room and praying he would stand up so I could find him. That was the era of good manners so luckily for me, he always stood up.

One week there was a movie playing at the local movie theater that I really wanted to see. My grandparents said they wanted to see it too so we all went together on a Friday night. It seemed like the entire high school was at the theater, talking and laughing and yelling, all in the front rows, so they didn't notice my grandfather storming up to the usher about three times and demanding that he silence those "obnoxious youths." I was petrified someone might see me sitting with my grandparents and realize it was my grandfather who was complaining. Looking back, I wasted a lot of energy worrying and being embarrassed about dumb things.

Our collie Baron roamed freely here too, mostly in the huge backyards of the three houses adjacent to my grandparents. His friend, a German shepherd mix named Duchess, lived two houses over and they loved to play, but Ridge Road was not a quiet neighborhood street and the land across from my grandparent's house was undeveloped. We caught Baron over there a few times and scolded him, but not enough. One evening at twilight we saw him exploring across the street and my grandfather called him, and being such an obedient collie, he came racing.

We all saw the car approaching and yelled in unison, "Stop, stop Baron!"

But he didn't. The car didn't kill him, just wounded him badly. I was sobbing and my grandfather, I think to prevent himself from sobbing, angrily told the driver,

"You were racing down this street and now you've hit a valuable dog. He has a long, long pedigree and you've been reckless. Didn't you see him running across that field toward the road? You are going to hear from my lawyer."

No lawyer was ever called and Baron recovered.

My parents had friends in Hartford as they had both grown up there. They decided to have a New Years Eve party in the finished recreation room. It had a pool table, a fireplace, lots of furniture and a huge moose head on the wall. I have no idea the origin of that moose head. My brother and I loved to poke it and make huge puffs of dust fly out. I discovered that you could clearly hear conversation in the basement through the heating ducts and spent part of that New Year's Eve on my knees, ear pressed to the vent, eaves dropping on their festivities. All I learned was that adults get very silly and very loud when they are drinking.

I spent a few hours myself in that basement hiding out in a hidden corner of the furnace room sitting on a box reading *Forever Amber* and *Lady Chatterley's Lover*. I did know how you physically became pregnant, but that was about all I knew about sex. Those books weren't nearly as shocking as Phillip Roth's *Portnoy's Complaint* which I read in a bigger state of shock when I was an adult with children!

My grandfather retired at the start of 1950 and he and my grandmother decided to go to Fort Meyers right after Christmas for three months. My mother was not feeling well at all and often didn't have the energy to even get out of bed. My father told me years later that she suffered from a nervous breakdown. Once my grandparents left, he hired Mrs. Hopkinson, a practical nurse, to primarily take care of Mother and three year old Cynthia, but also to do the cooking. She was probably under sixty to have taken on the job of caring for three children and an ill parent, but Billy and I thought she was really, really old.

After a few weeks the doctor decided Mother was not improving as much as he had hoped and he recommended that she relax in Florida with my grandparents for six weeks. My father was still working in Philadelphia so he was only home on week-ends. Mrs. Hopkinson had us all to herself. She told us to call her Hoppy and as the weeks progressed and we liked her less and less my brother referred to her in private as Hopalong Cassidy. I found an essay I had written about Hoppy in high school so I don't have to rely on my memory. I wrote it when I was fifteen. I think I would be kinder now.

" *Hoppy was not fun. She was cranky and opinionated and bossy and I tried to avoid her at all costs. She had a really round face that matched her apple shaped body. A huge spurt of gray fuzzy hair shot up from the top of her head. She wore rimless reading glasses and my brother or I were constantly sent looking for those glasses. She had ill fitting false teeth causing her to lisp and spray spittle if she talked fast. We learned to keep a three foot distance if we wanted to stay dry. My brother confirmed this one morning when he raced in to tell me that he had just seen her teeth sitting in a bowl by her bed. Her cooking did not redeem her. It was horrid and that is using a kind adjective. Hoppy went to bed early which was her only redeeming attribute."*

Dad spent the last couple of weeks with mother and his parents in Florida. When our parents came back home we were ecstatic. Mother looked relaxed and happy to see us. She had what we then called a healthy tan. Billy and I were as elated to see that baby sitter go as we were to see our parents return. My father was offered two different locations for managing a branch office of Connecticut General. One was Springfield, Massachusetts, close to Hartford and the other was Seattle, Washington which only my grandfather had ever visited. Discussing the pros and cons of each engrossed us for weeks. My mother and I were apprehensive about the climate in Seattle. We liked four distinct seasons. The books on travel that we read said it rained there a lot and there wasn't much sunshine. I worried my hair would always go straight in the drizzle. And it was very far away.

The winner was Springfield. My father started working there immediately so no more commuting six hours to

Philadelphia on the week-ends and living in a rented apartment. He made the commute from my grandparent's house in 40 minutes. My parents started looking for a house right away. The plan was to move in the summer so my brother and I could start our new school in the fall.

4

Longmeadow, Massachusetts: 1950-1953

I was excited to be moving to New England. All my grandparent's ancestors on my father's side had emigrated from England to New England in the 1600's and now we would be only forty minutes from my grandparent's house in Wethersfield. My parents decided they wanted to live in Longmeadow, a suburb of Springfield. It is still a charming, beautiful old town with the tall white spire of the Congregational Church in the center, so typical of New England. It was settled in the mid 1600's and became a town in the late 1700's. When I lived there the population was under 7,000, but now it's triple that figure. The center of town is called The Green and there are many houses built before 1900 centered around that Green. There are still two large parks with tennis courts and play grounds. In 1950 there were no school buses. Everyone rode their bike to school. At each cross street, on one side of the sidewalk, the concrete curb was shaped into a ramp for the benefit of the bikers. You even saw tricycles being ridden to kindergarten. Riding your bike was the thing to do and you did it even if you lived a block away.

My parents started immediately looking for a house. I came along to see some of the final contenders. The house I liked the best had just been built on a street near the Longmeadow Country Club that I thought my father would like since he had just joined. What I loved was the family room. We had never had one of those. We also had never had new bathrooms and a new kitchen.

My father wanted Colony Hills, an area of older homes, mostly brick and mostly big with beautiful tree lined streets which were so curving you could only navigate around by memorizing the location of the different houses. The house we could afford had been vacant for two years. It was another house that needed everything! The style was Dutch Colonial, built in 1920, and my mother fell in love with the charming outside and she did keep it white! There were three rooms downstairs, the living room with a fireplace, the dining room, the kitchen with a butler's pantry and an unscreened porch off the living room. No powder room, no eat-in kitchen, no family room, all of which the house I liked had. But it was located in one of THE best areas in Longmeadow and that mattered to my father. Location, location, location- I guess that's always been the mantra. So they bought it – 19 Brittany Road.

My brother and I took a scrub brush to the narrow, long front porch as the roughness of the large painted white rocks on the façade had captured the dirt for what looked like thirty years. In the kitchen there was a huge painted metal cabinet with large built-in sifters the size of a gallon of milk on each end. My mother said this was for sifting sugar and flour. The only place with space for a refrigerator was an alcove by the door to the outside. The butler's pantry was lined with glass cupboards and deep drawers. It had a certain charm and was very useful. We did get new appliances and new cabinets.

Upstairs the master bedroom had its own bathroom which was considered spacious in 1950. The bedroom next door was also large and being the oldest I always got to pick first and I always picked the biggest bedroom. My new bedroom had yellow wallpaper with large flower bouquets thrown all over it. It certainly was nothing I would ever pick, but the previous owners had put it up just before they put the house on the market so there was no way my depression era parents were going to take down new wallpaper.

My sister had the smallest bedroom and my brother's was over the garage, very narrow, with two built in bunks and cedar paneling on all the walls. To me it seemed very dark and claustrophobic and I didn't like it at all, but I think my brother thought it was masculine and rugged. There was a third floor that had been partially finished into two rooms. We ended up putting my parent's former, ornate, antique double bed upstairs. I contemplated making that area my own domain, but never did.

Charming as Longmeadow was, it had one big drawback. It had no high school. There were four high schools in Springfield which were designed in the twenties with the concept of separating students as to their interests and ability. There was the Catholic high school, the Commercial high school, the Trade high school and the largest, the Classical high school for the students who were going on to college. I enrolled at Classical. I was there four days. I only remember climbing up and down three flights of stairs to get to classes. I don't recall another thing about that school. I was only there four days because of my grandfather. He insisted my father pull me out and enroll me at McDuffie School for Girls, a private school also located in Springfield. I have a feeling he probably helped pay the tuition.

My brother Bill, (He left "Billy" behind once we moved to Longmeadow) was five years behind me in school and in the first graduating class that had attended the newly built Longmeadow High School for all four years. When they built the school they chose land that was undeveloped. In fact this undeveloped land was on a road that was a favorite parking place for necking teenage couples. The road had been named in the 1700's and the many traditionalists in New England did not want the name of that road changed. They won and it wasn't. So on all the official literature regarding the new high school, the address was and still is, Longmeadow High School, 95 Grassy Gutter Road.

Fortunately for me, MacDuffie started the school year two weeks later than the public schools so I had missed nothing. I had to take a bunch of tests and sit through a couple of interviews. You did not have to wear a uniform. There were boarding students, but over two-thirds were day students. It went from seventh to twelfth grade. There were thirty- five girls in my sophomore class. The headmaster was Ralph Rutenber, who was stern, brilliant and very caring. He knew everybody in the school. I soon knew everybody's name because the day started with all of us in the assembly hall and a morning roll call followed by announcements of the day and any wisdom Mr. Rutenber wanted to impart.

I don't remember having any choices about classes. Perhaps Latin was an elective, but I don't remember anyone not taking it. The physical plant was pathetic. The school later started buying up old homes nearby as they came on the market, but when I was there we had all our classes in one old building. If you bought lunch, which I did, you went up to a large former home that also housed the administrative offices and you ate whatever lunch was served that day – no choices. A teacher sat at each round lunch table of six or eight and good manners were expected. I once elected not to eat a repulsive looking desert of plain rhubarb and was intimidated into finishing it. All but one of my friends brought their lunch and ate in peace in a classroom in the main building. I stayed with the formal dining room because Dawn Ide, who became my best friend by the start of our junior year, also did and I could sleep ten minutes longer in the morning if I didn't have to make my lunch. I never thought of making it the night before which I certainly did for my children.

There were a few other rules. No makeup which meant no lipstick as that's all we wore and no strapless dresses at the proms. We all solved the last one by tacking onto the dress the skinny straps that come with strapless dresses to keep them from falling off the hanger. No pants or jeans were permitted. Men's shirts were not allowed and the powers that be could tell it was a man's shirt by the side the buttons were on. Wearing men's shirts was then considered very cool.

For gym class we changed into a one piece weird looking outfit, but no showers due to no shower room, no lockers of any sort until my senior year when they built some shelves partitioned into boxes big enough to hold a few books. I guess we hung our coats on hooks somewhere. Funny I don't remember a detail like that. I think the school only offered one after-school sport a season. The boarders were encouraged to participate, but most of the day students rushed out of school when that bell rang.

Senior year one of my good friends, Boo Garlock, joined the basketball team and stayed after school three days a week for practice. We were all in a state of disbelief that she would want to do that. Her real name was Barbara and the school stenciled on the back of everyone's ugly gym uniform their initials. Her initials spelled BAG. I was amazed her mother didn't realize when she chose the middle name Ann that her daughter would never want to have anything of hers initialed. I guess putting the last name in the middle, when initialing a towel or jewelry, was not commonplace then because it never occurred to my mother and me. I helped my parents pick out the names for my two sisters and we always checked out what the initials would look like.

Being a private school, there were no school buses so transportation was up to the parents, most of whom organized a car pool. As soon as we got our licenses, we begged our mothers to let us have the car on our car pool day. The minute that school bell rang at three thirty, the members of my car pool raced out the school door, ran up the hill to the street where the car was parked, yelling all the way, "Dibs on the front seat."

The school was extremely tough academically and had an excellent reputation with colleges. English was my favorite class and one of the hardest. You had to write a creative essay every week, the title of which was assigned by the teacher. The first week she gave us the title, "I am a part of everything I have met." We were to write at least two full pages on this subject. I came home in a state of panic. What would I write? I didn't know how to begin. My mother stayed calm and gave me some suggestions. I begged her and begged her to give me the first line,

"Just the first line, please, please. I just don't know how to start. I'll be fine once I have that first line."

She gave me that first line. I finished the paper and writing every week gradually became easier and easier. I still have all those essays I wrote at MacDuffie. We had to put them in binders and hand in the binders every week which the teacher lugged around. She didn't have to lug them far as she lived on the second floor with all the boarders in her own apartment shared with another teacher. Both teachers were older and overweight and unattractive and we were sure they were lesbians. This thought was just whispered among our friends in the fifties, but never discussed openly. I just retrieved my binder from the basement. The suspense over that first line was too much. It only has three words. I'm guessing my mother also gave me the four word second line, "Shakespeare was wrong. Parting is not sweet." As you can guess I went on to describe my moves from school to school.

Senior year we got a new English teacher, Mr. Harris. He was male and young and had some new ideas. Before, if we wrote an unfinished sentence or a run-on sentence, we automatically got an F on our paper. He didn't think these infractions were that critical and emphasized creativity and fresh ways of expressing ideas. He continued the once a week paper, but senior year we also had to write a research thesis with every fact and thought that wasn't ours being acknowledged in a footnote. I wrote about Joseph Conrad's *Heart of Darkness.* It's over 20 pages and is also now in the basement.

Mr. Harris only lasted one year at MacDuffie and moved on to teach at Purdue. He contacted me in the summer and asked if he could use my Heart of Darkness paper as a sample for his freshman English class that fall as he understood that most of the students had never written a research paper. I sent it right away and in December I received a nice note back, along with my paper, from the head of the English department at Purdue. I am going to quote directly,

> *"I have read your research paper a number of times here and it has been read in New York. It is with deepest regret that I am returning it to you. Paradoxical as it sounds, it is just too good a paper to serve our purposes, both in length and in subject matter. The space we have is around 2700 words and I estimate the length of your paper at around 8100 words, without footnotes and bibliography, and I should not like to see it cut. Most of the users of our handbook, also, are not English and/or literature majors, and we have, rather regretfully, decided against using a "literature" subject for the example.*
>
> *For those of us in the English Department your paper is most interesting, shows great labor and pains-taking, is beautifully written, and makes fascinating reading. I can only repeat my regret that, for the reasons given above, I must send it back to you."*

I'm sure he was being politically correct. He had to know, like me, that my paper, without question, was one of the most boring papers he had ever read. I can certainly understand why they wouldn't want to use it as an example. It would cause a revolt in the classroom. To feel confident that my disparaging opinion of my paper was correct, I asked my husband to read it. He couldn't get past page five.

The absolute most boring paper I ever wrote was my senior thesis at Vassar which was seventy pages long with four pages of footnotes. It was on the sense of humor in three to six year olds. Sounds like it would be interesting. I thought so when I picked the subject. It is so unbearably boring that I have never been able to get through rereading more than three pages. It is also stashed in the basement

My father knew it was hard to start at a new high school knowing nobody and wanted to help me make friends. He decided that for my fifteenth birthday in December, he and Mother would take me and any two friends I chose to a play in Hartford followed by dinner at the private and rather fancy Hartford Club which he had just joined. My grandparents had also belonged and when I was much younger we often went there for dinner. I loved going there. The waiters were African American, "colored" was the word we used then. They all wore tuxedoes and always addressed my grandparents and me by name. They made me feel very important. The foyer was small and there was a gold rotary phone on a tiny table by the wall. I had never seen anything except a black telephone and was in awe of that gold phone. It wasn't shiny, but a dull rich looking gold, like old jewelry.

I thought it would be fun to go back to the Hartford Club and especially to see a play at the Mark Twain Masquers where my mother in her early twenties had been the leading lady in most of their plays. But I didn't know about inviting two friends who I hardly knew. I'd only been at the school for less than three months. Would they think it was weird to go out to dinner and a play with my parents? I didn't want to be different. What if they were too embarrassed to say no, but didn't really want to go. I finally got over my apprehension and asked two of the girls who had been especially friendly to me, Marty Wallace and Sue Norris. They both seemed pleased with the invitation and Sue told me years later that it had been a very special night for her. They gave me a silver bracelet which I still have in my jewelry box.

Many of the students at MacDuffie were from Longmeadow. There was a clique of about thirteen girls that I desperately wanted to join. Nine of the thirteen in the clique went to MacDuffie and the rest to Classical. The majority of them belonged to a high school sorority called SSS. What those letters stood for was a big secret. There were two other sororities, Triangle and Rhombus. Triangle was only Catholic girls. This was not religious prejudice. Three of those members were in the clique. It was culinary prejudice. The sororities always met every other Friday after school at different member's houses and had hamburgers or hotdogs or anything the host parent wanted to cook. The Triangle members always had to have a tuna fish noodle casserole because it was Friday. I guess it was assumed you didn't want to eat that tuna fish casserole unless you had to. And you only had to if you were Catholic. The hostess could have served salmon or trout, but that gets pretty pricey when you're feeding twenty or so girls. The third sorority was Rhombus and it had mostly girls from Classical High School with only a few from MacDuffie.

The three sororities all organized a formal dance every year which I heard was really fun, but you had to belong to one of the sororities to attend. I finally got up the courage to ask Marty, who I really liked, if she could see if I could join SSS. I had been invited to join Rhombus, I told her, but I really wanted to join SSS. Weeks went by. I had a feeling I knew the answer. I finally got up the nerve to ask her. She gave me some excuse and encouraged me to join Rhombus because of the dances. I did and I loved the dances, but I hated every other Friday when I went to a Rhombus meeting and the girls who did finally include me in their clique and became my best friends, went to their SSS meeting.

The RST (Rhombus, SSS, Triangle) dances were held different places, usually hotels, but always formal with a large band, with the girls in long gowns and the boys in jackets and ties. The girls did the inviting as we were the hosts and bought the tickets. A friend of mine who also went to an all girl's school asked how I ever met boys to invite since I hadn't even grown up in the community. This is how I remember it. The first year I invited my boyfriend, Scott Carson, from Wethersfield. You do meet some new boys when your friends put your name on their dance cards. You can invite them to the next dance as long as your friend doesn't object. We also had a group of boys that we hung out with who primarily went to Classical High School. And there were Open Houses where you met a lot of new people as they all congregated for a night of partying. These were the houses of willing parents who agreed to have a huge, "anyone can come party," usually outside. The parents provided snacks and soda pop, but of course, no liquor.

I made the mistake of talking my parents into hosting an open house and we learned the next morning that there were many who didn't just drink coca cola. My father told me when I woke that he had just spent an hour cleaning up throw-up on the front lawn. Obviously some brought alcohol with them.

We also went to parties over the Christmas holidays, another great way to meet potential beaus. I only dated two heart throbs in high school. One was short lived, like three months, but I was crazy about him. His name was Dick Healy and he had been invited to tryout in the minor baseball leagues in the spring. I heard that he didn't make it and had returned back home from Florida, but I never heard from him again. My other heart throb was Terry Premo who I went steady with for over a year. Going steady is the way to go if you don't like stressing out over getting a date.

It was expected that the boys would bring a corsage for their date, and if they were really clued in to the proper etiquette, they would ask their date the color of her gown. By senior year we had all learned to ask our dates for a wrist corsage, having found the ones you pinned on got crushed during a slow, romantic dance.

We had dance booklets smaller than a playing card with a tiny pencil attached by a ribbon to the card. The expected protocol was to dance with your date on the first and last dance and the dances before and after intermission. The girls filled in these dance cards days before the event so the boys had no choice of dance partners. If you really liked your date you filled in that dance card very sparsely.

Before the RST dances and even more so before the MacDuffie junior and senior proms, some of the parents would invite their daughter's friends and dates to a pre-dance dinner at their home, their Club or a restaurant. Typically our dates were one or two years older than us so by sophomore year most of the boys were driving. Usually couples double dated. Nobody went to a dance without a date.

After the end of one of these dances my date stopped first at my house because I had the earliest curfew. The couple we had double dated with waited in the car. My father wasn't usually waiting by the front door for me, but this night he opened the door as we walked up, greeted my date and said,

"I bet you kids are starving. How about coming in for scrambled eggs and bacon?"

My date, who seemed very excited over the thought of eating, replied that we drove with another couple and they were out in the car, so my father said,

"Wonderful, I bet they're hungry too. Why don't you all come on in."

Everyone came in, but I was uneasy. I had never heard of any other fathers cooking breakfast at almost midnight and I didn't want my family to seem different. I just wanted us to be like everyone else. My father proceeded to cook a delicious pre-midnight brunch, talking to the boys who gathered around him in the kitchen the whole time while we two girls sat in the living room gossiping about the dance until the boys announced that breakfast was served. It was a festive ending to a fun night. I felt proud of my father and silly for always worrying what other people thought.

Sophomore year I visited my grandparents in Florida. It was my first time on an airplane and I was traveling by myself. My father purchased the plane tickets which were non-refundable at that time and then was informed by the headmaster, Ralph Rutenber, that it was MacDuffie policy that if a student took any days off at either end of a vacation she would get a zero in every subject for those missed days. I was really upset, but not enough to want to cancel the trip. I got dressed up for the plane trip as did all the other passengers. I bought an insurance policy from The Fidelity and Casualty Company of New York at the airport. It cost twenty-five cents for $5,000 worth of coverage. I found the policy in an old scrapbook and in reading it I see it not only covered loss of life, but dismemberment of my hands or feet and loss of sight.

"Make It a Girl, Gracie"

My grandparents now went to Lake Worth on the East coast instead of Fort Meyers on the West coast where they went in the forties. Every year they would look at real estate for a couple of weeks with the intention of buying and then decide renting was easier. I developed a huge crush on Tom Bird, the boy next door, who was home from college. He was blond, played football and worked out every morning. He was a big flirt and especially liked to flirt with my grandmother who thoroughly enjoyed it. I was determined to get a good tan in that one short week and lay out in the sun way too long one day and spent the next three days inside feeling miserable with swollen lips, puffy ears and beet red skin on most of my body. I have a feeling this really bad burn contributed to my many subsequent basal cell cancers.

We did not have a dishwasher in 1950 and my brother and I had the job of doing the dishes after dinner. I did the washing and Billy dried. He always wanted to listen to The Lone Ranger on the radio which we did most of the time unless I was mad at him for some reason and then I would insist we listen to something else even though I didn't mind The Lone Ranger. He would retaliate by handing back dishes that weren't fully clean to be redone instead of just wiping off the streak of food which was our custom to speed up the job we both hated.

He had a paper route every afternoon and when it was rainy or snowy he worried that he would start wheezing which he often did and would ask me to drive him around his route. Was I a gracious chauffeur? I can't believe how mean I was to him. I hated doing it and let him know it. When I recently mentioned the guilt I had carried all these years, he said he didn't even remember me being mean.

We had an old, upright piano that my brother and I had taken lessons on. My mother decided she would like to play the piano and take some lessons. The elderly gentleman teacher came to our house once a week. My mother faithfully practiced and really enjoyed it. After a year or so of lessons, my father said we should get a nice spinet instead of that old, upright and so my parents went shopping together for a piano.

The music store also sold small Hammond organs newly designed to be appropriate for a private home. My father became intrigued by how you could plug in any kind of accompaniment to your playing – a brass band, a string quartet, anything! The salesman, I gather, was really good at explaining the magic of this organ and illustrating personally how easy it was to create beautiful music. My father, having been an outstanding salesman, was always impressed by someone of similar abilities. They bought the organ.

You don't really need lessons when you play the theme with one finger and hit different buttons to play all the other parts. My mother seemed to enjoy the new organ, but she had loved those lessons with her delightful teacher and now they were over. Her teacher had been so excited that they were buying a new piano. I don't know how my mother had the heart to tell him the sorry news of no more lessons.

Every year the seniors had to write a one-act play. The class would then vote and the writers of the two plays that received the most votes would produce their plays. This meant the winning writers auditioned who they wanted for their cast and crew and they were the sole director. The plays were put on for the entire school. It was considered a big deal. My play was one of the two selected. I was ecstatic. I purposely wrote a play with an all female cast. The plays from the year before had a lot of male characters and I thought girls dressing up as men lent an unintended comical aspect.

My mother gave me the basic idea. I titled it, "Just a Remembrance." In a one sentence plot description, a bunch of married women are having an outing at a snazzy hotel without their husbands and go overboard keeping souvenirs, such as towels, ashtrays, even silverware and many repercussions follow. I loved being a director and strutting about with my clipboard and pencil, giving judicious advice to my cast and feeling very grown-up.

The fall of my senior year was the 1952 presidential election. All of our parents were Republican so all of us were Republicans, no independent thinking there. The Republican Party based much of their campaign on the need for a change, stating that there had been a Democratic President since 1932, eighteen years, and that was long enough. We all pinned to our coats, a three inch long gold colored little broom which signified, "Time to sweep out the old and let in the new." We heartily supported five star General Dwight Eisenhower, not just because our parents did, but because we felt we knew him. We had heard his name all through elementary school - he helped us win the war!

That reminds me of another political incident during my high school years. When General MacArthur was fired by President Truman, it was all the newspapers talked about for weeks. There were intense emotions on both sides, some hating Truman for firing a war hero and some feeling Truman had no choice and admired the courage it must have taken to do that. General MacArthur was scheduled to give a farewell speech to the nation and Dr. Rutenber arranged to have it piped live into our dining room while we ate lunch, as he considered it a historical event worthy of our attention. I still remember MacArthur's hoarse sounding voice and the dramatic ending when he declared, "Old Soldiers Never Die, They Just Fade Away."

Sue Baldwin, who we called Baldy much to her mother's horror, invited our clique and the group of boys we usually hung out with to an all day picnic and outing at her family's cottage at a lake about an hour away. A reporter stopped by to take pictures of this "healthy, fun, youthful gathering of friends" as he said at the top of his entire page of pictures published in the following Sunday newspaper. They were flattering pictures and we all did look youthful and healthy and it was obvious we were definitely having fun. However, Nancy Mosshammer's picture was taken with a cigarette between two fingers of one hand. Most of us smoked and our parents knew it, but Nancy's father was a minister and he did not know it. She tried punching a tiny hole in the paper with a pencil tip right where her hand was holding the cigarette, but he was wise to it and that pretty much ruined the fun of that day for her.

In the fifties you dated a lot, usually a twosome, but sometimes a double date. The typical date was going to the movies followed by a hamburger. There were no fast food restaurants then and pizza was still a novelty. Typically you went to a drive-in restaurant where a waitress, called a car hop, clipped a tray to the side of the driver's window, took your order and when she returned with your food, she placed it on top of that clipped on tray. You couldn't drive away until she came back to remove the tray. That must have given some forward thinking people ideas about opening a restaurant where you drove up to a window, got your food and then could immediately leave!

Dates were usually initiated by the boy calling the girl on her family's telephone. No private cell phones then. The anxiety over that telephone ringing or not ringing was intense. All of us had a curfew. Mine was either eleven or twelve, and on rare occasions one am. Going steady was a common state of affairs. I went steady my senior year with Terry Premo. He was going to The University of Massachusetts in the fall so we both knew we would not be seeing much of each other after the summer and I was fine with that until he broke up with me in July for Nancy Breck. Even though I knew our break-up by mutual consent was inevitable, I was devastated. She was one of the attractive daughters of the man whose Springfield company made Breck shampoo which was the only shampoo any of us would even consider using. All his attractive daughters were pictured in the Breck ads. Nancy was pretty with curly brown hair and considered quite a catch. I didn't have a chance. I wasn't sad to hear she dumped Terry a few months later.

The real head of our clique, Peggy Sanderson, went steady with different boyfriends at least five times in high school. We often played bridge at her house after school and she would weigh out loud the pros and cons of breaking up with her current steady beau. One Friday afternoon during one of our bridge games she was discussing breaking up with Stu who she was seeing that night. She decided she definitely would break up, but first she'd wash her hair. She started heading to the bathroom, still talking about Stu, so we all followed her. She bent over the bathtub, quickly shampooed and rinsed, dried her hair with a towel, ran a comb through it, all in less than three minutes and then led our little parade of three back to the bridge game.

This casualness over her love life and her hair washing was mind boggling to me. Breaking up needed a lot of thought and caused emotional anguish and washing your hair was a production that required prior planning. There were no hair dryers then. The only ones were in beauty parlors and they were huge, heavy contraptions that the attendant slowly lowered over your head. Most of us washed our hair no more than once a week. We let it air dry partially and then rolled it up wet into circular coils tight to our head which we secured with bobby pins. We called them pin curls. Now you know why photos of girls in the fifties have hair that looks glued to their heads.

Peggy and date and Terry and me

Peggy was the first of us to get her driver's license. Her father was a doctor and her mother, who had a flamboyant streak, had emblazoned on the side of their wood trimmed station wagon the words, "My Mink II." It had replaced a similar wagon with just "My Mink" on the side and when I was in college, "My Mink III" emerged.

There was a big basketball game and we all wanted to go and Peggy got permission to drive. Elation all around – our first all female outing with no parent driving. Station wagons were roomy, but not nearly as roomy as mini-vans. No one had ever heard of seat belts. We managed to fit ten girls into that car. Peggy's license was one week old. To put this in today's perspective, it was as though Peggy was driving and talking on ten cell phones at the same time. She misjudged her braking distance at a stop light and bumped the car in front of her. The angry driver stormed out of his car as we all quickly jumped out of Peggy's car. About five of us wisely started walking down the street like we had no association with that stopped car. The two drivers exchanged insurance information, the other driver left and we all quietly sneaked back into the car and rode in guilty self-enforced silence the rest of the way to the game.

When Peggy was much younger she had fallen and broken a large triangular piece of tooth off her two upper, middle front teeth so when she smiled there was this large inverted V of space in the middle of her mouth. I never could understand why she didn't get it fixed. I knew finances weren't a concern. I was in awe of the self-assurance and confidence she must have had in herself to not give that gaping hole a second thought. I probably wouldn't have left the house until the dentist repaired it. Before she went to college she did have both those front teeth capped.

One last story about Peggy. I went to a few fairs when we lived in Springfield with members of our clique, often including Peggy. Our goal was always to win a stuffed animal at one of the game stands. I don't think we ever succeeded, but Peggy always won with the "Guess your age" booth. She would hand us her watch, her rings, her purse, anything that looked like a teenager and then walk over to the booth and buy a ticket. We all slinked back in the background so the vendor wouldn't see us. I remember the guesses being twelve and thirteen years old. Then Peggy would pull out her license stating sixteen years old and we would all gather around and help her pick out her prize.

Senior year many of my best friends headed off to Florida with their families for spring break which was in late March. It was a dreary March and I had nothing fun planned. There had been notices put up at our school over a state wide exam endorsed by the Massachusetts Federation of Labor and given by the Central Labor Union. There was a first and second prize of scholarship money towards college. I decided I might as well take the exam and try my chances at winning since the exam was only an hour and a half long.

Four of us from MacDuffie signed up. I went to the Springfield Library and came home with piles of books and union pamphlets about the history of labor unions. I read as much as I could in that week of vacation with lots of skimming, much note taking and chart making of bills sponsored by the labor unions. I tried to memorize as much as I could. The exam was April 8th. There were 1009 students participating from 148 schools. I opened the test booklet and the exam was comprised of ten true and false questions, ten multiple choice questions and a choice of five essays. I chose, "What A Labor Union Can Do For Its Members," writing furiously to finish in the allotted time. When they made the final call for the booklets to be turned in, there were only three of us still in the room, none from MacDuffie.

Three weeks later I got a phone call from a union executive who told me I had won second place. First place was won by a boy at a very elite private school in Boston called Boston Latin. There was a certain irony in that the two winners of the labor union contest were students at private schools. I was invited to a celebration dinner at the Highland Hotel in Springfield with many union big-wigs, my parents and any teacher I wanted to invite. I invited my history teacher of three years, Miss Morris, who I held partly responsible for my win.

When we studied the union movement in class, Miss Morris emphasized how the unions not only helped its members economically, but gave them a sense of dignity and respect that made them feel more a part of the American dream. They no longer had to work seven days a week, they had time for their children, could even play golf on the week-end. These thoughts are what I emphasized and elaborated on in my essay. At the dinner some of the union executives were eager to talk to me. They said they couldn't believe how many congressional acts I described that had become law. Truth is, I didn't know which acts were important and which weren't, so I just mentioned every act I had memorized. They had probably never heard of them because they were of no importance, but the quantity that I listed impressed them.

My essay was what won the day. They said they were fairly confident I was a female from my handwriting. I remember all these details because I saved the article that was in the newspaper about my win which quoted four long paragraphs of my essay. My father and his golfing pals at the Longmeadow

Country Club thought it was hilarious that I won a scholarship from a labor union, but my father was proud I took the initiative and delighted I had won.

MacDuffie, like most high schools, had a formal dance junior and senior year. I was elected Chairman of the Senior Prom. It was just after Princess Elizabeth was crowned Queen so our theme was a "Coronation Ball." We transformed our ugly gym for these proms. We rolled out eight foot high rolls of pink paper and covered the walls and then glued onto the pink walls cutouts in shiny gold paper of coaches, horses, crowns, anything we could think of relating to royalty. We hung apple blossoms from the coach windows and encircled the blossoms around the horses' necks. We finished by hiding the ceiling with pink, white and green streamers.

I'm guessing ten of us worked on it and we all thought it looked elegant. Again, my memory is refreshed by an article from the newspaper I had saved in my high school scrapbook which is rapidly disintegrating. In the fifties, the two local newspapers, a morning paper and an evening paper, had long articles with elaborate details about local activities like the school dances, who attended, which parents gave a party beforehand, detailed descriptions of bride's and bridesmaid's dresses - all kinds of juicy details about everything.

We had lots of formal dances with live bands in the fifties. The biggies were the junior and senior proms, but we also had the RST annual sorority dance, coming out parties for girls turning eighteen or nineteen, dances at a nearby boy's prep school, and some I've probably forgotten. The girls that "came out" were not officially selected by some elite committee as in New York City, Cincinnati and other cities, but girls whose parents had the money and inclination to give a big party. Three of my friends gave one such party together and two friends gave another one. For most of these events you needed a formal gown. The boys wore tuxedoes for the proms, but could get away with only a suit or jacket and tie at the others. Buying all these gowns was a big endeavor. They were expensive and you wanted to be sure you didn't have the same gown as a classmate and there weren't that many retail stores in Springfield.

My senior year my grandmother said she had some beautiful yellow lacelike material she would like to use and asked if she could make a gown for me for my senior prom. She showed me the yellow lace and a melon colored material that was probably taffeta that she would use underneath. I loved the way the two fabrics complemented each other. Together we picked out a pattern for a strapless gown (with spaghetti straps added), with a full skirt at a mid-calf length. The finished gown was striking and I loved it and I loved that my grandmother was so talented she could create something this beautiful. When I was a toddler she made most of my clothes. In old photographs all my panties match my dresses and often there's even a matching bonnet.

My sister Cynthia was in kindergarten when I was a senior in high school. She had picture books with accompanying records that she loved playing. She didn't know how to read, but she had memorized all the lines from the record for each story so she could open her books and read them perfectly without any need for the record player. She probably had three or four stories in her memorized repertory. These record-books were put together by Disney and the record clued in the young listeners when it was time to turn the page by having Pluto go "arf." There was no picture of Pluto, but you knew he was doing the barking. There were big pictures so the writing was brief on each page. Her recital would go like this,

"The prince saw Cinderella and he was sure this was *arf* just the one for him. She was beautiful and delicate *arf* and he wanted her for his *arf* very own."

Cynthy used great animation in her recitation which made the *arfs* seem even funnier. She must have wondered why we always held our hands over our mouths when she read as we tried to stifle our laughs.

We had lived within an hour of New York City in Cedar Grove, but it was during the war, Billy and I were young, Pamela was just a baby and my parents didn't have lots of extra cash. So we kids mostly glimpsed the city when we crossed the George Washington Bridge on our way to my grandparents. My parents decided in the summer after my sophomore year that we should all spend four days in the city. I remember sightseeing on the top level of a double-decker bus and going to the huge, fantastic Metropolitan Museum of Art and The Museum of Natural History which my brother loved. All of New York was so exciting to me, even taking a taxi cab. We saw two big hits at the time, "South Pacific" and "Guys and Dolls." That was my first time in a theater in New York and I loved it and wanted to come back again and again. Now I have a daughter, son-in-law and three grandsons right in the city and I do come back again and again and I still love it.

When you lived on the East coast, going to the beach was what you did for your vacation. We went to Grove Beach, near Saybrook, Connecticut in 1941, when my brother was less than two years old. My mother once said it's lucky he survived because she was so absorbed in reading "Gone With The Wind" which had just been published, that she hardly paid attention to either of us. The next beach I remember was White Sands in 1945. It's near Old Lyme Connecticut, famous now for Lyme disease. We were told that Lucile Ball was staying there that summer. This was when she was a glamorous Hollywood star, long before she became a comedian. I had paper dolls of Lucille Ball and spent those two weeks hoping I would see her.

The summer after sophomore year, 1951, my parents and grandparents rented a cottage for a month at a beach in Connecticut called Giant's Neck. It was located on the Long Island Sound, like every cottage we rented, which meant the waves were not huge, but similar to Lake Michigan on a rough day. The cottage we had rented two summers before at Mulberry Pointe was very roomy and pleasant with a wonderful location across from the beach. That beach was sandy and inviting at low tide, but unbeknownst to us until we arrived, there was no beach at high tide which is half the time.

This time my father thoroughly checked out the high and low tide situation. I was told I could invite a friend for a week. I didn't have anyone specific in mind and I didn't want to hurt anyone's feelings so I mentioned it casually when we were all playing bridge one day after school. The only girl that responded was Dawn Ide who said she would love to come. She was in our clique, but I didn't know her very well. She had not made a point of being extra friendly to me when I started MacDuffie. I was quite apprehensive about it, but after this one week together at the beach we became best friends, then college roommates and now the only close friend I have had for over sixty years. Dawn has since told me she was really upset that I thought she was unfriendly and that she was just very shy in high school.

There were lots and lots of teenagers at Giant's Neck. Dawn and I were having a fantastic time. We hung out with a couple of boys who looked and acted like the boys we dated in Longmeadow, that fair haired, waspy look. Sometimes they stopped by the cottage and asked us to meet them at the beach or asked us if we wanted to drive to the Dairy Queen and get a cone. They never came inside our cottage and showed no interest in meeting my parents.

Two other boys, Sam and Dave, really pursued Dawn and me. They offered us a dozen options, the movies, bowling, grabbing a hamburger, whatever we would like to do. We remained very aloof. They didn't look like our type. They had really dark hair and olive, deeply tanned skin and at the beach their parents spoke a language we couldn't identify and were very loud and laughed a lot. They seemed really foreign to us. Looking back I can hardly believe we were such snobs. Dawn and I considered ourselves tolerant and completely without prejudice and yet we had this reluctance about going out with boys who looked, and we thought acted, differently than our social group.

But, it is exhilarating to be pursued so diligently so we finally agreed to go out with them. They arrived at the cottage, asked to come in and introduced themselves to my parents and Bob and Betty Decker who were visiting for a few days. They didn't just mumble their names, look at the floor a lot and immediately head for the door which was often typical of the boys we dated. They initiated a long animated conversation with the four adults. They seemed in no rush to leave. Finally we left, and drove to the Ocean Beach Country Club on the boardwalk at Ocean Beach Park. Sounds like a private golf club. It wasn't private, but there was golf, a miniature golf course. We set up competitions on each hole, laughed a lot and had a fabulous time. They were interesting, bright and fun. The next morning my father and Bob Decker commented that those two young men were the nicest, politest boys they had ever met. They were Greek and we hung out with them the rest of the week.

The next afternoon Betty Decker pulled me aside and told me to find something to do to keep Dawn away from the cottage that afternoon as my mother had been drinking. That was the elephant in the room that our family never talked about and you never knew when that elephant would show up.

I always knew the minute I came home from school whether or not Mother had been drinking by the arch in her eyebrow. Her face just took on a different look and I knew before she even said a word that she had been drinking. I never reproached her to her face, but inside I felt terribly sad, but that sadness was mixed with anger and disappointment. I didn't ask friends over to my house to play bridge after school because I never knew what to expect. My father also drank heavily, but held it well. When he did have too much he became irritable and unpleasant, but a stranger wouldn't have suspected alcohol was the cause. He regularly had two martinis before dinner and often another one or two at lunch during the week. In his business, going out to lunch for a leisurely hour was the norm. Drinking at lunch was not unusual. We never saw my mother drink except one cocktail before dinner and sometimes a glass of beer. I don't know for sure if she drank a lot or if her capacity to hold liquor was just low. I suspect she drank a lot.

I never mentioned my mother's drinking problem with my friends. I felt both ashamed and protective of my mother. We never discussed the situation openly in our family of five or with our grandparents who were like second parents to us. My dad was the logical one to instigate a family discussion about my mother's problem, but he never did. The act of an entire family gathering together to confront one family member over his or her problem, which was common practice later, especially with children who had joined a cult, was not done in the fifties. My father would make comments like your mother's been drinking so let's order in dinner tonight. I remember him telling our cleaning woman Marjorie when she arrived one day to keep an eye on Mrs. Gilbert as she had been drinking.

When my sister, eleven years younger than me, reached high school the situation had become much worse. She joined Alcoholics Anonymous for teenagers and luckily had a friend in the same situation and they went together to the meetings. Not surprising, that friend's mother was a good friend of my mother. Cynthia faced coming home not to an arched eyebrow, but a mother passed out on the floor and she was the one who had to call for the ambulance. She decided in high school she wanted to go to boarding school and found and loved the only coed prep school in the east, Northfield Academy.

Cynthia was only nine months old when Pamela died and only eight years old when mother's critical blood pressure crisis started. She was truly cheated out of knowing the wonderful mother I had known in my early years. Dawn recently told me she loved coming over to my house because everyone, especially my mother with her wonderful smile, was so warm and inviting and it was such a relaxed atmosphere and she had no idea my mother drank. And she said it wouldn't have mattered to her either!

I taught kindergarten every Sunday at St. Andrews Episcopal Church my junior and senior year. I really enjoyed it and decided I would like to become a teacher. My father loved discussing at length the importance of a woman having a profession even if she didn't end up using it. It was assumed I would marry, have children and stay at home raising them. That was the expected role of women and I was fine with it. He said you never know what life will bring and it's important to have something to fall back on if necessary. In his opinion the best options for a woman were to become a nurse or a teacher. Being a secretary was another possibility, but not as desirable as teaching or nursing. Hard to believe I didn't argue and rant and rave that a woman should be able to do anything she set her mind on. But I liked teaching and I liked the idea of all those vacations so I didn't give a lot of thought to the real lack of professional choices available to women in the fifties. I also assumed I would marry young and my career would be raising my children.

Junior year is the critical year for thinking about college. In the East, then and still today, you know the reputation and the elite index of every college in the Northeast. The most prestigious ones to attend were the Ivy League Schools for boys and the Seven Sister schools for girls. There were respected coed schools like Swarthmore and Middlebury, but they didn't carry the clout of Ivy League or Seven Sister schools. If you had really good grades, did well on your SAT, showed extracurricular activities and got good recommendations from your school, you would probably get in one of these elite schools. The competition then was nothing like it is in 2015.

In reading the college brochures I found that Vassar in Poughkeepsie, New York had an outstanding, highly regarded "Child Study" major that would entitle its graduates to a teaching certificate in the state of New York when they graduated which was honored by many other states. It became my first choice. I really thought I would prefer a coed school, but I was used to an all girls' school and I liked Vassar's program and I liked the prestige of going to a Seven Sister School and dating boys from Yale and Princeton.

In the fifties, unlike the mid-west, the state universities in the East had the reputation of being for those students who didn't have the grades or the money to get into a private college. Although the private colleges were more expensive than the public universities, they were not obscenely priced as they are now. Vassar cost $4000 a year in 1953. We were all advised by Ralph Rutenber to have a second choice, just in case, so I applied to Colby College in Maine. I picked it because it didn't have an application fee and those fees came out of my allowance. We had driven around Colby on a trip to Maine, but I had never had a tour of the campus. My brother actually ended up teaching at Colby for a few years.

My parents took me for an interview and tour of Vassar and I was impressed and liked the feel of the campus, but my mother was impressed by the double rainbow that spread across the sky as we drove out the main gate on our way back home. She said that was an omen I would get in and I would love it. Dawn also applied to Vassar, we both were accepted and were roommates all four years.

The summer before entering college, my father pulled a few strings and got me a job in the Service Department at Sears. I think it was called Sears Roebuck then. My job was to answer the phone, make a note of any problems customers were experiencing with parts they had ordered and promise those complaining customers that someone would get back to them with an answer right away. Now you see how long ago this lack of direct, immediate service with someone knowledgeable on the other line started! But, being conscientious,

I wrote copious notes and brought them immediately to the head of the department and where they went from there I do not know. I also went to each cash register on both floors two times a day to pick up receipts or some type of paperwork. That was the most fun part of the job because the sale clerks enjoyed talking to me and that made the time fly all the faster. They actually had lots and lots of sales clerks in Sears then. Perhaps they had too many since they usually had plenty of time to talk to me. Now if you find a clerk in Sears to help you, with the exception of the appliance department, it is a minor miracle.

I also enjoyed the company of everyone in my department. None of them had been to college and they seemed genuinely interested in where I was going and what my interests were. When the phone didn't ring and I had nothing to do, I volunteered to put the papers with updated parts descriptions that arrived daily into the huge notebooks they had for service parts. They had weeks and weeks of these sheets sitting in a stack just waiting to be inserted in those fat books. It wasn't a fun job and it was murder on your nails, but it was better than being idle and endeared me to the heart of the woman who had this task.

I forgot to describe the graduation ceremony at MacDuffie. The girls did not wear caps and gowns, but long white dresses and carried a bouquet of red roses. Everyone in our class was sobbing or at least teary except Dawn and me. We whispered to each other that maybe we should fake some tears. We could understand why the boarders were sad.

"Make It a Girl, Gracie"

They were moving away, but our friends all lived in town. We would still see them all the time. I enjoyed most of my classes, liked most of my teachers and was happy I had made it into the clique. I also liked all my classmates and enjoyed being with them, but I was excited to be leaving MacDuffie and moving on. At the end of that summer the SSS sorority planned a two week vacation at a cottage on Cape Cod and I was invited to join them even though I wasn't a member. I had finally, really made it!

Dawn and me

5

Vassar: Fall of 1953 to spring of 1956

Vassar started in the middle of September. I quit my summer job at Sears Roebuck after Labor Day so I could get organized and packed. This was the era of the wardrobe trunk. My mother and I went out and bought one. It was over four feet tall and opened into two sections. One section had hangers and the other had four drawers. I put the clothes I was taking into this hefty piece of luggage. A week before college was to start my mother called a delivery service to pick up the trunk at our house and deliver it to Main, the dorm I was assigned.

When I arrived at college, the hallway was filled with huge trunks and there was mine, sitting upright outside my room. As soon as I emptied it, it was whisked away to be stored until I needed it again in June. I don't remember if I used the trunk every year. What amazes me now is how I fit everything into four small drawers and a hang-up rod of twelve inches long. I must have supplemented with other bags.

This is what I packed for college. A few dresses, usually tailored sheaths which were slim fitting and would look appropriate today. No pants or slacks as they were not worn on the east coast in 1953. In place of pants, Bermuda shorts were worn, wool in winter, cotton in summer, always with knee socks. Above the Bermuda shorts, button down collar shirts were worn under crew neck sweaters. This outfit was like a uniform. Jeans were called dungarees and were baggy and rolled up mid calf. They were seldom worn. Lots of skirts, either straight or pleated, paired with the same shirt and sweater that was worn with the Bermudas. To dress up a little, a skirt was paired with a cashmere or wool cardigan sweater over a dressy blouse.

It was important to have skirts because we had to put one on for dinner every night. We whipped off our Bermudas, slapped on that skirt and we were appropriately dressed to enter the dining room. Anything could be worn for lunch and we could be in our bathrobe for breakfast if our dorm voted that no boys were allowed as visitors for breakfast. Most dorms preferred the bathrobe to the boys.

Sweatshirts were prevalent, but no one had cute workout clothes or sweat pant outfits or any of the attractive casual wear so prevalent today. A camel hair coat was typical which was often adorned with a long, machine knitted scarf from one of the boy's colleges. Ski type jackets were rarely worn because of the bare knees protruding between the knee socks and the Bermudas. Even with a long, camel hair coat, when riding a bike to class the knees were exposed and stayed red and dried out looking all winter. Either knee socks or stockings were worn with the skirts. Panty hose, knee high stockings and tights were not yet on the market. A garter belt held up your stockings and dug unmercifully into your thighs. On further reflection, I guess I could fit everything in that trunk.

My parents drove me to Vassar with a car stuffed with blankets, comforters, towels, lamps, huge aluminum boxes to fit under the bed for storage and a phonograph with lots of records. A chair, a loveseat and a couple of small tables were soon to follow. The college provided the beds, dressers and desks. Dawn and I were in the building called Main. It housed all the seniors and about a third of the freshman plus the post office, the book store and probably some other businesses. Our room was long and narrow, like a bowling alley, with only one window at the far end. It was on the fifth floor which had a manned elevator, but only until 8pm. It was not a pretty room, but we put a lot of effort into jazzing it up. Compared to the small rooms my children had at large universities, our room was spacious.

Orientation sessions were scheduled for a few days before classes began. One orientation talk was on sex. It was given twice to accommodate the four hundred freshmen. It was assumed we were all unknowledgeable virgins and that was an accurate description of me and my friends. Virginity was the Holy Grail then. We were told by our parents that there were two types of girls. The ones the boys took out to "fool around with" and the ones the boys took out who were "wife material." You didn't want to be in the first category and if you did get pregnant before marriage, you had better "visit an aunt" for those last months of pregnancy and give up the baby or marry the father even if you didn't like him. There was no such thing as a single mother who could hold up her head in our social class.

Most of us, despite our high school dating, were mostly ignorant about sex. I think there was a formal presentation first, probably about how to, or rather how not to, get pregnant. They probably described the ovulation process and perhaps birth control methods, e.g. the diaphragm and the condom, the only two known then other than the rhythm method promoted by the Catholic Church, but they certainly did not hand out condoms or advise you where to buy them. In the fifties through the seventies, if you wanted to buy a condom you had to ask the pharmacist who kept them out of sight in the back with all the prescription medicines. A proper woman was expected to be a virgin until she married and most of my friends were virgins. Looking back, by glorifying virginity, as the culture did in the fifties, independence was discouraged and early marriage promoted. Most of my close friends, from college and high school, were married within two years of graduation. After the formal talk on sex, the last hour and a half was open to questions and nobody held back. I never asked any questions, not because I knew it all, but because of my blushing situation. My face would have been the color of a stop light if I had raised my hand. All in all, it was very informative.

Another orientation phenomenon common to all the women's schools and infamous for its humiliation and absurdity, concerned the posture pictures. I think they were promoted as a way to diagnose scoliosis or other abnormalities that no doctor in our 17 or 18 years of age had ever happened to notice. We were assigned a time slot in the gym along with two dozen or so other classmates and told to strip down to only our panties. Maybe you had to take them off too. I'm amazed I've forgotten a detail like that. Once naked we walked out alone in front of three women sitting together in three straight back chairs who stared at us, telling us to turn front, back and sideways. I don't think we had to bend over which is the best way to spot scoliosis. An older male photographer with a huge camera on a tall tripod took pictures of us in all three positions. I still remember the sweat rolling down the inside of my arms during that dreadful incident.

Posture pictures were distributed to us that same week with comments written underneath them. Mine said I was too stooped and needed to stand up straight. I guess they expected us to pull our shoulders back and push out our breasts. I didn't have much to push out, but Dawn was well endowed and she also was accused of not standing up straight.

I'm sure it was our cover-up mechanism for privacy regarding our body parts. Nothing was said about scoliosis which it turns out I do have. In the spring there were rampant rumors that some boys from Princeton had absconded with the posture pictures.

What's really interesting is our acquiescence to something we felt was degrading and pointless. Our generation later became tagged as "The Silent Generation," and this would certainly be one example of that silence.

Classes began and what I noticed immediately was that every student called upon either knew the answer or gave an excellent attempt at an answer. No one ever said, "I don't know," as they often did in high school. I loved my classes and found the whole experience exciting and stimulating. Everybody was smart and we only had full professors teaching almost all our classes. At the start of every semester we filled out forms listing the classes we wanted and being a small school with a total of 1400 women we almost always got the classes and the time slots we selected. I didn't appreciate how wonderful this was until my children who went to large universities shared their frustration of not getting the class or time slot they wanted time and time again and having inept teacher assistants teaching the 101 classes. This was true of smaller, prestigious colleges also. My husband went to Yale, which has about 5,000 students, and never had a full professor until second semester sophomore year.

I enjoyed the Child Study classes and never wavered in my enthusiasm for that major. I had to take a science class so I selected Physiology with little enthusiasm. I ended up loving it. Perhaps I would have enjoyed being a nurse if you didn't have to give shots or handle blood. I still subscribe to medical newsletters from the Cleveland Clinic, Mayo Clinic, John Hopkins, University of California and a couple more. I keep meaning to cut back on those.

Philosophy turned out to be my favorite subject and the professor who I had for four semesters tried to talk me into changing my major. I have a feeling there weren't enough philosophy majors and he was worried about his job. Sadly, I've retained almost nothing from those classes. The class I looked forward to the most was taught by Reinhold Neibuhr's nephew, Richard Niebuhr. It was called Christian Ethics and was really just like a philosophy class. He was brilliant and his class was mesmerizing. It didn't hurt that he was unbelievably handsome. One of our friends, Polly Lindert, babysat for him once a week. He had two toddlers. He and his wife usually didn't go out when she babysat, but had a quiet dinner alone in their dining room with a linen tablecloth, sterling silverware, crystal goblets, the works. At the time, age 19, we all thought this was the most romantic thing we could imagine. A decade later, when I had two toddlers, it didn't sound romantic at all. Did she cook the dinner? Did he clean it up? Who had to iron the linen tablecloth? Who hand dried the crystal? Why didn't they just go out? Vassar was only able to keep him for three years and then he left to teach at Princeton.

There were a lot of rules in the fifties, especially at women's colleges. In the first semester freshman year we could only leave the campus a limited number of week-ends. There were curfews at each dorm and the doors were locked after the curfew. I think it was eleven pm on week-nights and one am on week-ends. I don't know what you did if you were late. There were no cell phones to call for help. No private telephones were allowed in the rooms until senior year when you still had to make something up like a sick parent who might need to desperately call you in the middle of the night. To reach you, parents and friends had to call the main desk in your dorm and the paid student answering the phones during that time slot wrote down the message on a small white slip. When you returned to your dorm you always checked the front desk for those precious slips. Then you had to find a pay phone to return the call. Communication has come a long way! The advantage to the old days is my mother and grandmother wrote me letters almost every other week when I was in college. I saved many of them and just reread all their wonderful letters full of news and events. Those letters brought my grandmother and mother alive to me again. No reminiscing like that with cell phones and emails.

The bed sheets were provided by the college and every week you exchanged your bottom sheet for a clean sheet. You then put your old top sheet on the bottom and the new sheet on the top. No such thing as fitted bottom sheets yet. Cars were not allowed unless, senior year only, you had a very legitimate excuse. I didn't know anyone who had a car.

Dormitory food did not have a good reputation. We had a limited choice at breakfast and lunch. Dinner was whatever meat or fish the chef had decided to cook with some choices for vegetable and dessert. About every three weeks he cooked liver and onions, to save money I guess, as only a very few showed up on those liver nights. We could have seconds on anything except meat. We went through a buffet line, but the food was served onto our plate by a kitchen worker. Once we sat down at a table, we were expected to wait until everyone in our group had finished eating before we left the table. Everyone had to take on a volunteer job of some sort. I don't remember if we had any choice or if it was only freshman year, but I do remember vividly one job which involved wiping the food off the finished plates and stacking them up, while wearing a mandatory hairnet.

After dinner everyone went into the sitting rooms of their dorm where huge coffee urns were set up on tables with sugar and cream and a stack of demitasse cups. Many of us would relax before getting back to studying by playing bridge for an hour after dinner. We would all plop down on the floor, sit Indian style with our legs tucked under us and drink our little demitasse coffee and smoke. At least two-thirds of the students smoked. How we tolerated those fumes circling around our heads with four cigarettes lit in one tight square of bridge playing I don't know. I can't stand one single lit cigarette anywhere near me now.

Unless we had to go to the library, Dawn and I studied in our room, not at our desks, but in chairs or couches we had brought from home. Like many students we always played classical music on our stereo when we studied. It didn't distract us and made noise outside our room less noticeable. We didn't have keys for our rooms. There wasn't much to steal. No one had any of the following in their room: small refrigerator, computer, printer, television, microwave, hair dryer, Ipad, Iphone etc. Other than television, none of these items were yet invented and the programs on television then were minimal. When there was some very special program we could go to the student center which was a half mile away from our dorm and watch on the one television set there. Restaurants and bars were much quieter then with no televisions blaring.

There wasn't a charming college town near Vassar, but within walking distance there were some boutique style dress shops, a handful of bars that also sold food, a movie theater that only showed one movie at a time and probably some other stores that I don't remember. The drinking age in New York was eighteen so all of us could legally buy a drink. I did have to wait until December to be legal. Whenever our parents visited we always went out to a nice restaurant. Dawn and I would pocket the rolls and any other uneaten portable food to bring back to the dorm. We were always hungry at night and there was no place to get a snack. Rachel, a friend of ours who was Jewish and from New York City kept a roll of salami under her bed and assured us it didn't need to be refrigerated. Dawn and I were a little nervous about that, but it was a moot point because Rachel rarely offered to give us a slice.

The movie theater, only a block away, cost fifty cents for admission. They usually played art movies. We saw all of Ingmar Bergman's movies there. We went often and I still remember scrambling around to find 50 cents. I was on an allowance that included clothes and I was always broke. There were no large national credit cards like Visa or Master Card. Each store had its own credit card. You could not get your diploma until you had paid off all your charges at the local stores. This was a challenge at the end of senior year, but at least you didn't graduate with a fat credit card bill hanging over your head.

Most of the girls on our floor were freshman like us and a group of them remained our best friends for all four years. Our room was at the end of a short corridor and the only room within twenty feet of ours was occupied by a senior. It was a single room and she would come and go silently, never saying a word to us. She was the only senior on the fifth floor. We found out she was going to medical school after graduation. We decided she didn't want anything to divert her attention away from her studies so picked the fifth floor away from other seniors. Out of curiosity, Dawn and I just wanted to take a peak to see what her room looked like. What a shock – she actually locked her door. We didn't even know the doors locked.

One of the girls on our floor, Patti Breckir, lived in White Plains just outside the city. Her father was a psychiatrist and Patti asked if any of us would like to go into the city for the week-end. It wouldn't cost that much as we could sleep for free at her father's office. Merrill Moss, her roommate, and I accepted. I don't remember any details about the sleeping arrangements, but I'm guessing extra couches might be a necessity for a psychiatrist in case there's a sudden need for an emergency vertical consultation.

We took the train into the city, about an hour ride along the Hudson River, a beautiful train ride especially in the fall. What I remember is the exhilarating thrill I felt at being in New York City with no parents, just my friends. It was a giddy feeling of freedom and sheer happiness and an overwhelming realization that all the possibilities life offered were out there for me.

There was a long line to get half-off theater tickets, but we were patient and were excited to get tickets to *The Immoralist* staring Geraldine Page and Louis Jourdan. After the show, Patti, the drama major, insisted we go back stage to see if we could meet any of the stars. I felt sheepish and embarrassed as we passed one person after another backstage saying, "Excuse me, excuse me," but we all followed Patti closely and she and went right up to the door with Geraldine Page's name on it and knocked. Then much to Merrill's and my complete amazement, Miss Page opened the door herself and invited us in. We had a nice conversation with her or Patti did as she did all the talking, but Merrill and I smiled sweetly as Patti rambled on. Miss Page signed our programs before we left. I couldn't believe it was so easy to meet a famous Broadway star!

I don't remember what else we did. I know we stopped by to see Rachel. She lived on the west side of Central Park and was home for a cousin's wedding. We went to her apartment and it was the first apartment I'd ever been in except my grandparent's rentals in Florida. I was amazed at how huge it was. It seemed just like a regular house except you took an elevator to get to the front door.

Our choice of shoes for our week-end in Manhattan was lamentable. We didn't have a lot of alternatives. We all owned a pair of loafers and a pair of sneakers. We usually wore socks with these. For casual, semi-dressy fare we wore Capezios. To get even more dressed up we wore a two or three inch high pump. With the Capezios and the pumps we either went bare legged or wore stockings. The advice given by friends was to buy Capezios one size too small because they would stretch out. They looked like flimsy ballet slippers, offered no support at all and that stretching out period was one month of agony. We wore Capezios on the train, but then changed into heels for our city adventures. We felt that if we were going shopping and out to dinner and then attending a play in Manhattan we should be dressed up. That was a bad decision. I remember finally slipping my heels off at the theater because of the pain and then when the play was over, struggling to get those torturous shoes back on again over my swollen feet.

On the weekends during the fall, the campus seemed half empty. There was a major exodus to the boy's schools for the football week-ends. My children who went to large universities asked me how I met boys when I went to an all girl's school? I reminded them that the boys were in the same situation, no girls on their campus. Typically, a friend of yours would be invited by her boyfriend or maybe a boy she just knew from high school and that boy would ask her to find blind dates for his friends. I had nineteen blind dates at Vassar. I counted them up once when I was feeling depressed. Some were dreadful, some started long relationships and some ended in marriage, like mine.

To get to these boy's colleges and most of them were Ivy League Schools, we took taxis. Different students would take the initiative and arrange for a cab on Friday afternoon at a time slot that fit their academic schedule. They would state the time the cab would leave and the college destination on a piece of paper with lines numbered for the available spaces and post it in the main entrance of their dorm. We would check out these lists and sign up for the one that best met our time frame. The same passengers returned together by cab late Sunday afternoon. This traveling wasn't only in the fall. Two of the favorite week ends were Winter Carnival at Dartmouth and Williams. There also were spring formal dances and other events often sponsored by the fraternities. We paid for the cab ride, split five or six ways, but all the rest was out of our date's pocket. I'm guessing seventy percent of our social life was at a boy's school.

To save money, the boys would pay for their date to stay in a bedroom in a private home. Many residents were anxious to make money this way and it was cheaper for the boys than paying for a hotel so it worked out well for everyone. Dawn and I had dates at Princeton with two guys who were also friends so they had us room together. The house was on a street where all the houses were in a line and really looked alike. I wasn't with Dawn when this happened. She was as near sighted as I and also took off her glasses on a date. After the football game her date drove her to the house to change for the evening while he waited. He mistakenly parked in front of the wrong house and Dawn rushed up the walk to quickly change. She opened the front door, saw the family sitting in the living room, said, " Hi," dashed up the stairs which were open to the living room and into the bedroom where she had put her suitcase earlier. She put her hand out for where she remembered the light switch was and it wasn't there. She squinted further into the dark room and the beds were arranged differently. She was in the wrong house. She quickly turned, ran down the stairs, saw they were all frozen in position staring at the staircase, so she quickly shouted, "Goodbye, sorry" and ran out the door. The correct house was two houses down the street.

I kept a scrapbook of mementoes from some of my activities in college. I pulled it out when I started these memoirs. All the scotch tape has turned brown and lost its stickiness so everything tumbles out, but it helps refresh my memory on some things I've forgotten. For instance I had no memory of my first week-end away at a boy's college. It was Yale. There in the scrapbook was the Yale-Dartmouth football program and a note about my date. It was a blind date and there was his name, Henry Winkler, and a notation from me next to his name, so with a big gasp I yelled at my husband,

"I had a blind date with Fonzie freshman year and I wrote in my scrapbook that he was a big jerk!"

Then I decided I'd better google Henry Winkler. I was hugely disappointed to see he was born in 1945, so I didn't have a date with Fonzie.

My next week-end away was in New York City again. Pat Johnson's high school sweetheart, Champ, was a freshman or what they called a plebe at West Point. They start school in the summer and in the early fall get their first week-end pass. The boys come from all over the country so very few plebes know any girls from the east. Champ had the perpetual job of finding dates for his friends which meant his girlfriend Pat had that perpetual job. I think three of us went. We saw the Army-Duke game somewhere in New York and then went to dinner at Mama Leonas, a very popular tourist place with Italian food and very reasonable prices. Also, with very long lines, especially on a Saturday night. Our dates were in uniform and looking quite spiffy and hauled us up to the front of the line. Upon seeing the uniforms, the bouncer at the door yelled into the restaurant,

"Mama, we got some more at the door."

Mama came right over and exclaimed over the boys, as she led us to a table,

"I so happy to see you. Come in come in. Ah, such pretty girls. I have a very special table just right for all of you. Please,

please sit down, sit down right here. I have some very, very special food for you tonight. I hope you do some fun things in this beautiful city."

The boys chatted away with Mama while we three girls smiled widely. After Mama left, Merrill asked,

"How long ago did you have to make the reservations?"

Champ replied, "Oh, we never have to make them. She doesn't even take reservations. Her nephew went to West Point so she always lets anyone who shows up in uniform go to the front of the line."

After dinner we went to Jimmy Ryans. Listening to jazz at Jimmy Ryans was considered the "in" thing to do. We three girls shared a room at the Madison Hotel on E. 58th Street which is probably not still there. I don't remember where the boys stayed.

We were allowed four week-ends away first semester freshman year and I had one left. Pat was again anxiously trying to find some girls willing to go on a blind date to West Point. Three of us agreed to go. None of us had been there and we were curious to see what it would be like. West Point is only an hour from Vassar so we knew the taxi fare would be reasonable split four ways. The Academy sponsored dances, called Hops, with a full band for the plebes every night of the week after the upper classmen went home for their long Christmas break. The plebes were not allowed to go home for Christmas. We were there Friday and Saturday night with a different band each night, but the same date. My date gave me a 25 page booklet called the "Week End Pointer" with an inscription underneath saying, " Hand Book for Army Femmes." He made comments in the margins throughout the book which livened it up a bit. It has brief chapters on Accommodations, Clothes, What to Do, Cadet Vocabulary (military stuff, not swear words), and such. West Point is a very disciplined place. I do remember the beautiful grounds, but I don't remember my date or what we did.

All the freshman living in Main, about a third of the class, have to move to the other dorms their sophomore and junior year. They are replaced in Main by another third of incoming freshman and the entire graduating senior class. We were allowed to sign up for dorm preferences as a group. Ours was a group of seven and we requested any one of the four dorms that faced each other around a quadrangle. We thought they seemed charming and cozy after Main which housed hundreds of students. A few weeks later we learned we were assigned to Cushing. Our reaction was similar to hearing the sky had fallen. We were distraught. Cushing was the newer dorm, but not new enough to be exciting. It was way off to one side of the campus and had mostly single rooms which we were sure mostly attracted weirdoes and loners. What to do? We decided Patti, the drama major, should visit the Dean's office or whoever made this very bad mistake and plead our case. Patti, despite her oratorical skills and overly dramatic gestures, failed at the task.

We were all put together on our own corridor which helped ease our anguish. With only singles in Cushing, most roommates used one of their rooms for a bedroom and the other for a living room, study room combination. Mary Ann Connolly and Rachel Mehr elected to stay in their own single room. Dawn and I were assigned one large double sized room with its own bathroom, originally intended for a house mother. At first we were excited to have our own private bath. Feeling very clever, we wrote in colored pencil on the underside of the toilet seat, "It's so nice to have a man around." Colored pencils do not have the longevity of permanent magic markers which weren't yet invented. They do not do well in a moist environment. We soon abandoned our cleverness. The thrill of the private bath soon wore off. The bathroom on our corridor was only used by our friends so it was like a semi-private bathroom. So the next year Dawn and I asked for two singles and did the bedroom-living room split. My grandparents offered even more furniture, comfy, but not coordinated so the living room where we did our studying was an eclectic mix of styles and colors. The only furniture I remember is a formal pink and maroon striped loveseat, a non-descript couch and a light green arm chair with a noticeably sagging seat.

My grandparents encouraged me to visit them in Florida over spring break and said they had enough room for me to invite two girls. Dawn couldn't go, but Beth Vandenberg and Nancy Lowe accepted. The memorable event of that week was cruising on the inland waterway on a huge yacht owned by Mr. and Mrs. Roberts, friends of my grandparents. That evening the Roberts took all of us to dinner at the Everglades Club in Palm Beach, which my grandfather said was very exclusive and very, very expensive. Mr. Roberts told us that the chef, who only worked January through March, made $60,000 a year. That meant $20,000 a month. We were shocked. All three of us were studying to be teachers and the starting salary then averaged around $3,500 a year.

The boy I dated three week-ends at Princeton in the fall of my sophomore year was Steve Swensrud, who I also met on a blind date. He wrote me a letter in November and invited me to join a group of five girls, two of whom I knew and ten boys, all belonging to his eating club (similar to a fraternity) at Princeton called Cap and Gown to go skiing for a week after Christmas in the Laurentian Mountains near Montreal. There were two sets of parents going so it was well chaperoned and the ability to ski was no prerequisite. He said he'd only skied once.

All the girls were sleeping in a separate cabin from the boys and breakfast and dinner were included and I would not have to pay for any of that. I was really excited. I had a huge crush on Steve and was in awe of the fact that his father was the CEO of Gulf Oil Company. But I had only skied once and that was on a tiny hill near our house in Whitemarsh. I did own some skis and boots from 1948. I also didn't know then that skiing is a very expensive sport.

My father liked the idea of the two couples chaperoning and thought it would be a fun experience for me so I told Steve I would love to go. One of the girls in the group, Ann Moser, only lived a block away from me. Her boyfriend Gordon, a friend of Steve's and also a member of Cap and Gown, was going and would drive all of us to Montreal. We were to meet at Ann's house.

I didn't have any real ski clothes, just dumpy looking baggy leggings and a nylon pullover. Luckily my parents had not yet bought their Christmas present for me so we went shopping for a ski outfit. My father said I couldn't take my skis as they didn't have steel edges, but I could use his. Steve came up from his home in Pittsburg and slept in my sister Cynthia's room the night before we left. Previously I had sent him a letter regarding some details about the trip. His address was Park Mansions, Pittsburg, Pennsylvania, so exclusive that there was no need for a house number. Steve and my father really hit it off. My father pulled out his ski boots for Steve to try on and when they fit perfectly he urged Steve to keep them as he wasn't skiing anymore. Steve kept insisting on paying my father who finally replied, "Oh, Just send me a bottle of Scotch."

My father told me three weeks later that he received two bottles of Chivas Regal in the mail from Steve. In Steve's next letter to me he said he received a nice note from my father thanking him for the Scotch and that he was so relieved my father got it as sending liquor through the mail is strictly illegal.

The morning of the big ski trip, five of us headed out in one car for the six hour drive to Montreal. The next day we got up early, layered on our ski clothing, had a quick breakfast and drove the short distance to Mt. Gabriel. I remember mostly being more nervous than excited. I put on my father's six foot three inch skis and promptly fell before I moved two feet. I don't remember if I used my ski boots and adjusted my father's bindings to fit them or what I did involving boots. What I do remember too well is that I continued to fall and fall and fall. The skis were exactly a foot taller than me and I had no idea how to maneuver them. The only ski lifts I remember riding were T-bars with two people on each T. They worked well if the person you rode up with was about your height. The T-bar was an inverted T with the top of the T going under your fanny and the stem of the T being what you held onto. You leaned back on it lightly as it pushed you up the hill. But if the person on the other side of the T-bar was taller, the bar hit you in the middle of your back and at an angle. When you're five feet three almost everyone is taller, but what's worse is being paired with a child. Then the T-bar hits you in the back of your knees and you have to pray double that neither of you will fall as your survival to the top depends on you both staying upright.

First I was a nervous wreck attempting to get my skis lined up to be in the right position to get on the T-bar. When it started moving, I spent each agonizing minute being pulled up the mountain praying I wouldn't fall down. Once I reached the top I gazed out at the slope for at least five minutes, pretending to be waiting for someone. Finally I started traversing across the ski slope until I ran out of space and had to turn. I couldn't turn. The skis crossed over each other or started sliding down the slope. I could only be assured of stopping if I fell on my side. Then I scrambled up and turned my skis in the new direction. I often lit a cigarette and stayed immobile for awhile to calm my nerves.

This sad description I just gave of my typical ski day began two hours after we arrived at the slope. The first time I went up that dreadful T-bar and skied down the mountain I was in the company of friends or maybe instead of friends, I should say in the company of the girls who shared my cabin. When I finally managed to make it to the bottom, a few minutes after all of them, but not that many minutes, one girl suggested that we just meet at noon for lunch at the main lodge, and off they all went, quietly sliding away on their skis. Steve, who obviously had skied before, spent the next few days skiing with one of the girls in our group who was an excellent skier. I didn't blame him. I didn't like skiing with me.

At lunch it was suggested that I take a lesson. I signed up for a group lesson that afternoon. After our beginner group reached the top of the lift on one of the easier slopes, our instructor told us in his heavy French accent that he would ski down about ten feet and we were to follow one by one. By sheer grit I did manage to ski down ten feet and then turn enough to be in good formation with the two skiers who preceded me, but then when I came to a stop I toppled over and bumped into the person next to me who then bumped into the person next to her and like dominoes all four of us fell to the ground. It never got any better.

I have to think the instructor must have told me to rent some shorter skis, but he had a very heavy accent so if he did perhaps I didn't pick up on it. This also was the era when you were advised that the correct ski length was determined by holding up your arm and putting your hand across the tip of the ski. This method of selecting ski length didn't make my six plus foot skis freakishly tall for me at all. Many years later shorter skis were recommended, especially for anyone just learning to ski. I remember being worried I'd run out of money if I signed up for private lessons so I probably thought renting skis would also be too expensive. There were no Visa cards then. It occurs to me now that the only son of the CEO of Gulf Oil could have insisted I rent skis and even paid the fee! I was so clueless about the needed financial output for that sport.

The last day of that very long week we all decided not to ski. Steve was attentive and sweet and romantic and I sort of forgave him because I knew it was no fun to ski with someone who falls down all the time. When my husband was in graduate school and we lived just outside Boston, we skied many week-ends in Vermont and New Hampshire and I started to love skiing. Once we had children we took them skiing weekends in Michigan and out west over many Christmas vacations. It is a wonderful sport, but like all sports the key to success is not just determination, but the right equipment, the right instruction and the right amount of money. One final word about that infamous ski trip to the Laurentians. The black and white colors on my brand new expensive and sophisticated ski jacket ran together when they got wet. By the end of the week the ski jacket looked like a black and white tie-dye job that had run amok.

Skiing was not the only sport in which I was a novice. We had to take physical education classes freshman and sophomore year. I decided to make the most of it and become as athletically proficient as I could. Every semester I signed up for a different sport, all at the beginning level. The ones I remember taking were tennis, badminton, archery, field hockey and bowling.

Our bowling instructor was the head of the athletic department and probably in her seventies. She also was one of the judges who watched us parade half naked in front of her for the posture pictures. She said it was unladylike for girls to wear pants bowling. We typically wore Bermuda shorts which count as pants so we had to wear a skirt when we bowled! And this was the era before tights so when we squatted down to heave that bowling ball there was a lot of bare thigh exposed above our knee socks. So where is the logic there?

Even more absurd, if you wanted to swim in the pool you had to wear a bathing cap because hair might get in the drains and clog them up AND you also had to wear a bathing suit supplied by the college so lint from your own suit wouldn't enter those precious drains and cause havoc. I didn't know anyone who swam in that pool! Fortunately when Vassar went coed all those absurdities disappeared and a good athletic facility was constructed because the boys demanded it.

The only sport I was really good in was field hockey which I had played in high school. I was an aggressive player and a big scorer much to my surprise. In one game a puck hit me in the forehead above the eyebrow which was a very bloody affair. It was a Thursday and I was leaving for Princeton on Friday so I was very concerned it would puff up and look awful. Unlike male athletes, my teammates encouraged me to leave the game immediately, apply ice and just take care of myself.

I continued to see Steve after the skiing vacation. He came to Vassar for a couple of events and I went back to Princeton in the spring. We corresponded regularly and I saved all his letters which were funny and witty. He graduated that May and immediately started his mandatory two year stint in the Army. In the late fifties, every male after completing his education had to spend at least two years in one of the armed services. The last letter I received from Steve was postmarked Tokyo and I don't remember if I replied. I reread all his letters a couple of months ago and then googled him and discovered he was in the same class as my husband at Harvard Business School. I read that he was one of the early innovators in the venture capital community in Boston and went on to do the kind of financial things you can do when you have lots of money at your disposal. I was sad to read he died in 2011 after a long bout with cancer.

In 1954 at the end of the summer and just before my sophomore year, my father rented a cottage for two weeks at Point O Woods, another one of the Connecticut beaches on the Long Island sound. This time we were right on the water and it was a huge cottage. We needed more space because my grandparents were coming for one week and Mrs. Larson, mother's practical nurse, would also need a private bedroom.

My Mother needed a nurse because in January of my freshman year she was diagnosed with life threatening hypertension which put her in the hospital for weeks. She endured dozens of tests, but still no cause was found. The doctors learned that her pressure came down when she was at home and not confined in the hospital so they released her with the promise not to exert or stress herself in any way and to take a handful of pills many times a day. There were very few effective pills for hypertension then. To make sure Mother didn't do too much, Dad hired Mrs. Larson, a practical nurse who usually wore her white nurse's uniform, white stockings and white shoes. She came to the house every day for six months, not only to care for my mother, but also to help take care of Cynthia who was only eight years old.

I was given permission to invite Dawn for the whole vacation. My father rented a small motor boat for fishing and Dawn and I brought up our phonograph and many of our records. We had beautiful weather and loved being right on the beach. We invited Dig and John Ansty to come over for a few days. Dig was my current love interest and we had double dated with Dawn and John many times. John was not Dawn's love interest, but he was fun company. I don't know where the boys stayed or what we did, but I do remember we had as much fun as we had at Giant's neck.

We all celebrated my father's birthday on August 26th. My only recollection about that birthday celebration is one of the gifts. Mrs. Larson had bought Dad a present at one of those touristy gift shops they have around beach resorts. He opened all his gifts with everyone assembled around him. Her gift was a wooden placard, with the saying emblazoned in bold, bright letters, "Old golfers never die, they just lose their balls." My father managed to keep a straight face and thanked her, saying,

" What an appropriate gift. It is so true. I am always losing golf balls every time I play. Thank you, Mrs. Larson. I will put this up in my locker."

The rest of us had to hold our facial muscles rigid in fear of laughing and my dad never dared look at any of us, but he pulled it off brilliantly.

I 'm not sure what we did that first week, other than lie in the sun and dash in the water when we were too hot. We went fishing one day, but caught nothing edible. The Sunday morning at the beginning of that second week, Dawn and I were abruptly woken up by my father rushing into our bedroom, going over to the windows, pulling up the shades and nailing the windows shut with the head of his golf club.

"Dad, what are you doing?"

"I just talked to the neighbor in the cottage next door. He's heard there's a big storm coming and I'm trying to keep the windows from rattling and maybe breaking. You girls better get up."

It was windy, but the sun was out and we hoped it would clear up. When we finished breakfast the wind was much worse, dark clouds had come in and it was starting to rain. We couldn't find any news on the radio that sounded alarming. A few minutes later the same neighbor banged on our screen door and said he heard on a special radio channel he had that tied into the weather bureau, that they were now predicting a possible hurricane. He told us he was leaving right now and he advised us to leave right away too. He said he had owned his cottage for over a decade and had learned from past experience that it's best to leave immediately when a bad storm is predicted.

We only had the Studebaker at the cottage. There were seven of us including my mother's parakeet in a cage. We didn't take the time to pack anything as our neighbor had scared us. We collected everyone and headed outside to pile in the car. The wind was now so intense it was hard to walk and the rain was coming down sideways. My dad, mother and Mrs. Larson sat in the front seat and I, Dawn, my brother and sister squished together in the backseat with mother's caged parakeet being handed back and forth between us.

After about five miles down the road the rain had become a deluge and it was hard to see the road even with the wipers on full blast. The wind was also noticeably pushing the car around on the road which was frightening. My father said we would drive to my grandparent's house which was only an hour or so away.

After another ten minutes of scary driving the car started to make sputtering sounds and then just stopped dead in the middle of the street. That wasn't a problem as there were no other cars on the road. My father tried again and again to start it to no avail. We were in front of what looked like a farm house, the only house within sight. So draping a beach towel over his head, my father dashed toward the front door. I still have that picture in my mind of my father, a flapping towel like a shroud over his head, splashing up puddles of water as he ran up to that house. It was hard to see what was happening because the rain was so intense, but we couldn't see him at the front door anymore. After just a few minutes he came running back and jumped in the car, sopping wet, so furious he could hardly talk.

"What happened Dad, what happened?"

"I am going to buy the land next door to that God damn house and put up a pig farm. It would serve that woman right. She is a disgrace to the human race."

"What did she do?"

" Oh, my God that rain is fierce. First she told me to go around to the back door so I wouldn't get her hallway all wet. Then when I got to the back door she said I couldn't use her phone because she was waiting for an important call. I told her the wind was blowing us off the road and the car wouldn't start and I had six people in the car including children and she had the gall to say she was sorry, but she couldn't help me."

My father turned the ignition key in great agitation, stomped down on the accelerator and the car started. He later told me he was worried for our lives.

The storm was given a name, Hurricane Carol, and the weather bureau was lambasted for not giving any warning until a few minutes before it hit. The neighbor who had advised us to leave right away, had retreated to a nearby friend's house high on a hill with a view of the entire beach. His house was the end house on the beach, right next door to ours, and as he looked out his friend's living room window, he saw his house picked up by the wind and water like a child's building block and tossed head over heels, so to speak, down the canal that ran behind his house. It finally came to a stop over a block away from the beach.

We went back the next day and our cottage was the only one still standing in its original spot on the beach. There was nothing now to the right of us where our neighbor's house had been. All the beach front houses to the left of us had been pushed back all the way across the road that ran behind them and piled into the houses on that side of the road so nobody on that beach escaped without massive damage. Our cottage was the oldest one with a beach front location. The rest had all built huge cement breaker walls in front of their cottages to protect them from hurricanes. Our cottage was built up on telephone poles allowing the ocean to seep or rush underneath the house when a storm or a hurricane hit. It was still basically intact in the same spot. However, the long, front porch, the entire two story front wall and the side wall by Dawn's and my bedroom were missing. Our phonograph records and the phonograph itself were nowhere in sight. The only clothes we lost were the ones we hadn't hung up. The closet was still standing, just missing its door, with our clothes neatly hung up inside. The speed boat my father had rented for fishing was nowhere in sight.

Our insurance company only covered items damaged by the wind and covered nothing damaged by water. They said our clothes and records which were no longer in sight were water damaged, not wind damaged, so we couldn't collect anything. They won even though it seemed logical that the wind had blown off the cottage walls, not the ocean water. I don't know how the owner of the cottage did with his insurance company. The owner of the rented boat demanded my father pay him for damages. My father thought he would win the case in court, but felt sorry for the guy who lost everything and paid him what he asked. My father never did put up a pig farm next to that woman. He didn't even go back to tell her off which we all wanted him to do.

After I wrote this I went on the internet to learn more about Hurricane Carol. It started in the Bahamas so there was a lot of damage before it hit the Connecticut shore line. In New England there were over 1,500 houses destroyed and almost 10,000 badly damaged. Over 3,500 cars were destroyed and 3,000 boats. The deaths numbered 65 with 1,000 people suffering injuries and these statistics are just for New England. At that time, Carol was the costliest hurricane in the history of the United States. I knew they retired the numbers on the jerseys of famous athletes when they stopped playing, but I didn't know they did it with hurricanes. They do, and the name Carol can never be used again to name a hurricane. I imagine Katrina is retired now too.

In the spring I had a blind date in the city with Dave Pickard. He was from California, and studying architecture at the University of Illinois. Three of us, Nancy Lowe, Barbara Donavan and I took the train down from Vassar. I think Barbara had the connection and set up the blind dates. The boys had never been to New York so we felt very worldly showing them around. We went to the play, *Fanny* with Ezio Pinza and Walter Slezak. It was Easter week-end with beautiful weather and we all walked in Central Park and strolled up Fifth Avenue and felt very sophisticated. I had a marvelous time and really liked Dave who was on the diving team at Illinois. We corresponded and he invited me to the spring formal at his fraternity. I had no intention of going because of no money, but when I mentioned it to my father, he said that would be a wonderful experience for me to visit a big university and he would pay for the plane ticket. This, from a father who complained if I asked for a 10 dollar advance on my allowance.

So I went. His roommate picked me up at the airport as Dave had a big project due that day. Dave had arranged for me to sleep at one of the sororities, but I asked to sleep on the couch in their living room instead. I felt uneasy staying in a sorority house with girls I didn't know. I'm amazed I didn't worry about privacy or that I felt comfortable staying in a condo with two guys and only one bathroom. I'm sure Dave never expected me to fly out to Illinois, and I never expected to, but I did and we had a fabulous time although I have no idea what we did other than attend the Orchid ball and promise to write each other regularly.

Dawn and I were tired of having boring summer jobs and decided to answer a request we saw on a bulletin board for two babysitters, at two different homes, in Cold Spring Harbor, Long Island. The two mothers had gone to Vassar. We arranged an interview with the mothers in New York City and they liked us and we accepted the jobs. We arrived at their homes the last week in June and signed up to stay through the Labor Day week-end.

My family had three children, two boys, two and six years old and a girl of eight. In the interview I said I had babysat a lot. I had, but only for my own family. I rarely sat for anyone else. For this job I had to get up at seven for the early rising two year old and wasn't off duty until the eight year old went to bed at 8:30. It was a long day with no break at all plus I was miserably homesick which is an awful feeling. I don't even know how to describe its awfulness. I was only there four days when the parents went on vacation for a week and the children and I were moved to the grandmother's house. Now I'm even more homesick because the grandmother is not friendly and really acts like I'm a servant. I called my parents and probably cried on the phone and my father drove down to see me. I told the grandmother he was in New York for a meeting and could I just go out to dinner with him after I put the children to bed. She agreed.

My father was very sympathetic and consoling which is what I needed at that time. He said I certainly shouldn't quit while the parents were away and to remember I made a commitment and to try and see if I couldn't make it work. He wrote me a letter after he got home. I'm going to quote the first paragraph as it is typical of the advice my father offered me his entire life.

"David and Bobby sound like all kids almost six and two. Eight can be a tough age – the dawn of reason unrestrained by the eve of judgment. It's hard to grow up and share the stage with brothers and sister, particularly when you are old enough to realize what is happening. At eight you know what's happening and you rebel against it. Anyone who can help a youngster acclimate to this social inevitability, with the emphasis on the positive, has reason to be proud. What I am saying, Sally, is this: Bobbie needs a custodian, David has to be amused and Susan has to be

> developed. This is the challenge of your job. Anyone can be a custodian, most have the capacity to amuse, but very few indeed have the ability to inspire, encourage, lead and otherwise develop an eight year old. It is a lot of fun, and the job well done is very, very rewarding. When Susan gets through the 'trying out the new boss routine,' that even big boys and girls can't resist, I predict for you an interesting and satisfying two months. To help in the development of any human character is extremely rewarding. I know you're going to be up to the task."

I was not up to the task. I adored two year old Bobby and loved taking him on walks, giving him his bath every night, reading him stories. He was a delight like most two year olds. David liked to play games, especially card games and we did this when Bobby took his nap and after dinner. There was little television then, no DVD's, no easy entertainment. I remember knitting away at the argyle socks I was making for my new boyfriend Dave, while waiting for my turn at cards, and it would irritate David if I paused too long before resuming the game. And the pauses were long as I had all these plastic holders for the different color yarns bobbing away each time I crossed the knitting needles for another stitch. As I think about it, I don't blame him. Knitting argyle socks for your boyfriend or even your father was a very popular past time. I even knitted a pair for my grandfather. I was so unhappy that summer that producing a finished pair of socks somehow seemed important to me.

I just felt sorry for myself. I couldn't warm up to Susan, the sullen, constantly complaining eight year old. I wasn't that fond of the parents either. The thirteen hour days seemed unbearably long to me. The agreement was that I would get one day off a week, but I never took it as I wanted to have two, three day week-ends with Dave. My mind-set was just to survive the summer. I obviously hadn't absorbed a single sentence of my father's advice.

Dawn actually enjoyed babysitting with her family. The mother she worked for believed in life "au natural" and didn't shave under her arms or her legs. Luckily she had red hair so the legs weren't too bad, but when she raised her arm it was not an attractive sight. I don't remember the ages of Dawn's charges, but I do remember she liked playing games with the family. She wasn't homesick either. She hadn't even read my father's letter and she was following it perfectly.

Dave had to report to Virginia for his six week training for Naval R.O.T.C. and asked if I would like to have his car for those six weeks. Mr. and Mrs. Noyes agreed I could keep it on the side of their large driveway. When Dave delivered the car, we drove up to Longmeadow for a three day weekend and six weeks later when he came back to retrieve the car, we again went back for another long week-end. Hopefully I took advantage of having his car all summer, but I don't remember even having an opportunity to use it. Cold Spring Harbor is extremely hilly. The roads have sharp horseshoe curves all the way up the mountain just like pictures of the roads in

"Make It a Girl, Gracie"

Switzerland. The family belonged to a bathing club and we had to travel those curving roads to get there. Mrs. Noyes would never let me personally drive the children anywhere. It was scary driving so I don't really blame her. I was amazed that part of Long Island was so mountainous.

In the middle of those six weeks their family of five and I went for six days to what I would describe as a family camp in the Adirondack Mountains. I really enjoyed those six days. There was hiking and horse back riding and some other activities I don't recall and wonderful food. I had never had to diet or watch my food intake my entire life. I had a tiny waist and was confident I'd always be thin. The camp breakfasts were enormous with eggs, oatmeal, Danish pastries, French toast, bacon and more. I normally ate one piece of toast and a small glass of juice. Not at camp, I piled my plate high at breakfast. After hiking my appetite at lunch was ravenous. Dinner was even better and ended with wonderful desserts, even more wonderful than the delicious cookies at lunch. I was finding enormous pleasure in eating and eating and eating.

When we returned to their house, I had put on five pounds in six days. I now weighed one hundred and fifteen pounds, which meant two and a half more pounds in each thigh. I was only five feet three inches tall. I definitely looked fatter. I started dieting immediately. The first thing I gave up was sugar and cream in my coffee and I started drinking a lot of coffee to dull my appetite. The Noyes's didn't drink coffee in the evening so I was told to just save and drink the leftover morning coffee. It tasted just short of rancid, but I drank it anyway.

The first week-end I drove to Longmeadow with Dave we went to the Longmeadow Country Club to go swimming and that's when he put on a bathing suit and I saw his perfect body. He was a diver and a swimmer with wide shoulders, a tiny waist and hips and strong, muscular legs. Every proportion was model perfect. You might ask, "Why wasn't this spectacular body dating models of equal beauty?" His only flaw from physical perfection in the eyes of the world was his height, five feet six inches. I was only five feet three inches and that might be one reason he felt immediately comfortable with me on our first blind date. With those extra five pounds I gained, I felt fat and certainly not toned, but then toning wasn't a big thing in the fifties. We didn't even use that word. Nobody we knew worked out except professional athletes. You only walked when you had to get somewhere. Now I was seeing him in three more weeks and had these fat, jiggly thighs. I just had to take off five pounds. I don't remember if I succeeded with all five, but I do remember that I learned dieting is not fun at all.

I saved Dave's letters, about a dozen in all. They are funny and thoughtful about the trials of school, finding the time to practice with the diving team, the hard courses he had to take in architecture and such. He also discussed at length the problems with a long distance romance with me on the East coast and he on the West. But all of this was dwarfed by his protestations of affection and growing love for me and he even went into detail about why my personality was such a perfect match with his.

As I'm rereading all these letters a few months ago and only have one more to read, I think to myself, "Why did I break up with this guy?" He sounds so interesting and how wonderful to be loved like that. The last letter is one month after the one before which proclaimed how much he missed me and how we must figure out a way to get together soon. In this final letter, the first paragraph is chatty in a neutral way and in the second paragraph he tells me he is engaged, but proclaims that his fiancé is a lot like me and I would like her! I was as surprised rereading that now as I must have been when I first received it. I obviously wasn't broken hearted because I didn't even remember that final letter. I immediately jumped up and googled him and he did become an architect and he did stay in California and he did join his father's firm and his son is now the head of that firm. He also died two years ago.

One day before final exams in May of our sophomore year, Merrill went to the infirmary for an ointment for her rash and was immediately plunked in a hospital bed with German measles. We were all petrified we would catch it. Her first symptom before the rash was swollen glands at the back of her neck. All of us went around for a week with our hands constantly behind our ears checking for swelling. None of us got it and it certainly wasn't a serious disease, but sadly Merrill never returned to college. She didn't appear to dislike school. Perhaps the thought of restudying for all those exams did her in. She was my first friend with parents of a mixed marriage. Her mother was Episcopalian and her father was Jewish. He wrote her a letter EVERY single day at college. She never left her mailbox without something in her hand, unlike all of us. We asked Merrill what did her father possibly find to say every day and she said sometimes it was just the word, "Hello." Somehow, that made the letters loose some of their allure. Merrill had not been raised in either the church or the synagogue, but she was closer to her father. There also was a Jewish boyfriend from high school lurking around and that might have influenced her to quit school. She did marry him, but not for a few years.

First semester junior year I thought I would be very efficient with my time so I scheduled four of my classes in the morning, one right after the other, starting at 8 am. I figured I'd then have most of the afternoons free for uninterrupted study. I quickly learned it's hard to keep up your concentration on four subject matters for four straight hours all in a row with no break. Even worse, it's not enjoyable to then spend an entire afternoon studying with no interruptions. I also hated getting up early. Whatever had I been thinking!

I mentioned Dig Ansty only once, the time when he and his brother John visited us at Point O Woods just before the hurricane. Dig lived in a neighboring town twenty minutes from Longmeadow. He went to Manhattan College, a Catholic college in New York City. I never visited him at his college, but he came to Vassar many week-ends. He had the kind of sense of humor that makes everyone feel good. He never used his humor to put anyone down. He loved to talk and we would talk for hours.

One summer he came over to my house in Longmeadow at least twice a week and we talked and listened to music and probably made out a little and then he would hitch hike a ride home. I can't believe I didn't drive him home. Was I that lazy and inconsiderate? I remember I always offered, but I never insisted and he insisted there was no problem, he always found a ride. The fifties must have been safer and friendlier. Does anyone now pick up a hitchhiker?

During Christmas break, Dig and I took the train into New York to go to a jazz concert at Carnegie Hall with at least a dozen different bands. I was so excited anticipating it, but the concert was a disappointment to me. I was in college five years too soon. Jazz was the thing during my college days which I pretended to love when I was with a group or on a date with a guy who enjoyed reciting the background of his favorite sax player or drummer, but I didn't really love it. I did like Louis Armstrong, but my true love was and is folk music, but I had graduated by the time it became popular. The Kingston Trio is the first group I remember and I was out of college by then. They were followed by countless others and I enjoyed them all. Some are still around as senior folk singers, but most are long gone. My top favorites still are Simon and Garfunkel and Peter, Paul and Mary.

Dig wrote especially clever and funny letters to me in college. Of course I saved them. My plan was to read all these old love letters from past boyfriends when I was an old lady which explains why I'm reading them now! I don't still have Dig's letters. His wife died fairly young of a brain tumor. Dig and his brother John were visiting someone in Longmeadow and ran into Dawn's sister Jayne who still lived there. They chatted for awhile and Jayne told Dig he should look up Dawn as she was now divorced. Dawn lived in Boston and Dig in Providence, an hour or so apart and so they started dating.

They found they had a lot in common, both outliers, as Dawn puts it. It wasn't a long courtship. They knew they were in love and became engaged fairly soon. He had three older children and she had four, none living at home, so marriage would be just the two of them and they were both tired of being single. Naturally I didn't think it appropriate to save his letters to read in my old age since he was now engaged to and about to marry my best friend. So I told Dawn I would bring Dig's letters on our upcoming trip to Boston in two months because they were such funny and interesting letters. I thought he should have them to see how he described his thoughts and hopes when he was only twenty. She told me later that Dig was a wreck about those letters, not remembering what was in them. There were some mushy parts, but not that many.

On our long ride to Boston from Detroit I sorted the letters by date and of course reread each one. If Dig was embarrassed thinking my husband Ted might read them, he had nothing to worry about. Ted, unlike every woman I know, had no interest at all. So that night at Dawn's house I handed them over for Dig to read later in private. We all had a wonderful nostalgic time remembering all our adventures together and Dig put on a new record he had just bought by Louis Armstrong which brought back another sea of memories.

They were married soon after our visit. Dawn said those years with Dig were the happiest years of her life. He was diagnosed with chronic leukemia weeks before their wedding. He was told it's an unpredictable disease and he could live for decades. He lived only six years. Dawn now is also a grandmother to Dig's grandchildren and one of his sons lives just a few houses away from her in Dedham, Massachusetts. Dawn has retyped Dig's letters and put them in booklets for his children and grandchildren. Now, all you young people reading this, aren't you sad letter writing is a lost art?

I met Ted, my future husband, on, guess what, a blind date and I was a substitute blind date at that. It was an early weekend in October of my junior year, 1955. Ted's best friend Bob Raymond had just graduated from Princeton and Ted from Yale and both were waiting to go into the service. As I briefly mentioned earlier, in 1955 every male over eighteen had to register for the draft and then serve at least two years. The choices were waiting to be drafted as a private, joining R.O.T.C. in college which led to becoming an officer or enlisting in an officer candidate program which meant more than two years. There were exemptions if you were married or had children. Ted had applied and been accepted in the Naval Flight program which was a commitment of four years, but Bob had waited to be drafted so he only had to serve two years. Bob would start as a sailor and Ted would start as an Ensign, both in the Navy. Neither one knew exactly when they would be called up to report in, so didn't get a job that fall. They decided to have some fun and spend their time waiting to be called to active service by dating girls at different women's colleges.

Bob had the slim connection at Vassar. One of his classmates at Princeton had a sister whose best friend went to Vassar. The night of the double blind date, Mary Ann ended up in the infirmary and I agreed to step in for her. I remember when Rachel and I walked into the reception area to meet the boys, even though I couldn't see much, not wearing my glasses as usual, I knew I wanted to date the shorter one so I just angled up to him like it had already been decided. We had an enjoyable time and Ted asked if he could come back in two weeks to see me.

The whirlwind of college football week-ends, especially with blind dates, sputtered down to very few for the juniors and seniors at girl's colleges. We typically dated boys two years older and they had all graduated and most were off in the service. The current juniors and seniors at the boy's schools tended to date the freshman and sophomores or continued to date their girlfriends from their first two years. The flood of blind dating had dried up to a puddle.

So I was very available and ended up seeing Ted almost every other week-end that fall. At first he brought other friends from Yale who I then fixed up and we double dated. I learned more about Ted from those friends than from Ted himself. I found out he lived with his three much older brothers in the family home in Hartford and that he had been an orphan since he was ten years old. He had been very independent at a young age and was not that close to his brothers. He didn't have to account to anyone for his actions. That really intrigued me as I sure had to account to my parents and my grandparents. His friends told me Ted not only played the piano by ear at parties, but also played classical music and that he was the valedictorian of his high school class at Kingswood, an all boys prep school in Hartford. I knew he was a graduate of Yale and soon to be a Navy pilot. Wow! – I was impressed and smitten. I was also moved by how he had coped with no mother he could remember and a father, older than my grandfather, and then for only the first ten years of his life. I wanted to shower him with the love and affection he had missed growing up.

Over Christmas break Ted drove up from Hartford almost every evening. He went with me to all the Christmas parties and we had fun together. We also spent some of our days together and both professed we enjoyed the same things, going to the symphony, the opera, the ballet, the movies, attending plays. (In hindsight Ted might have lied a little about loving the ballet and opera.) Our thoughts were similar politically. We were both liberal arts majors and never ran out of things to talk about. And we were physically attracted to each other.

As our courtship continued, I managed to inch out of him more details about his life. His mother died of breast cancer when he was two. His father died suddenly of a heart attack when he was ten. His three brothers and one sister were nine to fifteen years older than him. During the Second

World War his siblings were either in the war or off in college so when his father died in 1944, an aunt and uncle moved into their house to take care of him until his older brothers returned from the war and his sister graduated from Sarah Lawrence. They were assisted by a housekeeper and a cook. When Ted was young he was raised by a string of nannies.

Ted's father was fifty five when he was born and his mother forty four. He was the surprise fifth child. In my letters to my grandparents I told them I was dating Ted Flynn from Hartford and it was a serious relationship. My grandfather became very excited. Both he and Ted's father had been officers in the Travelers Insurance Company and knew each other well. My grandfather was actually six years younger than Ted's father. My grandparents remember going to Ted's mother's funeral and seeing Ted, age two, being carried in for the service. My grandfather, who I adored, had a conservative waspy attitude about many things. He once told me Vassar was "pinko" when I was deciding where to go to college. And in the case of this serious boyfriend he said,

"Now, Sally, that's a Catholic family I wouldn't mind you marrying into."

He told me Ted's father was one of the most brilliant men he had ever met. He had formulated all the original actuarial tables still used by all the insurance companies. Many years after we were married I found out his father, Benedict Devine Flynn, had also been honored by the British government by being made a Fellow of the Royal Society of Actuaries. My sister-in-law told me that when Benedict Flynn died it made the front page of the Hartford Courant with a eulogy that covered half the page.

Ted left for the flight program in Pensacola, Florida in mid-January, but not before he met my grandparents. My grandfather peppered him with questions about relatives of his, asking how they were and what they were doing. Ted had never met any of them and didn't even know some of them existed. From then on whenever my grandfather referred to Ted he called him "that boy who doesn't know his relatives."

Ted and me at Vassar.

Sally at Gotthard Pass, Switzerland

6

The European Trip, Summer of 1956

The summer after my junior year five of us from Vassar signed up with a travel agency geared for students called SITA which stood for Student International Travel Agency. We picked them because they not only let us plan our entire trip, but arranged for a car and a guide-driver. The drivers were young men who not only drove, but read the maps, figured out the best routes, loaded the luggage which kept expanding on top of the car, confirmed the hotel arrangements and accompanied us on our adventures in the evening. In 1955 in

Europe, women usually did not go out in the evening without a male companion. It's considered safe, but it's not comfortable. For example in Italy you are followed by boys of all ages shouting, "Hello baby," or "Bellisimo, bellisimo." So having a male companion made it more pleasant for us. We were allowed to bring only one suitcase. I borrowed the biggest one I could find and bought a small selection of tan, black and brown outfits as our constant traveling meant anything needing cleaning had to be done in a bathroom sink. Our actual tour started July first in London and ended in Paris, August twentieth.

To get to Europe in the fifties you took a ship and they had ships just geared for students. To get to ours, the Arosa Sun, Dawn and I took a train to Montreal and then a boat train to Quebec where we boarded. Air travel was still a luxury, especially an overseas flight. The Arosa Sun was a large ship of 20,000 tons which took five days to cross the Atlantic, but those were five days full of fun and flirtations and drinking (ten cents for a whiskey sour) and sunbathing and talking to students from all over the country. It was exhilarating and fabulous fun.

There were classes in the morning on the history and customs of the countries in Europe and I'm not sure what else because we were rarely up before lunch. The five of us were in one state room with two sets of bunk beds and one single, very skinny bed. Our group was composed of Dawn and I from Longmeadow, Polly Lindert from Chicago, Nancy Lowe from Delaware and MaryAnn Connelly from Ludlow, a town in Pennsylvania so tiny her parents clicked a switch in their house to turn on the town's street lights. Honest! One of the deals with SITA was if the planner of the trip found four other friends to go with her, her fee was free. So we all split the saving of a free fifth person. In a sedan, we soon learned, having six in the car, five of us plus the driver, is a very close quartered event.

The second day we saw an enormous iceberg and I ran to get my brand new Christmas present camera. I had not used it yet and took a dozen pictures of that iceberg from lots of different angles. I had over fifteen rolls of film in my luggage so I decided to finish the roll by taking pictures of our room, the dining room, the deck, all of us. I knew my film had twenty-four pictures on each roll and I sensed I had taken a lot more than twenty four. I attempted to roll the film back up to remove it and the little metal wheel wouldn't budge. I went into a dark bathroom, opened the camera, felt around and didn't feel any strips of film. I had forgotten to put the film in the camera. We never saw another iceberg.

We had the second seating for dinner and we were all in love with our adorable waiter, Johan. The entire crew was adorable. They were mostly German or Italian. We were told it was against the rules for there to be any social interaction between passengers and crew.

There were three bars, a veranda and innumerable decks. I will quote a typical day from a letter to my parents. My parents and grandparents saved all my letters from Europe and rereading them has helped bring back so many memories of our wonderful trip.

> *"This is how our day goes. Arise at 12:30 pm, just in time for lunch. Eat quantities of food, there is quantity but not quality, and then feel half dead from still being tired and eating too much. Around 2:30 either play bridge, deck chair it, write letters, chat with others and so on. This really is the relaxing hour. At 4pm we go to tea and have tea and buns. Then we roam around a bit sometimes stopping in one of the bars. At 5:30 we go to an art lecture which lasts an hour. Then we go to our room and wash up and put on a skirt for dinner. Polly, Dawn and I just put on a skirt. Mary Ann and Nancy always get dressed to kill. You can wear Bermudas to dinner, but with only two pair in your suitcase you like a change.*
>
> *About 7pm we go down to one of the bars and have a drink before dinner. At 8pm we eat and are finished around 9:30. Next on the agenda is very likely a night of roaming and partying. We usually go to the aft bar and play a little bridge. Then everyone starts singing and so on and the party gets underway. At 12 pm the bar closes and everyone stocks up on wine bottles and goes to another bar, the room of which stays open. (Now try to understand that!) We discuss with all different students all kinds of things. Last night it was Napoleon and the French revolution. We are having the best time and the days just zoom by, probably because we get up after noon."*

We docked at Le Havre first and before we could even see land clearly, dozens of sea gulls flew overhead, giving me the most joyous feeling. All I could think of was that these were French sea gulls flying out to greet us from France and even though they looked like our sea gulls, they were French and I was about to spend six weeks in Europe. I was in a state of wondrous, intense joy. I was about to travel abroad for the first time. We disembarked the next morning in Southampton and took the train to London.

Nancy met an English boy, Andy Little, on the ship the first night and by the fourth night told us she was going to spend our four days in London with him. She was already pinned to Bob at home, but she declared that Andy and she were true soul mates. She was SO in love. We all had private rooms in our London Hotel near Piccadilly Square which was such a delight after being crammed five to a room on the ship, so we don't know what Andy and Nancy did and we didn't care.

The four days we were in London we saw everything a tourist still sees when in London. At St. Paul's Cathedral there was still extensive bomb damage from the war. They had constructed an elaborate mock-up in three dimensions of the repair work to be done to the altar plus an extensive addition to the church. We saw two plays, *The Boyfriend* and *Hotel Paradiseo*. We loved the matinees. At intermission they brought everyone a tiny tray with tea and a biscuit on it. What a delightful custom. We also saw a concert in the Royal Festival Hall just built in 1951.

After London we took the overnight train to Scotland, boarding at 10 pm. The next morning at breakfast, we reminisced over our ship activities and asked Polly wherever did she disappear to every night around ten or eleven. Polly had a funny, biting sense of humor and was always up for a new adventure. She said the first day on the ship she went to the ship's doctor for some pills for a stomach upset and the two of them really hit it off. Then, every evening around ten when the doctor got off duty, she would meet up with him and spend the next few hours with the doctor and the other officers in the huge recreation room just for officers. It had a liquor bar, a snack bar, ping pong tables, card tables, a phonograph with music and more. We were dumbfounded, sort of a combination of shock and awe. You weren't supposed to fraternize with the crew! And he was a doctor!

When we arrived in Edinburgh, we all commented on the vivid green lushness of the countryside. We later decided it was because of their typical cold, damp, rainy weather which we had the two days we were in Scotland. I'm going to quote from my letter again,

> *"The main street, Prince Street, is one of the most beautiful streets I have ever seen. On one side are the stores and on the other a deep glen like park with a cliff behind it on top of which is the Edinburgh castle. It's difficult to describe, but it's a beautiful sight. We saw the castle which is quite lovely, but not as awe inspiring as Windsor Castle. The most memorable part of the castle to us was a memorial built after the Second World War to honor the dead from both world*

wars. The "drawings" on the wall are made out of bronze and are of soldiers in uniform and usually in battle. The Scots wanted to commemorate everyone who partook in any way in both wars and hence, there was a picture carved into the stone of a canary and some mice with a brief inscription saying, 'This is in memory of all the canaries and mice that died in the First World War in gas experimentation.' That really brought tears to my eyes."

We had a heater in our room which operated only when the room's occupant filled it with coins every thirty minutes. Dawn and I would argue over how cold we had to be before we would fork over more money to that ravenous metal box. The other funny thing I remember is when we were in a small restaurant for lunch I asked for a napkin and was told it would cost an extra five cents. When we all looked aghast, the waitress, obviously with a sense of humor said,

"Well you do know you are in Scotland and we're known for being mighty tight with the money."

After two full days of sightseeing we took a day train, eight long, long hours, back to London to spend one night. The next morning we boarded a train to Dover, saw the white cliffs in a shroud of fog, and then got on a steamer to Ostend, Belgium where we were to meet our driver. The minute we got off the boat a porter who barely spoke English rushed up to me and asked where we were spending the night and I said Brussels. Fortunately a minute later we met our driver-guide, Roger, who asked where our luggage was and when told about the porter, broke into a sprint to a train on another track that was headed to Brussels. It was being loaded with luggage, including our luggage, if Roger had been less swift. Already we were glad we had a driver.

Our car was a Mercedes Benz which I called a Mercedes Bends in a letter to my parents. It took years before they stopped teasing me over that. We drove through Brugge and Gent, fascinating towns built in the Middle Ages. The houses were built practically hanging over the street. We had never seen roads almost narrower than a car. After dinner at our hotel in Brussels we went to a café with Roger and were mesmerized listening to him talk. His English was excellent and his charming French accent made him sound romantically foreign and possibly brilliant. He told us he had been in the French resistance during the war, but only embellished that fact with a few vague comments. During the winter he managed a professional theatrical group. He had been doing trips with SITA for about three years and enjoyed the traveling and meeting new young people.

After coffee at the café we walked a short distance and then Roger said we were to continue walking, but with our heads down and no peeking until we got to the middle of the square. Then he told us to stop walking and look up. We were right in the middle of a square, surrounded by tall buildings which were all indirectly lit with tiny white lights and we professed we had never seen such a gorgeous sight. We were used to outdoor Christmas lights with those large multi-colored bulbs. The buildings themselves also were spectacular. Gothic and Flemish Byzantine Roger told us, all trimmed with gold.

The next morning we had been underway only a few minutes when we saw the flashing lights of a police car right behind us. Roger pulled over and got out of the car. The policeman didn't look friendly at all. Roger talked for awhile, pointed to us in the car, talked some more and then the policeman threw his head back and laughed. He gave Roger a pat on the back, went back to his patrol car and took off. Roger came back to our car smiling, and said the cop thought we were German because of the Mercedes and when he found out Roger was French and we were American he wished us a pleasant trip. This was another reminder that the war was only a decade behind us.

When we left Brussels and starting driving through the Netherlands there was a dramatic change as the landscape suddenly became absolutely flat, but still very green. It was so flat you could see for miles and miles. We toured different spots for a day and went on to Amsterdam and fell in love with the beautiful canals trimmed with more tiny white lights. Even the ships in the harbor were decked out with strings of lights outlining their shape. It was the cleanest city we had ever seen.

That night Roger, who loved to talk and we loved to listen, started talking about Algeria. I spoke up and argued with him on several points. I could tell he was impressed by my rather extensive knowledge of the decades of problems between France and Algeria. I was pleased he was so impressed. This aura of brilliance I had going for me crashed down the next morning during our car ride when Polly announced to the passengers in general that Sally knew all that stuff because she had just written a term paper on Algeria for her history class.

We found a small restaurant in Amsterdam we loved called The Five Flies and went there both nights. We ordered Espresso, very new to us, served with a spoon lying across the top in which were two hunks of brown sugar. Brandy was poured over the sugar and lit. Great fun! Amsterdam was my favorite city after London. To quote my letter, "It had a certain foreignness and mystery of a romantic sort that London lacked."

I forgot to mention that when we returned from Scotland to London for that one night, Andy, the guy Nancy met on the boat, actually formally proposed marriage to her and gave her a week to give him her answer. The week was up and she had driven us nuts discussing all the pros and cons of marrying Andy ad infinitum. She decided to fly back to London and make the final decision. Hurrah – more room in the car and no more hearing about that Englishman's glories.

Our next destination was Bonn with a stop on the way in Cologne to see its spectacular church. We were all very sad because Roger had to leave us in Bonn. For insurance reasons, in 1956, just eleven years after the war, a Frenchman was not permitted to drive a German made car in France. In hindsight why didn't they just give us another car. Roger left us for another SITA job and was replaced by Klass Hille from the Netherlands. Klaas spoke four languages and was polite and seemed extremely competent and possibly dull. (Polly ended up calling him, in our company only, "that bigoted wooden shoe.") He did wear a variety of clean shirts every day. We had noticed that Roger wore the same blue dress shirt each day. It did not look like he laundered it overnight, but we still loved him.

Bonn had very few American tourists which was a nice respite. We did get to see Beethoven's house. Next on our agenda, Heidelberg, with a half day tour of its famous castle. We ate lunch at the Heidelberg University for twenty three cents. It was terrible food, but what a price! Only one night in Heidelberg and on to Rothenberg which I loved and I quote,

> *"Rothenberg was built in nine hundred and it has preserved that architecture with wide walls surrounding the city and the typical narrow streets with the houses hovering over the street. When you reach the outskirts of the town and walk on top of its walls which are built on a hill, you look down on a lovely green valley below."*

I can still pull up that picture in my mind. We had one night in Nurenberg and I will quote from my letter again,

> *" Nuremberg is an industrial town, but still rather quaint because of its age. I've never seen as much bomb damage*

> *as we did here. It's rather appalling because from the rapid construction which you see going on, you know how desolate it must have been ten years ago."*

We received a wire from Nancy telling us she would rejoin the tour in Munich. No rejoicing in our car. We enjoyed Munich. We each bought mugs at the original and enormous Hofbrauhaus, which made the luggage on the roof of our car grow even taller in height.

Salzburg, Austria, was one of our favorite cities and in 1956 no tourist knew about the Von Trapp family, made famous by the "Sound of Music." We took a cable car to the castle and again at night to a restaurant on the top of the mountain called The Winnkler. We drank wine and danced. On the continent, whenever we went out for the evening and always with Klaas, we were asked to dance by other men in the restaurant or cafe. It was simply the expected thing to do. I danced with a young German who wore the full lederhosen outfit and was in his last year of medical school in Vienna. He was working at the hospital in Salzburg for the summer. He asked if he could show me a castle called Heilbrun the next day. Of course I said yes. Now I will quote from my letter,

> *"The castle was built in the seventeenth century by an archbishop who loved to play practical jokes and experiment with water. Consequently, tourists, beware, water can shoot out at you from anywhere! He had one large stone table with*

eight stone slabs around it for chairs and in the center of each was a small eight figured design cut into the stone. By pushing a button under his chair he could cause water to shoot up out of this design in all the chairs except his. After the tour we didn't walk around the beautiful gardens because of the rain, but went to a nearby restaurant and had coffee with whipped cream while listening to a trio of a pianist, violinist and accordion player. They played the whole time we were there. What with the coffee, the music, the gardens, the soft rain, the magnificence of the castle and this adorable, charming German boy beside me I felt like I was floating on a cloud and I didn't want that afternoon to ever end."

We had timed our trip to arrive the opening night of the Salzburg music festival and had preordered tickets for *The Marriage of Figaro*. The female lead was Elisabeth Schwarzkopf and she had the most beautiful voice I had ever heard. I currently have a CD of her singing songs by Strauss and Schumann. Polly, Dawn and Mary Ann were all knowledgeable about music and preordered most of our tickets. Polly used to play the violin in the Chicago Youth Orchestra. Mary Ann sang in a group at Vassar that sang Baroque songs a cappella and Dawn played the guitar and the piano. Every August, still to this day, Salzburg has a world renowned music festival.

The next day we left for Innsbruck, Austria, and arrived mid-afternoon. We stopped in a café next to a park to get something cold to drink and quoting from my letter,

> *"It was Sunday so they had an orchestra in the park and everyone was dancing. So we danced and met quite a few young men. Two of them were policemen and two were electrical engineers and they asked to take us out later. We went to an outdoor drink and dance place which was fun."*

The next morning we left early for the seven hour drive to Lucerne. Now a quote from a letter to my grandparents.

> *"We stopped and bought cheese, bread and a monster bottle of wine for eighty cents and had a picnic in a grassy area on the side of the road. We felt very European and decided we would all try to return to Europe the next summer. Switzerland is just breathtaking. The horse shoe curves on the roads without any guard rails are also breathtaking. That night Klaas took us to a beautiful place on top of one of the highest mountains I've ever seen to hear a piano player and drummer he met while skiing in Switzerland last winter. They were marvelous and we listened to them for hours. The next morning I got my hair cut and then met the group at a watch place where they were madly purchasing watches. I broke down and bought a traveling clock for seven dollars which was no bargain.*
>
> *In the afternoon Klaas, Polly, Dawn and I went sailing on Lake Lucerne. What a wonderful time we had. We rented a sailboat and Klaas, the experienced sailor*

from the Netherlands, navigated. We stopped at one dock and went for a quick swim, but the water was too cold to be very inviting. That night we went to the movies to see an English film with German and French subtitles which was really amusing. I must tell you, Grandma, about the wonderful goose down pillows and goose down comforters. They are on every bed we have slept in. I am buying a goose down comforter as soon as we get home."

Polly on Lake Lucerne.

When Nancy left her "soul mate" in London to come back to the tour, she gave Andy half the money she still had for the rest of the trip. She rejoined the tour because SITA felt obligated to wire her parents that she had left. My husband later told me he dated a girl at her prep school and Nancy was notorious for constantly changing boyfriends. I felt sorry for her parents. They insisted she return immediately to the tour. She and Andy parted sweethearts, with the assumption Andy would travel to the United States to see her as soon as he could arrange it. Nancy felt they would probably marry after she graduated. If the details of which country they would then live in was discussed, I have no recollection. (Andy did come visit her that next year, but her parents had no interest in their only child living in England. Nancy married a stock broker from Delaware less than a year after graduation, introduced to her by her parents.)

Back to summer of 1956 - because she gave half her money to Andy, she told us she was a little short of cash. We saw the wad of travelers checks she had, but she insisted half of that had to go to buying her mother a watch in Switzerland. There was no such thing as a Visa or Master Card then. Your only resource was having money wired to you which is difficult if you change cities every couple of days. And I know she didn't want to tell her parents why she was so short on money.

So Nancy decided she would save money by skipping lunch. Our continental breakfasts and our dinners at the hotels were included in the cost of our trip along with all our sight seeing excursions so there wasn't much you could save on except lunch and gifts. The continental breakfasts were usually hard rolls with jelly and coffee which was not very filling so we were all ravenous by lunch time. We would all order our lunch and Nancy would say she'd just like water. Then she'd watch us eat, saliva practically dripping from her lips. If we paused for conversation near the end of the meal she would ask if we were going to finish that soup or salad or sandwich or whatever was on our plate. She was driving us nuts.

Nancy's roommate had left Vassar that June after our junior year to get married and Dawn and I, not knowing Nancy that well and being basically kind, thoughtful women, had asked her if she would like to join us as a third roommate.

Now we cannot believe we did that. How could we get out of it? We contemplated leaving Vassar. Not really. We were stuck and rather distraught over the thought of being with Nancy twenty-four seven.

Our next stop Interlaken was next and I'm going to quote from a letter to my parents again.

> *"Interlaken, Switzerland, is a delightful, quaint town really geared towards tourists. We took a horse and buggy ride for an hour and played Queen Elizabeth with a subtle hand wave. Only the children waved back. That night Klaas took us to a place called the Belvedere Bar where they had a lousy floor show, but the dancing was fun. I danced primarily with an Italian tourist who only spoke Italian and French. I managed to sort of talk to him by sputtering out some French words with my horrible accent despite taking French for four years. Since we both weren't French we spoke slowly and deliberately, carefully translating each word we wanted to say into the French word. The punctuation and grammar didn't matter, only the nouns and verbs. It sort of worked."*

Next day we got up at six am to go up the Jungfrau. I remember how those train tracks curved up the mountain just like the roads so you could wave to people in the train cars behind you as you coiled your way up the mountain. We arrived at the top, snow and more snow, and then went into the ice palace which was fascinating. We took a husky ride and I ripped my straight skirt. That ride was awful. We are suckers for any type of slightly different vehicle. We got back around 4 pm and Dawn, Nancy and I went swimming in a lovely city owned pool. You could float on your back and see the white Jungfrau in front of you and lush, beautiful, high green mountains behind you. Before we all got in the pool I surreptitiously, or so I thought, hid my wallet under my shirt and left it in a casual mound. When we got out of the pool a woman came over to me and said,

"You don't have to hide your money **here**. Nobody in Switzerland steals."

She emphasized the word here, implying that you do have to worry in America which of course is true. After dinner we had coffee in the park and then retired early for a change. Our room had a tiny balcony which overlooked a main street and Dawn and I sat there for an hour, fascinated by the antics of the people in the street, especially the boys trying to pick up girls. Milan, Italy is our next stop. Again quoting,

> " *Klaas spent the evening with an old friend so we decided to stay in and relax in our Bermuda shorts. We bought two bottles of wine, went up on a lovely balcony of the hotel, played bridge and felt very mellow after that wine. A couple of bellhops, busboys, whatever, came out to join us and it was really fun. The next morning we took a quick trip to see DeVinci's Last Supper and then we piled into our car with*

the luggage on top being almost taller than the car itself, and headed off to Venice."

We left the car at a garage outside Venice and took a gondola to our hotel. That gondola ride was a real thrill for all of us. That night we went to St. Marks Square and had coffee and drinks while hearing a band play. We had a tour of the city in the morning and decided to go to the beach, called the Lido, in the afternoon because it was really hot. When we got there we discovered the changing rooms were all taken and there were signs everywhere saying changing in the bathrooms was prohibited. None of us spoke Italian, but you could tell by the black arrows and the universal word toilet what they were saying, but we were so hot we decided we would illegally change in a bathroom stall anyway and if yelled at, say we didn't speak Italian.

The bathrooms had attendants and they must have peeked underneath those doors because we changed quicker than it takes to go to the bathroom, but they suspected something and banged on our doors, yelling in Italian. We just stripped, threw on our bathing suit, grabbed our bag of clothes and ran out with them screaming after us, but we made it to the beach. Polly, of all people, lost her courage and didn't change and she was even wearing sticky, hot nylon stockings. It's those stockings that probably did her in. They're hard to peel off fast on a hot day, especially with someone yelling furiously in Italian at you. The rest of us went swimming and that beautiful blue water felt wonderful.

It was a lovely beach, very spacious with soft sand. We left around 5:30 to head back to our hotel and change for dinner. I fell in love with the Italian ice cream they call gelato. We had never heard of it at home.

Our next stop was Florence. It was now July thirtieth and we're more than halfway through our trip. We all wanted this trip to last for months, not weeks. That night we went to the Uffizi Galleries which happened to be open. Florence was our most fascinating city. The art work was so special – the Medici Palace, Michelangelo's David, all the beautiful churches and a fabulous Mozart and Strauss outdoor concert one night. We all bought gorgeous leather gloves, a staple in one's wardrobe in the fifties, at a tiny shop right on a famous bridge over the River Arno. The bridge is called Ponte Vecchio and we were told it was the oldest bridge in Florence. There have been shops on that bridge since the thirteenth century. We didn't begin to have enough time to see everything we wanted to see and we all vowed that we must come back. We met someone who taught English at a Berlitz school the year after she graduated from college and we decided that is exactly what we would do. Polly's the only one who actually did it.

Everybody loves Rome and we were no exception. We had a total of three full days with scheduled tours three mornings and three free afternoons to do whatever we wanted. It was disappointing that the coliseum was off limits due to its deteriorating condition. At the end of each afternoon we loved sitting on the Spanish steps people watching, while licking a cone filled with that fabulous gelato. Now I am quoting from another letter,

> "On one of our strolls we met five Italian boys. Two could speak a little English, one a little French, (Joseph, the one I dated) and two only spoke Italian. They were very nice and walked us back to our hotel. Joseph, my date and Nello, Dawn's date, were students at the School of Architecture in Rome. Two others worked and I don't remember what the fifth did. We made plans to see them after the opera that night."

We saw Puccini's *Turnadot* at the Baths of Caracalla. What a beautiful and impressive spot for an opera. It's the biggest stage in the world and it's outside. It used to be the elaborate baths where the Romans bathed. The grounds facing the stage hold 20,000 people. The stage itself is between two high towers and going out from each tower is a wall. Everything looks really ancient, which of course it is. We enjoyed it so much we got tickets for Verdi's *Aida* the next night and that was even better. In fact it was absolutely spectacular. They had live horses and even camels and elephants on the stage. During intermission we had hot coffee with Brandy in it, so European we thought.

Our last night our new Italian friends took us to a lovely place with a huge patio outside where everyone danced. Joseph and I talked in pigeon French to each other which worked well as both of us just literally translated our Italian or English word into the French word. It was still a rather sparse sharing of ideas, but it worked.

Sunday morning we left early for Sorrento and traveled all day, stopping in Naples for lunch and Pompeii for a few hours, not nearly enough time. It had not been that extensively excavated in 1956, but enough to make us awestruck by the details

Mary Ann, Nancy and Klaas.

of that demolished city. You could see the plumbing pipes which brought water to all the houses. It was amazing to us that they had running water so many centuries ago. Each house had a courtyard in front. Hard to imagine the horror of their sudden death in 79 AD as Mt.Vesuvius erupted wiping out the entire town and its people in 25 hours, but preserving them under twelve feet of pumice and ash until excavation began hundreds of years later.

We arrived in Sorrento at 6pm. SITA had screwed up for the first time. The hotel had no record of our reservations and was full. Klaas called up SITA and got approval to get our room in Capri one day early and to rent a private boat to take us across to the island. We were ecstatic over the error. Dawn and I shared a room in a small villa with a private bathroom and a roomy terrace and we planned on doing nothing but lying on the beach for two days. Now I'm quoting from two postcards,

"This postcard shows the square in Capri where we have coffee at night and watch the most fascinating people you've ever seen walk by in the strangest outfits you can imagine. We went to Gracie Fields pool today and I have a bright red glow and hurt."

I can still clearly remember Gracie Field's pool. It was on a hill like all of Capri and from the pool area you looked down at the ocean below. It wasn't large, about the size of a pool at a country club. I remember how relaxing it was to not have any tours lined up and to be able to just lie in the sun and do nothing. We rented lovely lounge chairs next to the pool and hardly moved out of them for two days. I just reread SITA's brochure with suggestions for Capri, "Suggest a climb to Tiberius by donkey." That was not even considered!

We took a steamer back to Naples and headed for Orvietto, a charming walled town that I loved. We were only there a half day, but I remember it like yesterday. But I will quote from my postcards and letter to my parents,

"Orvieto is a walled town built on top of a huge rock that used to be an Etruscan town before the Romans and then became a Papal refuge. It was very important during the crusades. The cathedral is lovely with striped maroon and white walls and pillars. It was originally built to

commemorate a miracle – a disbelieving priest suddenly being overwhelmed with the feeling that Christ's body was actually in the communion and when preparing it, he found blood not wine on the napkin.

Our hotel is very old and neither the guests or help speak English, a kind of fun change. Even Klaas doesn't speak Italian. We ate dinner out on the front porch at a long banquet type table, very thin in width owing to the narrowness of the porch. It was like sitting in the middle of a main street. We celebrated Nancy's twenty-first birthday here with a delicious heavily flavored rum cake, four bottles of Orvieto wine and two bottles of champagne. We finally left our banquet table at 11:30 and stumbled up to bed, sweetly smashed. The next morning at breakfast we saw a funeral processions from that front porch. It was all on foot, at least a hundred people with women all wearing black dresses, black stockings and waist long thick black veils. Even the children were wearing black. The coffin was carried through the streets by four men. It was really quite a somber moment."

The next morning was an all day drive to Pisa to see the leaning tower and it sure was leaning. I read that they have now stabilized it. We saw the tower and the Baptistry and church and that was it. Now, we had another long drive to Rapallo on the Italian Riviera but we broke it up with a visit Sienna on the way. I have no letters or postcards about Sienna which surprises me. My husband and I visited it about fifteen years ago and found it to be a charming, delightful town. Now I'm quoting again,

> *"Our hotel in Rapallo was magnificent with a huge private balcony. We went swimming immediately from a very rocky beach. The ocean was that beautiful deep blue color of the Mediterranean. We decided to get pizza for dinner on our last night in Italy. All through Italy they only seem to serve individual pies, with a diameter of about ten inches, nothing like the big ones we have. You also have no choice of toppings, but most of them have tomato, cheese and a little meat. We also learned it's socially incorrect to eat it with your fingers as we do at home. Klaas also informed us that it is a gross social error in Europe to go to the wash room, as he called it, after finishing a meal. For the past few weeks the minute we finish lunch at a café or restaurant or dinner at our hotel we all get up and troop into the ladies room. He could have told us sooner.*
>
> *I've loved Italy, especially Rome and Venice. The poverty in Naples was appalling. The toddlers all run around the sandy streets with no pants on. The countryside in southern Italy looks so sun baked and dry. The hills are yellowish*

Dawn in Rapallo on the Italian Riviera.

brown with few trees, but strangely it also has a certain beauty and tranquility, especially along the sea."

I must tell a story a guide told us about a home in Tuscany. Residents are not allowed to make any exterior changes to their home to preserve the ancient feel of the area which is what brings the tourists in droves. His four hundred year old house was way too dark so one year at night he painted the outline of a window on one side of the house. The next year he painted shutters on each side. This time he waited two or three years so all the villagers were used to seeing that "window." (I guess they tattle on each other if someone makes an unauthorized change) After five years he cut through the brick and had a real window that let in real sunshine and nobody was the wiser. It might be an apocryphal story, but I loved it never the less.

Nice was our next stop. It had another rocky beach, but you can rent these mattresses that lie on a platform and it's really comfortable. Now I'll quote,

"The aquamarine water is gorgeous. The girls all wear bikinis and they have scrumptious figures. (Only a foreigner or an exhibitionist wore a bikini in the United States in the fifties. A two piece bathing suit in America then, always covered the naval!) *We went to the casino at Monte Carlo and were disappointed. It was nothing very special. The second night we went to the casino in Nice where they had dancing on a floor about*

15 feet by 10 feet and there were 60 or more couples trying to navigate around that tiny dance floor. All you could think about were the hot, teaming mass of sweating, smelly bodies. Joseph, the boy I dated in Italy, had told us to visit The Hot Club in Nice as they had great jazz. Some boys we met at the casino said they would take us there. We finally found it and the jazz was a phonograph with records. Big disappointment! It was a dark, mysterious looking room about the size of our living room with tiny tables all around. On the walls was what looked like soot to my myopic eyes with letters scribbled all over the soot. The boy I danced with most of the time said, and thank goodness he spoke English so I can repeat what he said, that when you have a particularly enjoyable time you are to scrawl your initials in the soot on the wall.

At the casino I had danced with a French boy and in my best French asked him what I thought was a typical small talk question and despite my four years of taking French, he couldn't understand a thing I was saying. At The Hot Club, every time I uttered a French phrase, in my most cosmopolitan manner, the boys would all laugh uproariously. I decided I would only speak French to clerks and waiters who at least are polite enough to ask you to repeat it in English instead of laughing. But we had a fun, fun evening."

A long drive to Avignon, saw the Palace of the Popes, and now I'm quoting again,

> "Three of us have a fascinating room. It looks old and has a badly peeling ceiling. The walls are gold and red brocade with four huge, gold trimmed mirrors on the walls. There's a large marble circular table in the middle of the room, a mammoth couch, two smaller tables, a desk about five feet square, and a bureau. Two monstrously large windows have an elaborate valence at the top and red brocade curtains hanging down. Even Matisse couldn't paint something this colorful and wild. We just had coffee in the square after dinner and then returned to our delightful room and ordered a bottle of wine and wrote letters."

The next stop was Vichy and it took a full day to reach. Quoting again,

> "After dinner we took a stroll around town and ran into a parade which was celebrating some Catholic holiday the next day. The leader carried a giant sparkler and about two hundred people followed him around. They finished at city hall and set off a series of firecrackers. It was a spectacular sight. Vichy is charming and reminds me of what I've read about Sarasota Springs because of its Vichy water. We decided to skip the next stop, Tours, and drive directly to Paris. Klaas is excited because his girlfriend is meeting him there so we gave him a farewell party in our room with cake and wine we ordered from the hotel."

We all loved Paris. The first day we went on an all day sight seeing tour by bus, the city sights in the morning and Versailles in the afternoon. The next morning we shopped. I bought a black sheath dress for a fortune which the salesgirl pulled in at the back when I tried it on. She said alterations were free and would be done in an hour if I wanted to come back. I agreed because I loved the idea of owning a chic, black dress from Paris. We were rushed when we returned to the store so I didn't try it on until we were back at the hotel. It looked like a sack on me. That seamstress did not achieve the effect the salesgirl did when she wadded up a fistful of fabric at the back of the dress. I never wore it.

We went to the Eiffel Tower, wanted to go to the top, but you pay more for each level and we were all running out of money so we stopped at level one and had lunch. That night we went to the Folies Bergere at the Music Hall, a disappointment, and the night after to the opera to see *Boras Godunnov* which was great, but the Baths of Caracalla had spoiled us.

Another day of touring and hours spent at the unbelievable Louvre. Two of the girls, I think it was Dawn and Polly, decided to go to a spiffy Parisian hair salon and get their hair done. What the rest of us did I don't remember, but I do remember rushing back to the hotel to see how they looked. They hated their hairdo, came right back to the hotel and immediately washed their hair without even letting us see how sophisticated or funny it might have looked. We were really ticked off. We had looked forward to a good laugh.

After four busy days in Paris we felt seeped in culture and so very, very sad our wonderful, wonderful trip was over. We left for Le Havre via boat train and boarded our ship, the Arosa Star, the sister ship to the Arosa Sun. The Arosa Star was half the size of the Arosa Sun and everyone except Polly got miserably sea sick. The sea was so rough it took nine days to reach Montreal. We came over in five days.

I remember considerably less about the return trip. Everyone's mood was less exuberant. Our fun and wonderful adventures were over and most of us were returning shortly to college. I don't even remember our sleeping arrangements. None of us had a shipboard romance. Polly didn't fraternize with the crew. We didn't roam from bar to bar at night. We spent at least two days in our bedroom trying not to throw up. We were told it is better for sea sickness to stay up on the deck which we did. I took pictures of the boat dipping way down so you saw a wide ocean before you and then rising way up so you only saw sky. It seemed like at least a ten foot range to me. We did play bridge on the deck, but I don't remember partying and I doubt if they held any language or cultural classes. It was a long nine days, much longer than scheduled due to the bad weather conditions. It didn't rain, we just bounced up and down.

My parents met me in Montreal as planned as did Dawn's parents. My grandparents also came as a surprise to me. The plan was to have a welcome home dinner celebration in Montreal and then spend another day or two sightseeing before heading home, but tragedy struck. My grandmother suffered a minor stroke, but not that minor, just before they arrived in Montreal. They went to the local hospital and were told to get my grandmother home as soon as possible. I am fuzzy on the details, but I know we had two cars and my father drove like a madman and I followed him in the other car trying to keep up. The stroke partially paralyzed her left side. She recovered her ability to walk with the aid of a walker, but her left arm never functioned properly again. My grandmother was only sixty two and her vigorous, dynamic personality was taken from her. She still functioned mentally at a hundred percent, thank goodness, but she couldn't do much physically and she had always been so active and energetic, a real force in my life.

When I got back home there was a letter awaiting me from Josef who I had met in Rome. He spoke little English and we had conversed, so to speak, in French. To be honest he wasn't particularly attractive and the conversation certainly wasn't sparkling as we both mumbled along in rudimentary French, but I must have given him my address and he must have used an Italian/English dictionary to help him write it. I will quote,

> *"Dear Sally, Sudden excuse my horrible English. As for as I know probably this letter is for you indifferent, but I hope that you know how I think to you no how a friend but how a lover. Because sincerity I love you, and as for you no is so. Answer me and tell me that you think of me. My father is very happi if you in future go in Roma in my home. I*

know that to seem strange how I love you but I same no to comprehend why. I know only that truly is no and only this is important. I no speak in this letter of other because only for to write this is to fatigue very much.   A little kim, Joseph"

I must have written back because I received a second letter saying how thrilled he was to get a letter from me. I don't remember if I wrote back again, but I will quote from his third and last letter which shows better English and now friendship, instead of love.

" Dear Sally, A month ago I have written to you a letter, that I think you have not received because till to-day I have not yet received any answer. On the contrary I should be very sorry if you did not want answer me because I feel a sincere friendship towards you and I wish to know your news. How are you dear Sally? I hope very well, do you remember Italy and Rome? In your latest letter I knew that you was writing a book about the children. Your very interesting on it and I joy you my best compliments to you. I remember you, so especially now that it is 'Sad winter' and I spend many hours at home in my room to study than my mind goes to my best friendships. Remember to send me your fotographic, and please write to me as soon as jumble, I do not want to have a delusion also this time. Good-bye dear Sally, Good wishes for your studies and a little Kim from your sincere, Joseph."

All my photographs of the trip were developed as slides which was typical then as colored photographs were extradinarily expensive. I did end up with over three hundred slides which I put in trays that fit into my projector and showed them many times. When my two older children saw the slides they couldn't get over how uncrowded the streets in Europe were in 1956. Sadly I didn't convert them to DVD's in time and the slides are now badly faded with that century old sepia tint. I kept them in their cases in a dark closet, but I guess sixty years is old age for a slide.

Nancy and I at graduation.

7

Senior year, 1956-1957

Dawn and I arrived back at college before Nancy. All the seniors were in Main and our assigned room was a suite of three rooms on the second floor, a real improvement from our bowling alley room on the fifth floor freshman year. The bedroom was still long and narrow and we pushed our two beds parallel to each other with a night stand in the middle and shoved Nancy's bed and dresser to the other end. That act already made us feel better. One room just had two of the dressers and a wall of closets. The third largest room was our living room, empty until a formal request was made to have our stored furniture delivered. We remembered that

Nancy had a matching loveseat and chair and hassock in a red chintz fabric which we knew would look considerably better than our mismatched accumulation. When she arrived she asked if we could use her furniture. We enthusiastically agreed. Having her as a third roommate was losing some of its horror.

It was now possible to pay to have a daily morning newspaper delivered to you at Main which was left at the entrance to the dining room. I ordered The Herald Tribune instead of The New York Times because I was told it was a friendlier newspaper. I also arrived on campus with my first pair of contact lenses which Bob Decker had prescribed. He and his wife Betty had lived with us in Whitemarsh. I was his first contact lens patient. His inexperience was unfortunate as I had a terrible time with them and he was too far away for any adjustments while at college so I only wore them at dinner. It was a joy to see without glasses, but it hurt so much. Bob had set up practice in Watertown, Connecticut and he and Betty had two boys.

I was assigned as a practice teacher to a third grade class in Poughkeepsie. I was to assist the teacher and also to teach lessons I prepared myself. I went there three times a week for one semester. I enjoyed it but it was intimidating having the teacher sitting there staring at me and sometimes the stare looked more like a glare. Mine did a bit of eye rolling too.

I did one social experiment we had talked about in child study class at Vassar where each student in the classroom is to write down the three students they would most enjoy sitting next to and the three they would not like to sit next to. The intent was to understand the social dynamics within the classroom. Then I made this huge interconnecting chart with different colored lines going from one person to another which was supposed to give the teacher a mind blowing revelation of the social interaction among all her students. It took a lot of time and I proudly showed it to the third grade teacher who glanced at it briefly, then handed it back, saying,

"Hmmm, very interesting. Whatever are you going to do with it."

I had no idea really what I would do with it. It told me who was very popular and who wasn't, but as a practice teacher three times a week for only another month, she was right, I wasn't going to do anything with it. That semester was the extent of my practice teaching. It was not nearly enough experience, I learned the next year, when I took over a classroom in a rural area of Florida with forty-four fifth graders with IQ's ranging from sixty-five to one hundred forty-four.

The fall of my senior year I went on another blind date to Colgate College. Beth Vandenberg, a good friend, fixed me up with her boyfriend's roommate, John Ring. I honestly have no recollection of this at all except in my scrapbook are three football programs with Colgate playing Syracuse, Army and Cornell and John Ring's name next to all of them so I obviously went there three week-ends. I don't recall any romantic leanings toward John. I didn't even remember his name until I read it in the scrapbook. In one of my mother's letters she commented liking Ted so much better than that John Ring. When I read that letter before I opened my scrapbook, I thought, "Who is John Ring?" I now wonder how my mother even met him.

Beth was one of my favorite people. She was on a scholarship so other than freshman year she lived in Ferry Cooperative House, called Co-op for short. It was designed like a house and it was available only to scholarship students who had to request to live there and they all wanted to live there as it was a super arrangement. The students took turns buying the food for the dorm, cooking it, doing the cleaning, basically running a house and they got a huge reduction in their room and board expense.

Beth and Polly were from the same town outside Chicago, but decided not to be roommates. Beth was assigned a room in one of the dorms on the quad freshman year and her roommate, I now think, was probably autistic. We didn't know the word then. We all called her psychotic. It was a hard year for Beth and she came over to see us a lot freshman year. Beth had a twin sister and three older sisters. She was the fourth sister to go to Vassar on a full scholarship.

Her dad was a farmer and I remember when we were all talking about who had the worst summer job, Beth said her worst was the summer she had to help her dad plant or harvest, forgotten which, onion plants. She spent the entire day in the hot sun bent over at the waist. She won that contest. Senior year her dad sold the farm to a developer.

"Make It a Girl, Gracie"

The city had creeped up to his farm and it was now prime residential property. He wrote to Vassar Beth's senior year and said he wanted to take her off her scholarship because he could now afford to pay the tuition and he was so thankful to Vassar for being so generous to all his daughters. The college allowed Beth to stay in the co-op house for her senior year. We had all wanted Beth to come with us to Europe, but she couldn't and I've forgotten why and that's how Nancy joined us.

Beth married her Colgate beau soon after graduating and I have never forgotten his rhythmic sounding name and home town, Charlie Tillou from Nutley, New Jersey. He became a single engine jet pilot like Ted, but in the Air Force. They were stationed in Germany and Beth told me she couldn't get any prepackaged food like cake mixes and macaroni boxes and such. So I sent her what I called a Care package of all those foods. A few months later I got one of my letters addressed to Mr. and Mrs. First Lieutenant Charles Tillou, back in the mail with "Deceased" stamped on the envelope. My first thought was about the stupidity of the Air Force for making such a stupid and scary error. I had just received a letter from Beth! But I did feel a little uneasy and called Polly on the phone, just to confirm it was an error.

"Oh my God, I am so sorry. I can't believe I didn't tell you. I am so, so sorry. Charlie was flying over France and his plane was in a mid-air crash with a civilian plane that was way off course. Both pilots were killed. Beth is still in Germany packing up, but I'll call you when I know something."

I was devastated and broken hearted for Beth. It was my first death of a close peer. Beth decided to move to California and having been a child study major like Polly, Dawn and me, she found a teaching job immediately due to the explosion of people moving into California. She was single a few years and then met and married Ron Lyon, a professor at Stanford. Ron was six years older, divorced with two sons. He and Beth had a daughter and a son. Dawn and I have seen Beth and Ron at three Vassar reunions. They are a delightful couple. So this story has a happy ending.

Now that we all loved the opera, in gloomy November, Merrill, Dawn and I took the train into the city to hear "*Rigoletto*" at the Metropolitan Opera House. (I now know you're supposed to say "hear" the opera and not "see" the opera!) In my notes it said, "Saw the debut of Negro lead as Gilda. She was very good – Mattiwidda Dobbs." Negro was not considered a derogatory word in the fifties. In March, another dreary month, three of us went again into New York to hear "*Carmen*." We had really become fans of the opera.

My very first professional ballet was in January when I saw at The New York City Center of Music and Drama, a program that said it combined the highlights of *Swan Lake* with the highlights of *The Unicorn, the Gorgon and the Manticore*. Maria Tallchief danced the lead and it was a memorable night for my first ballet.

Dawn and I went into New York two different times to see the plays, *The Diary of Anna Frank* and *Too Late the Phalarope*. I loved the Anna Frank book and the play and had also loved the book of *Too Late the Phalarope*, but we both thought the play was too confusing. Whenever we went into the city we stayed at the Roosevelt Hotel, a huge hotel with a neglected third floor in terms of décor and private bathrooms. Two large bathrooms, one for each sex, were down the hall. It only cost nine dollars a night and for that we easily gave up the private bath. Vassar students and alumnae could get a discounted room at The Waldorf Astoria, but it was still fairly expensive.

Vassar had an outstanding Music and Drama Department. Both Jane Fonda and Meryl Streep were drama majors at Vassar. I have not mentioned any of the fabulous musical programs and plays that were put on by Vassar students in my four years. The majority of the musical presentations highlighted the classical composers. We had an all Mozart program, a Bach and Beethoven combo, a Chopin evening, all with Vassar students playing the instruments, but sometimes there was a visiting musical group.

There were two singing groups at Vassar who performed for us and other colleges. I cannot remember the name of their groups. The a cappello group wore identically colored dresses and were very formal and proper looking. The other group wore jeans and played the guitar as they sang. Polly and Dawn tried out for that group. For the tryouts they sang the song, *When The Saints Come Marching In*, and went up the keyboard on their guitars for each verse, playing it in probably five different keys. They practiced for our little group and we all thought it was marvelously impressive. They didn't make it into the group so we all decided it had to be political.

To help keep these memories alive, I'm going to list some of the plays we saw put on by our outstanding drama department : *Ondine* by Giraudoux, *Heartbreak House* by Bernard Shaw, *Six Characters in Search of an Author* by Pirandello, *The Three Sisters* by Chekov, *Amahl and the Night Visitors* by Minotti, *Him* by e.e. Cummings, and *Noah* by Andre Obey.

That reminds me of a dismal event my freshman year. I decided to try out for a part in a play the drama department was putting on. I didn't think I would like acting, but my mother had been such a star in dramatics I thought maybe I had a hidden, unrealized talent and I should find out. I don't remember which part I tried out for, but I'm sure it wasn't the maid with only two lines and that is the part I was given. I had a problem even with just two lines. I worried I would forget them or come in at the wrong time. I hated rehearsals as they were so time consuming I had to study until midnight to get my homework done. I didn't even like standing on the stage with people looking at me. I quickly learned I had absolutely none of my mother's dramatic desires or abilities.

Although I said 70% or the entertainment was at the boy's schools, Vassar did offer social activities. We had proms junior and senior year, mixers with all male colleges freshman year and sophomore hops or dances. There were a lot of lectures by visiting notables, but I don't remember much else.

Every student in their senior year had to write a thesis in their major. In Child Study we had to come up with our own subject. After much consternation I picked "Children's Sense of Humor." Vassar had an on site nursery school where we had all taught and were also allowed to just visit and take notes. I spent hours with my clip board listening to the three to five year olds at recess and writing down everything they found humorous. At this point I should have gone to my advisor for advice, but I didn't. I categorized everything in what I felt was a logical manner and it took countless hours. Next I spent more countless hours writing the very long first draft and then I went to my advisor, expecting praise and encouragement. Instead he told me my categories were not appropriate and it should be done such and such a way. I had to start all over from my original notes. It was especially horrible because I now hated my subject matter and just wanted to get it over with. I reorganized and rewrote and he gave me the go ahead and finally some praise. I hated that paper. It's over seventy pages long with pages and pages of footnotes and is deadly, deadly dull and it's about humor!

The only other thesis I remember in Child Study was Polly's. She took voice recordings of normal children and abnormal children (I don't remember where she found those children) and played the soundtracks backwards. Then by analyzing those swirly lines that are recorded to decode music or voices (sort of like the lines of an EKG for your heart) she could tell which children were disturbed from looking at those swirls and squiggles OR she couldn't tell from looking at them. I've forgotten her conclusion. No one I knew enjoyed writing their thesis.

For one of our child study classes in my senior year, we had to design and implement an experiment with animals. Beth was my partner. We ordered a pair of hamsters, an animal I knew nothing about at the time. Now I know a lot. My children had at least five different hamsters as pets. Their exploits deserve a chapter. The cage Beth and I were given to house our two hamsters was kept in the basement of the Science Building which was not accessible all the time. Our experiment started with us ringing a bell at the same time we put a pellet in their food chute. They learned to push a lever when they heard the bell and the pellet would be released. After a couple of weeks they got it down perfectly. Now for the experiment in mental torture: we rang the bell, put in the pellet, but also pumped and aimed strong bursts of air at them when they rushed over to push the lever to release the pellet.

This is when I knew I would be a lousy scientist. My heart broke for those little fellows. They became frantic at first and then so depressed and miserable that they would hide in the corner when we rang the bell. Our hypothesis proved to be correct: the hamsters became overwrought and anxious due to the ambiguity of two signals, one positive, the bell, and one negative, the air. Beth and I had turned these friendly bundles of fur into miserable, shaking, pathetic little creatures.

But our work wasn't over. Now we had to restore their psyches to their former happy state. We just repeated stage one, bell, pellet and no forced air over and over and they appeared to recover. They were then donated to the nursery school run by Vassar. They had not recovered. One of them bit a child's finger and they were removed from the classroom. I was also a forgetful and dangerous scientist, that is, dangerous to my subjects. In the middle of the experiment I forgot to go to the lab one Friday and forgot again on Saturday. I rushed over Sunday morning and found the building closed until Monday. If they had been mice they would have died from starvation, but hamsters are hoarders and they had squirreled away some extra pellets which kept them alive. I became extra loving to all the many future hamsters in my life.

Beth and I also teamed up on another endeavor. Every child study major had to write and produce a children's book, not publish, just have it in a finished format that any child could enjoy. Naturally pictures would be required. We evaluated our abilities and drawing was not one of them. Beth, who lived in Co-op, had access to a sewing machine so we decided to sew our book. It would be a wardrobe book with snaps and Velcro and zippers and buttons and anything else we could think of. Pockets – that was another addition. We thought it ended up looking more fantastic than we ever expected. We decided whoever had the first child would keep it. I ended up with it and my two oldest children played with it. I must admit it did not bring them the joy and delight that Beth and I envisioned.

I just remembered one more animal story from college. This took place in the spring of my junior year. One of my teachers, maybe English or possibly psychology, required us to write our thoughts in a journal. The entries didn't have to be long, but they were to be written every day. Her theory was that in writing every day we would get in the habit, sort of like brushing our teeth, and hopefully this habit would stay with us our entire lives. That was her hypothesis. Maybe some students wrote every day, but I was not one of them. At the end of the week I went into one of the small sitting rooms at the end of our corridor which was usually empty, shut the door, sprawled on the couch and tried to come up with five entries for my journal. It required a lot of day dreaming and gazing out the window, desperate for ideas to pop into my head. In one of my gazes, I saw with a jolt, that there was a yellow bird sitting on the windowsill. I quietly went over to the window and gently pushed it open. Luckily there were no screens on the window. It was just what I thought – a yellow parakeet. I put out my hand and he jumped right on. I pulled him inside and quickly shut the window.

My mother had three parakeets as pets in serial order so I felt comfortable holding this adorable bird. He jumped onto my shoulder and actually leaned over and kissed me! A parakeet kisses by jumping next to your chin and putting his beak up against your lips and making sucking sounds. This action could alarm some, but I knew this trick from my mother's parakeets. I gently put my blouse or sweater, something, over him and rushed the fifty feet back to my room, calling out for Dawn. This little bundle of yellow feathers even talked. I can't recall what he said, but it was an impressive vocabulary. Dawn and I forgot about studying, we had to create a temporary home for him until we could somehow get somewhere to buy a cage. We went down to the basement and found an old cardboard mailing box and an old window screen which we propped in front of the box. I don't remember what we fed him or how we offered him water, but he was suddenly our most precious pet.

The next morning we showed him off to our corridor mates, our buddies, and one of them had the cruelty to suggest that his owner might be looking for him and might be broken hearted. In our joy over this new addition to our room, we had forgotten about little Georgies' former residence. Yes, we had named him already. How would we find out? It was suggested that we buy a Poughkeepsie newspaper and see if there was an ad in it about a missing parakeet. I bought a paper two days later, praying I would find nothing, but there it was, "Precious pet missing. Yellow parakeet, comes to the name Buddy. Ten dollar reward." There was a phone number which I called and an older woman answered. Needless to say I filled her day with joy.

We arranged a time that would work for the two of us and met in the reception area of Cushing. I took her to our room and detected a gasp when she saw the paper box and the half broken screen housing her bird, but she was elated to see Buddy who burst into song when he saw her and then started talking and kissed her over and over. My mother had never had a parakeet this delightful. She offered me the ten dollar reward and I took it. My corridor mates, who were also my best friends at college, said she might be a poor old lady and I should not have accepted the reward. I had a slight twinge of guilt, but felt confident at that point that I had less money in my wallet than Buddy's mother.

I will now review the love affair that culminated in marriage, now ongoing for fifty seven years. Ted and I met in the fall of my junior year, 1955. We spent many week-ends with each other that fall at Vassar and at Christmas I saw him for a steady week. He was called to report for flight training that January. I did not see him again until four months later in May when he finally was able to get a pass for a week-end and we met in New York. Neither of us can remember what we did.

We corresponded constantly and I saved a pile of Ted's letters. But after we got married I tossed them out because they were not witty and clever and full of protestations of love. They were like a manual of what to do and not do for someone who wanted to learn how to fly with a brief declaration of love at the end. Now I wish I had them to review a few details. I was gone that entire next summer on our fabulous European trip of 1956. The following fall it was an especially rainy season with Ted's flights being constantly cancelled due to the bad weather during the week. They were told to stand-by which means don't leave the base as we'll be flying if it doesn't rain.

So the next time we saw each other after May was at Christmas when he had a long leave. He commuted back and forth to Hartford at the beginning of the vacation and then just slept upstairs on our third floor in that antique bed. We talked and talked and I learned more about his unusual upbringing. I am supplementing what I heard then with what I later learned.

I mentioned earlier that his mother died of breast cancer when he was two years old and his father died of a heart attack when he was ten. All the nannies, maids and cooks that worked for the family lived on the third floor of that large family home. Being the fifth child, with no more bedrooms on the second floor, he was of necessity put on the third with the help, but in his own private room. They all shared one bathroom. He never moved downstairs. The first nanny he remembers is Marjorie. She was very affectionate to more than just little Teddy. It was discovered that she'd put Ted in the backseat of her boyfriend's car, conveniently parked in the driveway, while she and the boyfriend necked in the front seat. That was forgiven because she was so caring and loving to Ted. But the next indiscretion was another story. She went out one evening with her boyfriend, returned home around eleven, said goodnight to Ted's father and then instead of going upstairs to bed as she implied, she slipped out the backdoor, climbed over the fence and met up with another man. For this proper Catholic family that was the last straw, out she went.

Mary was her replacement. She was from England with a clipped English accent. She didn't last very long. Christina was next in line. She was from Denmark and more prim and proper in demeanor than Marjorie which was desired, but not nearly as much fun. She also had a brief stay and was replaced by Peggy who grew up on a farm in Berlin, Connecticut. Her parents had emigrated from Germany. Ted visited the farm once when they were throwing and pitching the hay up into the loft. He remembers it being hot and dusty and desperately wanting to leave. Shortly after Peggy moved in, her sister Edie was hired as the cook. After another year Tillie showed up, a third sister. Ted has no idea what Tillie did, if anything. He thinks she just needed a place to live. Peggy was with them a number of years.

As Ted grew, the era of nannies was over, but not the need for a housekeeper, a cook and a laundress. Another Mary was hired, this one from Ireland. She was grouchy, a terrible cook and couldn't drive which was a problem for Ted with after school sports. I was amazed that Ted could recite this long list of caretakers. It seemed like a lot of change and a lot of nannies. I couldn't believe he remembered all their names. Now when we leave a party we will say to each other, "Who was the woman in the blue dress?" or "Who was the guy with the mustache?" Neither one of us ever has the answer.

It was near the end of summer camp when Ted's father died in August. The head of the camp told him his father was ill and one of the counselors would escort Ted on the train from New Hampshire to Hartford. The camp knew his dad had died suddenly from a heart attack, but they wanted the family to tell Ted. After he was given the sad news at home, he was told he would not be going to the funeral, but was to stay at the family cottage in Westbrook, Connecticut for the next week with his Uncle Eddie, his mother's youngest brother, and Eddie's wife, Aunt Phyllis. They were staying at the cottage that entire summer.

It was soon decided that instead of Eddie and Phyllis returning to their apartment in Hartford, they would move into Ted's family home for the next year to oversee the care of Ted until his brothers returned from the war and his sister from college. Ted's father was fifty-five when Ted was born. He doesn't remember ever seeing him without his suit with vest and tie on. The only exception was when they were all at the shore at Westbrook. He never came to any of Ted's athletic games at school. He was a brilliant mathematician, played the violin and did admirable pen and ink sketches.

I have felt very sad about Ted's childhood, so different from mine, but also sad for his father. His wife, who was the light of his life, died in her early forties, leaving him with three teenage boys, an eleven year old daughter and a two year old son. He had to manage it all. Fortunately having money helped, but then the war came and he had three sons in the war. He wrote copious letters to his sons all during the war, especially the eldest, who was his namesake. His daughter Jean's fiancé was killed in the war. I think he had run out of the energy you need to enthusiastically raise a young boy.

Near the end of that Christmas vacation Ted proposed and I accepted. We both had a fair amount to drink the night of the proposal and in the morning I wasn't sure, since I always had vivid dreams, if he had really proposed or if I had dreamed it. Dawn and I had talked about moving to California after graduating and teaching in one of the towns around San Francisco. So my acceptance of his marriage proposal was a game changer that affected the direction of her life as well as mine.

Ted and I drove to Hartford to buy the engagement ring and see my grandparents and Ted's much older brothers to tell them the news. Two of the brothers, George and Norbert, were bachelors and still living in the family home on Kenyon Street in Hartford. The oldest brother, Ben, was married to Priscilla and they had toddler, twin boys and lived in West Hartford. Ted was raised a Catholic, but stopped going to church in high school. My family belonged to an Episcopal Church in Longmeadow where we all had been very active so there was no question between Ted and me that the wedding would be in my church. His brothers were shocked. They had no idea Ted had left the church. It was an awkward meeting.

Ted then went back to Pensacola and I went back to college. I wrote up the announcements for our engagement which would appear in the Springfield paper, the Hartford Courant and the New York Times. I used my college graduation picture. The newspapers then only printed a picture of the bride in engagement and wedding announcements. The announcement came out in the papers on March 17, 1957, Saint Patrick's Day, which was a coincidence. I took my ring out of the jeweler's box and put it on my finger. We talked on the phone. It was sad to be thousands of miles apart. It certainly didn't fit my image of a romantic engagement.

In my second semester, senior year, I decided to sign up for an art course which sounded like fun and it wouldn't matter what grade I got as it only carried one credit. It did not involve studying great art of the past centuries which I had taken and loved, but creating art. I basically knew I had no artistic talent. I could copy other's ideas, but I didn't think I had a creative streak. There were three mediums – wood, plaster and charcoal. My wood piece started as a large dowel of wood, like a really fat rolling pin. I gouged out a face on the top half that looked very primitive which I liked. I polished it up and even displayed it in the first home we owned. If anyone asked I was going to lie and say it was an artifact from Ethiopia where my brother had been in the Peace Corp. No one ever asked. At times I used it as a hammer when I didn't feel like going into the basement to retrieve one. I thought I had thrown it out, but saw it the other day in a closet in the basement behind an old flour canister. I don't think anyone would even give it the prestige of coming from Ethiopia.

The second challenge was molding a body from plaster. I guess it was plaster. I think we started with a tall metal dowel shoved into a block of wood with lots of soft plaster wrapped around the dowel which we were to create into something beautiful. I did the body of a Greek woman who had lost her arms and her legs above the knees "over the centuries." It really didn't look that bad. I don't know where her ultimate demise occurred.

The last medium was charcoal. We were each given a huge pad of drawing paper and started by drawing items the teacher put on the front table, a bowl of fruit, a vase with flowers, an assortment of objects of different sizes, that sort of thing. Charcoal does not lend itself to precision and she emphasized free flowing strokes so I actually had fun drawing with relative abandon.

The last week of class she told us we were to sketch a human figure and the model would be at the next class. There was a certain amount of excited anticipation. We all sat in class, poised over our pads, waiting for the model to come in. She entered wearing a long, white robe and asked the instructor where she should sit. I remember thinking at that moment that the model didn't need to wear that long robe as we were all girls and used to seeing people in their underwear. The model got up on the table, took off her robe, arranged herself in the position the instructor wanted and she was stark naked! And I had to draw her! Charcoal is very forgiving. I mustered through somehow and the teacher even said, "Nice line." I loved that class, but knew without a doubt that I had not missed my calling. At graduation the Art department displayed the work of their students and there was my wooden head and my woman, without all her limbs, perched on a table.

That spring at Vassar dozens of girls became engaged. The most frequent party on campus was bridal showers. Our mail boxes were also fuller with a wedding invitation coming about every other week. I was now daydreaming about living in Pensacola and enjoying the beach and all that warmth and sunshine. In the lecture hall for the music class that I loved about the master composers of prior centuries, I would turn my hand at different angles while I listened to the music, mesmerized by the way it sparkled in the high domed auditorium.

I thought I would see Ted that spring or summer. Again, another dreadful rainy season and cancellation after cancellation of all week-end passes. We now had a telephone in our room at college so we could talk fairly easily, but he was living in the officer's bachelor's quarters and could only use their pay phone so the length of our conversations depended on the popularity of that pay phone. But we made up for the shorter lengths of conversation with the frequency of the calls.

In June through August Ted was stationed in Memphis for final training in single engine jets prior to getting his wings and there was no way he could leave base. Why didn't I fly to Pensacola early fall to see him? It was not done by proper girls. Another favorite written-in-stone saying of my father besides, "Never Lie," was, "A girl's reputation is the most valuable thing she owns." I actually don't remember discussing flying to Pensacola by myself probably because I kept assuming that each week-end Ted would be able to get a pass, but every Friday at the end of a rainy week they cancelled all the leaves. Even if I had flown down there he couldn't legally leave the base. I didn't see Ted again until Friday, October fourth, the night of our rehearsal dinner when he left the base without a pass with his commanding officer screaming at him that he could not leave. That story is on another page.

In May of my senior year I received two happy letters. One was a letter of congratulation informing me that I was going to graduate with honors. I was thrilled with that news. There were times when I thought my thesis might do me in. The other letter was an invitation to join the Junior League of Springfield, Massachusetts and I was excited about that too.

Our weather wasn't rainy on graduation day so it was held on a gently sloping hill on campus, the same hill we went to with our baby oil and bath towel to lie out and get a tan. Since it was outside there were no restrictions on how many you could invite. My parents, brother, sister and grandparents came. Vassar has a hundred plus year old tradition of a daisy chain at graduation. It used to be the prettiest girls who were selected or so the rumor was, but now it was the girls who had contributed the most to the campus. Polly would be eligible either way and she carried those daisies well.

Dawn and I decided early in the spring that we would like to set up a summer nursery school after graduation for pre-school children, ages three to five years. Dawn's home was a regal turn of the century house on over three acres and Mrs. Ide was in full agreement with our idea. Linda, Dawn's younger sister who was in the same grade as my brother Bill, was our secretary and she and her friend Lee

"Make It a Girl, Gracie"

Ericson took over running the nursery school the following summer. We circulated a flier describing our school. We called it, The Yard. We advertised having swings, slides, climbers, toys and athletic equipment. We collected from different sources most of this equipment, but had to buy some of it. For rainy days we went inside to the Ide's spacious playroom stacked with dolls, dress-up clothes, blocks, trucks, rhythm instruments, art supplies and such. We also offered mid-morning snacks. The best part was the hours 8:30 to 11:45 for a period of nine weeks. Short as those hours were, they gave the mothers time to play nine holes of golf, go shopping, whatever. We didn't know a single mother who worked and needed full time day care. The Yard was hugely successful and we had a most satisfying summer running our own school. We considered ourselves entrepreneurs on a very small scale. Linda and Lee went on to run it successfully for two more summers.

I was determined to see clearly without my glasses at my wedding so my goal was to conquer those uncomfortable contact lenses. In the fifties there were only hard lenses and it took a long time to get acclimated. You not only needed your eyeballs to adjust to them, but your eyelids had to build up a soft callous on the underside so the lenses didn't irritate them when you blinked. Mine were miserably uncomfortable. I started wearing them an hour at a time and every day I added another half hour. I'd go for a walk or do an errand at the drugstore, anything I could think of to distract me from the discomfort. My mother kept saying, "I don't know why you put yourself through all this misery. You look just fine in glasses." I gritted my teeth even more at this unwanted advice.

Gradually they felt better and better and, halleluiah, by the day of the wedding I was wearing them the whole day long. I am still wearing them the whole day long, almost fifty eight years later. I still wear hard lenses, but they are now gas permeable so are much healthier for my eyes than the old ones. Now almost everyone starts with soft lenses as they need no breaking-in period. They are more expensive because they're disposable so constantly need to be replaced and they don't correct for stigmatism nearly as well. Nevertheless, my ophthalmologist says only people over fifty are still in hard lenses.

8

The Wedding: October 5, 1957

Those short hours running the nursery school gave my mother and me plenty of time to plan my wedding. There was so much to do. I had always wanted a candle lit

Christmas evening wedding because I had been to one the previous year and thought it was so romantic. That was the plan until the end of June when Ted asked why are we waiting so long? How about a fall wedding? No reason not to everybody agreed. My dad said we needed a church bigger than St. Andrews in Longmeadow so our minister contacted the Episcopal Cathedral in Springfield to check the availability and Saturday, October fifth was open. My dad called the Longmeadow Country Club, also available, so October fifth, my mother's forty-fifth birthday, would be our wedding day. I still wanted an evening wedding even though the fire department would not allow the center aisle to be lit with real candles which was a blow to the romantic scene I had pictured.

I wanted to sew something for my trousseau. That was a tradition still talked about. You should come to your marriage with enough clothes for an entire year. I bought a pattern for a cotton robe. It turned out okay. It's hard to screw up with a free flowing robe. Then I decided to practice cooking. I thought Ted's favorite pie was lemon meringue. The first time I baked one it looked like a puddle of pudding on the plate. It tasted okay, but looked pathetic. Determined to succeed I tried again with the same recipe and got the same results. I gave up on lemon meringue pie. I think I might have forgotten the cornstarch.

My mother and I went shopping for the bridal gown. Forbes and Wallace, owned by the father of my good friend Marty Wallace, and one other department store were the only large retail stores, but I'm sure there were small bridal stores. I don't remember where we bought my dress. The newspaper described it elegantly, *"The bride wore a formal gown of faille taffeta fashioned with an empire waistline, re-embroidered lace and a seed pearl yoke with portrait neckline, brief sleeves and a full skirt terminating in a chapel train."* It also had about thirty tiny satin covered buttons going up the back. My youngest daughter, Jenny, wore it at her wedding thirty-nine years later.

The bridal gown wasn't my only concern. Two thirds of the way through the reception the bride and groom change clothes and leave their expensive reception, while their friends continue to enjoy all the food and drinks and dancing. An odd custom when you think about it and I think it's now very optional. There is one nice side to that custom. All the bride's and groom's attendants go with their glass of champagne to the separate rooms where the bridal couple are changing for a final whirl of conversation and goodbyes. Since the wedding was in October, I not only needed a dress, but a coat, a matching purse and of course a hat because the bride is always dressed to the nines when she leaves the reception. So silly since it was a night wedding and we would be leaving around 10pm and going directly to a hotel. Ted only had to put on a suit and it didn't even have to be new!

Picking my bridesmaids was easy. I chose the four girls I went to Europe with and my sister. Dawn was my maid of honor. I had asked a good friend from high school, Marty Wallace, but she was pregnant and in the fifties that gave you an excuse to not have to buy that gown and walk down the aisle. My sister would be a junior bride's maid. We found autumn looking green dresses for the bridesmaids and a small velvet green hat that looked like an oversized headband. In the Episcopal Church you had to have your head covered.

My sister was only ten, but she was tall and could wear the same dress as the other bridesmaids.

So much to figure out: the invitations, the cake, the flowers for the church, the flowers for the club, the flowers for the bridal party, the band, the food and drinks, the photographer, the guest book, the limousines, white gloves for the ushers. It just went on and on. Good thing I was only working mornings.

In that era the bride displayed all her gifts in her home. We set up card tables in the room my dad had built in the basement and put long white tablecloths over them. It was a custom for friends and relatives to come over and look at the array of displayed gifts. On the wedding day an off-duty policeman was always hired to sit in the house during the wedding and reception, the assumption being that since the wedding is usually mentioned ahead in the newspapers, it could alert the crooks.

Another task was going to the photographer's studio weeks before the wedding with your gown, veil and shoes in hand for the formal shot that would appear in the newspapers. I guess the newspapers laid out the society pages days ahead of publication because they not only wanted your picture weeks ahead, but a detailed description of your gown, usually provided by the bridal department of the store; a list of the entire bridal party and their gowns; a description of all the flowers at the church and reception; the name and occupations of the parents of the newlyweds and of course a blurb about the bride and groom. My father played golf with the editor of the Springfield paper and he whispered to my father at the reception that I would be full figure in the center of the front page of the Society section the next day.

Ted ran into a snag with the ushers. All the men were called ushers then. At least in Springfield no one had heard of the term groomsmen. Ted had three brothers, three Catholic brothers. The Catholic Church then was very unforgiving of any transgressions. Ted didn't care as he had stopped attending church ten years before, but his brothers, who never missed a Mass on Sunday, were told by their priest that participating in a ceremony in which their brother, raised a Catholic, was being married in a Protestant Church, was an unacceptable thing for them to do. It was probably more ominous than "unacceptable" because his brother George did not participate. Ben and Norbert took weeks to decide and being sure they would say no, I told Ted, who is thousands of miles away and now learning how to land a plane on a moving ship, that we just HAD to have five ushers to match the five girls in my bridal party.

His best friend, Bob Raymond, who was on our original blind date, was being discharged from the Navy on our actual wedding day and couldn't make it in time. Most of his other close friends were in the service and stationed nowhere near Massachusetts. I'm getting more and more anxious. Ted starts asking anyone he can think of who could make it to Springfield on October fifth. With no affirmative replies coming in, we ask my brother, who agrees to be best man, and my cousin Sandy, who is my brother's age. Then we ask Dawn's boyfriend, Dick Austin, who we do know well as we often double dated at Vassar. Now we have three. Two boys Ted knew at Kingswood say they are available. Now we're in perfect shape with five, all we need, but a fellow ensign with Ted who just flunked out of flight school and was heading home to Vermont, says, "Yes." One of his roommates at Yale now working in New York says, "Yes." Now we have more than we need – seven ushers. Then, three weeks before the wedding, Ben and Norbert, after much soul searching, have decided they will be in the wedding. There will now be nine ushers and five bridesmaids. In the final wedding picture of the bridal party, with the bridesmaids in green, me in white and my mother in beige, we females are mere specks of color in a sea of black and white.

The custom was for the groom's parents to host the rehearsal dinner. That obviously wasn't possible. My grandparents said they would like to be the hosts. It wasn't the huge rehearsal dinners my children had. I think my daughter Julie had over a hundred and fifty people at her rehearsal dinner. We had around twenty. One week before the wedding Ted called me and said he can make the wedding, but he won't be able to make the rehearsal dinner. I didn't faint, but I know I screamed. I told him I had not seen him in ten months because of that blasted Navy and he better make this dinner or I didn't know what I would do. I repeated again and again that the dinner was very, very important. I had this feeling of "the world will end" if you don't get here that night and I successfully got that idea across to him. He made the dinner. He left the base without authorization. I think he figured the Navy had too much money invested in him as a pilot to kick him out for going to his rehearsal dinner.

I must have been in a daze on our wedding day because I can't recall any of the details. I could write pages about all four of my children's weddings and my sister's, but not mine. This is all I remember. I forgot to bring the white gloves for the ushers to the church. Ted couldn't find the studs for his shirt so he borrowed some from our next door neighbor. I aimed my bridal bouquet at Dawn, my best friend, but Mary Ann who was taller, grabbed it. Ted went up on the balcony at the club and threw the garter down which was caught by the tall usher who had just flunked out of the flight program who Ted hardly knew. When we cut the cake, with great merriment, I shoved a piece with lots of frosting into Ted's mouth. I didn't I know that he hated frosting. I danced with my father, brother, grandfather and Ted. This I know because of the pictures. We were all upset after we saw the proofs because the photographer never took a picture of my beloved grandmother.

I do remember that we left in the middle of our reception and drove to a hotel in Hartford for our wedding night. We got there late – why did I ever want an evening wedding? I took off my hat before we entered the hotel and tried to look ultra blasé as I casually perched on our suitcase while Ted registered us at the desk. I didn't want people to know we were newlyweds of a four hour duration. The next morning we discovered our plane was delayed for hours, meaning we missed all our connections. Ted was now going to be four days AWAY WITHOUT LEAVE!

I was now Sally Gilbert Flynn and about to start on a most exciting adventure, fifty-eight years long at the time of this publication, as a wife, a fifth grade teacher, a kindergarten teacher, a nursery school teacher, a mother of four, an active community volunteer, an avid tennis player, a successful realtor of twenty-two years, a grandmother of nine and now a retired lady of leisure who loves to play bridge.

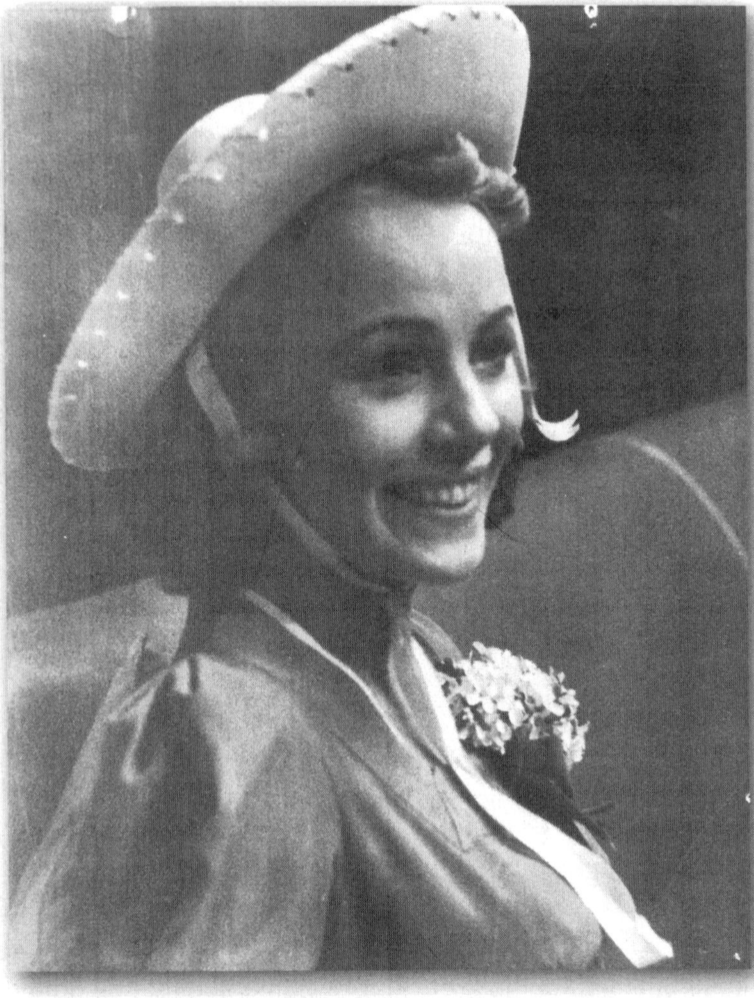

9

My Mother, Grace Hildegarde Reinholdz Gilbert

My mother was born on October fifth, 1912 in Middletown, Connecticut. She was the second and last child of Emma and Albert Reinholdz. Both were from an area in Sweden (like a state in our country) called Varmland. Both were born in 1883 and didn't meet until they emigrated to America. Albert Reinholdz Andersson was born in Hagfors and Emma Lovisa Westbon in Bjornborg. The two towns were in different areas of Varmland. Emma emigrated in March of 1900 from the port of Goteborg to New Haven,

Connecticut. When Albert arrived in America his name was Albert Andersson and he decided to make his middle name, Reinholdz, his last name because of all the people emigrating from Sweden named Andersson. He was right. I tried to find his exact date of emigration from geneology.com and there were hundreds of Albert Anderssons. My mother always wished he'd kept his name Andersson, just with one less "s," as the name Reinholdz sounded German and for the early decades of her life everyone hated the Germans.

I don't know how Emma and Albert met, but I do know that after my mother was born, Albert, and a year later Anton, moved to Dayton, Ohio to work for the National Cash Register Company. They soon moved back to Hartford and bought a house at 145 Flatbush Avenue. Their first child, Arnold, died at age two. Dorothy was born a year later and my mother four years after that. Albert worked for Hart-Haggeman Tool & Dye Makers in Hartford and Emma was a stay at home mom.

My mother and father met when they were both fourteen. They each dated other people until they were married, but according to my father, they both knew at age fifteen that they would eventually marry. When my mother was twelve and her sister Dorothy sixteen a young man from Sweden stayed with them briefly. He was on a graduation trip to Europe and the United States as a gift from his widowed mother to her only child. Typical of wealthy Swedish families, the sons traveled abroad before settling down and often stayed with relatives or friends abroad who had emigrated from Sweden.

I don't know how long he stayed, but it was long enough to fall in love with Dorothy. Albert told him his daughter was too young to marry as she had not even finished high school, but did not discourage him. The story always told was that he returned two years later to officially propose and they married as soon as Dorothy graduated from high school.

Dorothy spoke fluent Swedish as her parents had primarily spoken Swedish at home when she was young. By the time my mother came four years later, her parents insisted on only speaking English so my mother never learned any Swedish. The bridegroom's name was Eric Ragnar Sundquist. The newlyweds settled in the Hartford area and within a year, had a son. They named him Frederick because that name is pronounced the same in Swedish and English.

When Frederick was a toddler his Grandmother in Sweden begged her son to come home with his new family for a long visit. So in 1928, Dorothy, Eric and Frederick left for Sweden to visit Eric's mother. They never came back. My parents theorized that Eric's domineering mother threatened to not leave him any money if he didn't live in Sweden. The sad part is they never even returned for a visit and my parents never visited them in Sweden. There were good reasons. First was the depression, soon followed by the Second World War. By the time ocean travel was feasible my mother knew she suffered from extreme seasickness. By the time airline travel was possible my mother soon became too ill with high blood pressure to do any extensive traveling. I don't know why her sister never came back for a visit. They never saw each other again.

Emma, my mother's mother and my grandmother, became ill with breast cancer my mother's senior year in high school. Mother's high school English teacher wanted her to apply to Mount Holyoke for a scholarship as she was an excellent student, but senior year all thoughts were about Emma, not my mother, and nothing was done. My mother graduated in June,1930 and seven months later, January, 1931, Emma died. Albert married again just nine months after Emma's death. Her stepmother, Helene, who never had children, was well off financially and owned several cottages which she rented on the Connecticut shore. She and Albert spent most of the summer before their marriage at one of the cottages and she made it plain to my mother that when they returned to Hartford and married in the fall she would prefer to live only with Albert.

My mother moved out and stayed at the YWCA, a popular destination for young unmarried women. It had curfews and restrictions just like the colleges had at that time. My mother worked for the Superintendent of the Hartford Schools, but her avocation was dramatics. She had three things going for her, she was beautiful, she had a photographic memory and she loved to act. In early photographs she looked a lot like Greta Garbo. She joined the Mark Twain Masquers, a new amateur group in Hartford, founded in 1932. They are still active and have enjoyed an outstanding reputation in the Hartford area for decades. My mother was the leading lady in most of their productions.

At some point my grandfather invited her to live with him and my grandmother on Linnmoore Street. He had known Mother since she was fifteen and was very fond of her. He was furious over the treatment she had received from Albert and his new wife. He told Mother she was like a daughter to him and he hoped she would have nothing to do with her own father again who had treated her so badly. At one point my father implied that Mother had suffered from a nervous breakdown before they were married. That might have precipitated the invitation from my grandparents. Also she was now a well known actress in the Hartford area and my grandfather had loved acting in college so that might have also influenced him. In any case, she moved in with her boyfriend's parents. Her boyfriend, my father, was then a junior at the University of Maine.

My grandfather had been very active in dramatics as a student at the University of Maine. He was short and played most of the female roles because a proper lady wouldn't act on the stage in those days. For years they had a picture of him playing Ophelia hung up in the hallway at the University. He loved theatrics and spent hours helping Mother rehearse her lines. She truly became the daughter he always wanted.

My father came home for Easter vacation in March of 1933 and he and my mother said they were going to New York to see a play, but actually their plan was to elope. They were married in a civil court and planned on keeping it secret for awhile. Mother went back to work the Monday after Easter and Dad went back to college. Some reporter who read legal government marriage announcements saw the names and recognized the name Grace Reinholdz because of her prominence at the Mark Twain Masquers and put the marriage announcement in the Hartford paper.

My grandmother came down to breakfast that morning, prepared her cinnamon toast and orange juice, picked up her morning newspaper to relax and read,

"Special to the Hartford Courant from New York, April 2. William Henry Gilbert Jr, 21, a student, and Miss Grace Reinholdz, 21, both of 89 Linnmoore Street, Hartford, Connecticut, were married here Friday afternoon in the city chapel by deputy city clerk and so on."

Further down the page an article focused on my mother with a huge picture of her dressed for her role in "He," put on recently at the Avery Memorial with the write-up underneath saying she has been prominent in amateur theatricals and is employed at the local board of education. I doubt my grandmother finished that cinnamon toast.

Many anxious phone calls ensued. Mother left work and came right home, which of course was also my grandmother's home. Many years later my mother told me my grandmother's first question was, "Well are you pregnant?" I think that's a very logical question, but my mother, even years later, felt it was insulting. My father who was now back at college was called and explained to my grandmother why they felt they had to elope. He said that he and my mother knew there was no way my mother's father, Albert, was going to put on a wedding for her and it would be too awkward for his own parents to sponsor a formal wedding; in fact, it would be too awkward to even have Albert and my grandparents at the same wedding; so they both felt it best to elope.

My grandfather was in California on business when the elopement occurred. In the thirties, when you crossed the country on business, you stayed there months at a time because the train trip took days and days and it was very expensive. He finally arrived home June first, told his son that since he had made the decision to marry, he now had a wife to support so he'd better find a job and not worry about school. Today this would seem ridiculously harsh, but this was 1933, the middle of the depression and children were not coddled. To me, my grandfather was a sugar daddy and I could do no wrong, but I had been told he had the reputation of being tough and unyielding.

My brother, who has done exhaustive research on our family, said my father was on probation his first semester at the University of Maine and trying to get an acceptable C average second semester, so perhaps academics at that point seemed less appealing to him than the prospect of making money. He was aware of my grandfather's rule that once you married, you were on your own financially. They might have paid all their bills, but they lived with my grandparents at least three times in the early years of their marriage when my father changed jobs.

My father finished out his junior year, but did not return for his senior year. He got a job at The Travelers Insurance Company where my grandfather worked. He told me years later that there were all these subtle insinuations from his peers and bosses that he only got the job because of his father, which was probably true. He thought this perception of favoritism would hurt rather than enhance his chances of success at the Travelers. He found a job fifteen months later with an insurance company in Chicago. Mother was six months pregnant with me at the time and my grandparents insisted she continue to live with them on Linnmoore Street until the baby was born.

All during the pregnancy my grandfather kept asking my mother to please, please have a girl. He was one of two sons, his father was one of two sons and his grandfather was one of two sons. There had not been a girl born in his family for three generations. They both brought Mother to the Hartford Hospital after labor had started. As she was being wheeled down the hospital corridor to the delivery room, my grandfather cried out,

"Make it a girl, Gracie"

I was born on December eighth, 1935. My grandfather was thrilled and urged my mother to name me Mary. I'm not sure why. I think he just liked the name and he could be very persistent, but he didn't win. My parents had already decided a girl would be named after his wife, my grandmother, Sally Hamlin Gilbert. My mother quit work and became a full time mother. My grandparents managed to convince her that it would be unhealthy and unsafe to travel with a baby so young so she should stay with them a little longer. She gave in to all that pressure until I was four months old. Then my mother and I boarded the train for Chicago, accompanied by my grandparents, for the long train trip. My father would soon be seeing me for the first time.

The first night in my dad's apartment I wouldn't stop crying. My parents were beside themselves. They called my grandmother at the hotel for advice and she came right over, rushed into the room, picked me up and said,

"Why she's roasting to death in all these blankets. We've got to unwrap her and let her move her limbs about and feel the fresh air."

That did the trick. I stopped crying and everyone went back to bed. He loved telling this story about the first night he spent with his first child.

I have snapshots of my mother and me, seven months old, enjoying the sunshine on the roof of the Kenmors Shore Apartment Hotel in Chicago. We all came back to Hartford for a visit in the summer of 1936 and stayed with my grandparents.

In 1937 my father took a job with another insurance company and we left Chicago for New Jersey. The first rental house was in East Caldwell, followed by a slightly larger house at 500 Eagle Rock Avenue in West Orange followed by a really large house at 30 Grover Lane in West Caldwell. My parents decided to share this house on Grover Lane with two good friends of my father's who were bachelors. The house was white stucco with pillars on each side, a red tile roof and a large balcony on the second floor. They hired a live-in maid named Julia. The story I remember hearing is about the railing on that balcony which was four inches wide at the top, just like a gymnastic beam. One day when I was four years old I decided to practice walking on that railing. My mother spotted me from the lawn and just about fainted, but it was Julia who calmly walked out on the balcony, talked to me quietly as she strode towards me, and then quickly grabbed me. I have no recollection of this at all. I'm just amazed I once showed such a lack of fear of heights and such prowess on the beam!

A close friend of mother's was Regina Davison, married to Marshall Davison, who played the leading man opposite Mother's leading lady in the productions put on by the Mark Twain Masquers. Regina was stunning looking and used to say she never wanted to become thirty years old, the beginning of old age. Mother always assumed she was joking, but at age twenty-nine, Regina came home early from work and swallowed an entire bottle of sleeping pills. That is the story Mother told me. My brother said our father told him that

Regina killed herself with a gun. In either case, Marshall came home that night and found his wife lying across their bed, dead by her own hand. From the vantage of my current age, I'm sure she was probably bipolar or even schizophrenic. Marshall married nine years later to Connie who was ten years younger. They had two daughters and a very happy marriage. My parents stayed good friends with them their entire life.

My mother's extended family had taken sides when she abruptly moved out of her home when her father remarried. Most sided with her father. My mother once told me it was because of greed. His relatives thought they could get a deal on renting one of the cottages his new wife owned at the shore if they stayed on good terms with Albert and his new wife, but Albert's younger brother, Anton, and his family sided with my mother. Anton's wife, my mother's aunt, was named Gouda and her daughter, my mother's cousin, who she was close to, was Gunhilde. She married Robert Preston and their children had very American sounding names. I remember going to birthday parties at their house and playing with them. They lived in Hartford so we saw them infrequently. Sadly I don't recall ever seeing them again after I left grammar school.

For some reason living in the lovely house with Julia doing all the work ended and my parents rented a modest house at 253 Grove Street in Montclair. That is where they lived when my brother was born on November 30, 1939. My father must have changed jobs or lost his job because by the fall of

1940 we were living with my grandparents in their house in Wethersfield. I went to kindergarten at Chester Elementary school diagonally across the street from them. I can tell from pictures that we already had Lassie, our collie, but I don't recall when we bought her. My father took a job next with the Prudential Insurance Company in Newark, New Jersey. At the end of the summer we moved into a larger house he had rented at 52 Overlook Road in Cedar Grove and stayed there for five wonderful years. This was the sixth kitchen my mother had to set up in eight years of marriage.

When I was in elementary school I loved it when my mother visited school. She was always the prettiest and usually the youngest mother of all my friends. I was so proud that she was my mother. She told me a story that embarrassed her about having baby pictures taken of me when they were living in Chicago. The photographer came to the apartment to take the pictures which was convenient since she had no car. When he returned with the finished photos he insisted on being paid right then or he wouldn't leave the photos and he implied he didn't know when or if he would ever be able to come back. She had no cash on hand and I guess no check book and there were no credit cards then so he talked her into giving him a small gold ring on her finger in exchange for the photos and she did. She felt ashamed she was so naïve to have agreed to that.

Many years later when my sister was in preschool, I temporarily took over a job my mother loved. Every year in early December she went to all the different stores that had a

Santa Claus to pick out the one she thought not only looked the most genuine, but had the best rapport with children. My sister was eleven years younger than me and seven years younger than my brother so the whole family worked diligently to keep all the fantasies we grew up with vividly alive for Cynthia. Finding a good Santa was one of our top priorities.

So one December when my mother ran out of time, she asked me to take over the Santa search job. I treated it with as much importance as Mother did, taking detailed notes on the look and demeanor of the four Santas I observed. I was to meet Mother and Cynthy at a children's shoe store, quietly relay my information to Mother and then off the three of us would go to the chosen store to meet the perfect Santa. I arrived at the designated time and they weren't there, but Mother wasn't known for her punctuality so I wasn't concerned. After twenty minutes I was getting concerned, when in they walked. Cynthy was beaming and ran over to me with a sticky candy cane in her hand and said she had just talked to Santa and told him everything she wanted and he said, "Yes, she could have it all." Mother whispered to me that they stopped in the bank on their way to meet me and the bank had a Santa who just wandered around greeting the customers. Cynthy's eyes lit up when she saw him. She ran over to him, started talking and had his exclusive attention for fifteen minutes. I was disappointed and so was my mother because there was no photographer in the bank so she wouldn't have a picture of her daughter sitting on Santa's lap.

In our family my father was the dominant force, not my mother. I don't remember them having other couples over for dinner, but I do remember different couples coming for the week-end. Usually the husband was going to play in a golf tournament with my father. The Friday before they arrived, my father, not my mother, would put on one of mother's aprons and vacuum the entire downstairs. My mother rarely had to cook for these events as dinner at the club was always part of the celebration. Unlike my father, who enjoyed playing or watching sports, my mother was not an athlete. She did love to read. She was not a joiner or an active volunteer. I do remember her being on a committee to organize a fashion show in which she and my sister, age five or six, modeled mother-daughter outfits. The event was captured with a picture of them in the newspaper wearing their matching spring dresses.

I wonder if there were very few snack like things in the stores during the war or if my mother just didn't buy them because I don't remember ever munching on anything after dinner. Many times when we were hungry at 9pm or so and felt energetic we would make fudge. We all loved chocolate fudge and there was a certain art to making it. What I recall is the importance of a soft ball forming when you dropped a small bit of the liquid chocolate into a bowl of cold water. If that chocolate liquid didn't form into a ball, the fudge was not ready to be poured. It sometimes took a really long time of gentle boiling to make that ball appear and we would have to stir and stir so the chocolate wouldn't burn. We all salivated in anticipation of pouring out the fudge on that waiting sheet of wax paper and cutting it up into pieces. We never waited for it to completely cool. My mother's favorite was penuche fudge, but we only had that when we could buy it.

My father won lots of contests put on by Connecticut General for reaching the sales quota the home office had set for his office. The typical prize for the winning managers and the very top salesmen from around the country was a fully paid four day week-end trip with their wives to the Greenbrier or the Homestead, two very elegant resorts in the south. My mother enjoyed these trips. She had become friends with the other wives and they always provided side trips and entertainment for the women while the men golfed. She also loved just relaxing and sitting around the pool. In March of 1956, my father's office won the "Outstanding Agency" award, meaning one of the top agencies in the entire country, with the prize being a week's trip to Nassau. At the end of that trip they went to Lake Worth, Florida, to celebrate my grandfather's seventieth birthday.

A sore back plagued my mother as long as I can remember. When they moved to Longmeadow they installed the twin beds my father had bought at an auction in Philadelphia. She had been told by her doctor it would help her back if she put a board under her mattress to make it harder. (How medical advice has changed!)

In Longmeadow we had a cleaning woman, Marjorie, who came two times a week. I still remember that she was paid $15 a day. My mother would often tell us to leave the dinner dishes as Marjorie was coming the next morning. This brings envy to my mind as I now spend an hour picking up the entire house before my cleaning woman comes and then only once every two weeks

My mother was not a shopper. She rarely bought anything for the house and didn't shop that much for clothes. I remember Betty Decker, known for being extremely outspoken, coming for a visit and exclaiming with disbelief, "I can't believe you still have those ugly lamps on your dressing table."

I loved to watch my mother sitting at that dressing table putting on her makeup. In high school and college the only makeup any of my friends wore was lipstick. My mother had these small, skinny boxes about three inches long by one inch wide with a tiny brush that fit inside. They were sold by Maybelline. She rubbed the brush against the dark strip of mascara paste in the box and then flipped the brush up and down on her eyelashes. She had loose powder she applied with a fluffy powder puff. I don't think she used any foundation. She only used one perfume, Toujours Moi. She preferred using the oil to the liquid as the scented oil lasted much longer on her body. Whenever I hugged her that fragrance would fill my nostrils and give me a happy feeling. I bought the perfume once after she died in a nostalgic mood, but felt uncomfortable wearing it. That scent meant my mother and it made me sad. Some of our best talks started when she was sitting on that upholstered, extra long stool in front of her dressing table with the ugly lamps, carefully applying mascara, while I sat on the bed watching.

My mother hated sewing. I should say hated mending. She never did any sewing. Her explanation was the trauma she experienced in a home economics class her senior year in high school. The assignment was for the girls to make their graduation gowns and it took half the semester. Her teacher liked Mother and sensed her lack of manual dexterity with a needle and even worse with a sewing machine so always picked Mother's gown to demonstrate the next step in the process. Finally, when every piece was in place and sewed together her teacher felt comfortable having Mother clip-off the basting threads. The ceremony was in two days so the girls had completed their project just in time. Mother said she carefully hovered over that gown, gently snipping away those basting threads or so she thought when suddenly there appeared a huge hole in the middle of the front of the gown, a hole that had no easy repair. Her teacher spent that evening remaking the entire graduation gown. From then on, Mother tried to never pick up a sewing needle.

After we moved into our house in Longmeadow I bought some yellow pleated curtains for my bedroom window to hang from a traverse rod. They were too long and too wide so I altered them by hand. The material was very tough and resistant to a sewing needle. I kept leaving a trail of tiny droplets of blood as I progressed across the hemline. I begged to get the curtains cleaned, but my mother said that was ridiculous as the blood was hidden under the seam, but I said I knew it was there. She won and I got over it.

There were only two items I remember my mother getting from her parent's home. One was a copper tea kettle with a matching sugar and creamer, each with its own little copper stand. My mother's mother had brought the set from Sweden and I have it now. The other item was a wooden rocking chair, visible in some of the early photographs of her father sitting in it holding my infant mother. I remember vividly when it met its death. The electrical power had been down for a few days in Cedar Grove and it was really getting cold in the house. My father kept stoking the ongoing fire in the living room fireplace from our pile of firewood and when that ran out he grabbed scraps of wood he found in the garage and that's when he spied the rocking chair. It had been in the garage for months because a couple of slats had fallen off and it needed repair. To him it was the last piece of wood in the house that was expendable. I was in third or fourth grade and remember being really upset as he took it apart because I thought it came all the way from Sweden. It hadn't, my mother said, but I said it had come from my mother's home and she had been rocked in it as a baby and I didn't want it burned. I seemed to care more than my mother and into the fireplace it went.

When I came home from college freshman year between semesters I was sitting at the table having breakfast with my mother when she said,

"You know what's really odd. I can feel the blood racing through my blood vessels."

"What, what do you mean you can feel it?"

"It's like a whooshing feeling. It pounds sometimes or throbs. I have this funny flop-over feeling."

"That sounds weird. Have you seen the doctor?"

" I'm seeing him Monday. I'll let you know."

I went back to school that Sunday and Dad called me the next night. My mother was in the Springfield Hospital. She had been sent there directly from the doctor's office. Her blood pressure measured 320 systolic over 200 diastolic. Normal blood pressure is 120 over 80. Her doctor had never seen anything like it.

They put her through every test imaginable. They said the kidneys and adrenal gland were fine. Maybe it was caused by a kidney infection that had cleared up. They had no idea. Mother was forty six years old. Her blood pressure would not come down. There were few medications for blood pressure in the mid-fifties. She told me they had found a miracle drug in 1953 and wasn't she lucky this hadn't happened sooner. The miracle drug didn't touch that pressure. Because of the rules they imposed I'm assuming the doctors thought it must be caused by some kind of emotional stress. Mother was not allowed to get out of bed except to go to the bathroom, always with an aid in attendance. She was forbidden to watch television or to talk with friends on the telephone. She could not have any visitors except my father. She took thirty-four pills a day which did little for the blood pressure, but made her face puffy, gave her nausea and terrible headaches. I'm going to quote at length a letter my mother wrote me from the hospital.

> *"Dear Sally, If I could write a boooook, as grandma's cleaning woman used to say I'd make Irene one of the principal characters. She is sort of head maid on Chapin 5, my area and floor. There is quite a caste system among the help. She has black hair pulled straight back with a neat round pug in the back and speaks beautiful English with a heavy, charming accent. She came to America as a refugee less than two years ago and I don't know whether she was a Russian Countess or a Czechoslovakian Princess, but she loves America and everyone here loves her. I always feel better, the day she is here. She regales me with wonderful stories and old world proverbs and is so proud of her English that I hate to ask her to repeat if I don't understand some word or phrase. When I feel particularly miserable she looks so worried and is very quiet and can't do enough for me.*
>
> *One morning she said she had told her family about me, "So Yong, so bee-yew-tee-fool, so seek," and when we became good friends and I showed her the pictures in my wallet of all my darlings she became dramatically overwhelmed and*

simply couldn't believe that I had a daughter eighteen and in college. She said she thought I was "twenty seex, maybe." Do you wonder why I love her.

One day as she and another maid were cleaning my room, they were discussing a male patient down the hall, complaining about the peanut shells he drops all around his bed on the floor. I haven't even thought of peanuts in the husk since I was a child, but suddenly I wanted a bag of them more than anything in the world. Not knowing my fellow sufferer down the hall, I wrote them on my list for Daddy to bring me, which he did the next night...two bags! I think he would borrow Bob Wilson's ladder and bring me the moon if I asked for it. Good thing I didn't crave Planters Nuts in the can as I'm on a completely salt free diet.

The next morning I told Irene, with a twinkle except I can't twinkle, but that is the general idea of how I said it, that I would love to throw the peanut shells all over the room. I wouldn't really because I have suddenly become as persnickety neat as Aunt Betty. Dr. Pease says that neatness affliction goes with acute hypertension. Irene said quite seriously that if I felt like doing it, to go ahead as she and her assistant Betty would love to sweep them up for me 'For you, we do anything you want.'

Betty is also very sweet to me. She waters my plants, arranges my flowers, brings me extra tea bags and a whole lemon sliced every few days because she read that lemon is a good substitute for salt. She arranges my cards every time she dusts the bureau, placing her favorites in the first row and my favorites facing me. They both tell me the entire floor is worrying about me and Irene says, 'Everybody lofs you.'

Well imagine the first day they both had a day off together and their replacement was a woman who is very old, nervous and doesn't do anything except go from room to room carrying a dust rag and begging for slips from plants and anyone's old pots of withered daffodils, tulips and hyacinths. I had an ice bag on my head, it was one of my bad days, and when she walked in she didn't even look at me, but asked how my plants were doing. She noticed two new ones and took away a couple of old ones, 'Oh, you gotta gardenia plant,' she said indistinctly through her ill fitting double dentures.

'Yes, from my children,' I said under my ice bag.

'Oh, you got children,' And then she made the most unkindest cut of all,

'Dey all growed up?'

'Oh yes, all grown up and married and I have several grandchildren.' I didn't say it, of course, but it's what I wished I'd said after she left. I should draw a picture of me on this fancy art paper I am writing this letter on. I look something like Fred Allen, worse though, because even my eyelids are puffy. I have drawn pictures on sheet after sheet of this art paper of all my plants and flowers. Called "Still Life" – that's me.

Love from your old Maw"

I wrote Mother weekly and tried to keep my letters uplifting and humorous. I succeeded because she always wrote back that my letter had lifted her spirits and made her laugh. I wish I could reread all the letters I wrote. They were discarded like so much else when my father sold the house.

She was in the hospital nine weeks and then sent home with instructions to remain completely inactive. Basically she was to follow the same restrictions as at the hospital. They had concluded that the most likely culprits, her kidneys and adrenal gland, were fine and they were all out of options and ideas. Even on Mother's Day she couldn't come downstairs or talk to anyone on the phone. Mrs. Larson, a practical nurse, was hired to come to the house daily to care for Mother and Cynthy who was only in second grade. Mother wrote me that despite her pleading with the doctors they told her she could not go to Cynthy's school to see her act in the play put on by her class.

The months passed and the blood pressure came down a little, but it still was at a dangerous level, so in January of 1955, one year after she was first diagnosed, she was encouraged to go to Peter Bent Brigham Hospital in Boston. They put her through the same awful tests with the same, "We just can't understand it," results. She described to me one of her preparations before some new test. She had to drink a half cup of castor oil which made her throw up all night and then was given an enema in the morning. But these Boston doctors gave her more freedom. She could shower, use the phone, watch television and go out to dinner with my dad who tried to come to Boston every week-end. They discovered her pressure went down when she left the hospital and went out to dinner with her husband. I'm going to quote another letter from my mother,

> *"I am so excited. The doctor is allowing me to go out to dinner with Daddy tonight, I can be gone 5 hours – from 4-9 and I have a pass! I feel like a school girl on her first date or a parolee from Sing Sing. Dr. Emerson wants to see the effects on me of 'getting out in the world' while I am still under this strenuous care. Your letter came as I was writing and I can't tell you how thrilled I am to have such a smart daughter. If you were a man you'd be a 5 Star General. It is snowing today in Boston, but I have my boots and as it is 2pm think I'll start getting ready. Don't know where we'll eat and I don't care as long as the food is hot. Daddy is going to wear his new suit.   Much love, Mother."*

The doctors concluded she should go home and be active within reason. They also took her off temporarily all her medication except aspirin and sleeping pills, perhaps to give her body a rest. Quoting another letter written six days later,

> *"I was released last week and Daddy took me to Hollidge's in Wellesley – new dress, new petticoats, new gloves, rope of pearls, earrings, pocketbook, stockings, hat !!! We had cocktails at the Stagg's and dinner at the Simpson House, then saw a darling play called 'The Grand Prize.'*

The next night we met the Staggs at the Ritz Carlton (fabulous) and had dinner at a French restaurant called The Café Vendome – delicious and gorgeous. My blood pressure was 225/115 before I left. When I returned it was 180/90. So I've been going out ever since I got home! Friday was Daddy's agency party with wives at the Sheraton. I had a wonderful time and wore my new petticoats and such.

I have to keep going to Dr. Pease every week for a few months and Dr. Emerson in Boston wants to see me in April. As Daddy may have written you the diagnosis was practically the same at Peter Bent Brigham as it was in Springfield – benign hypertension which can be almost controlled with drugs. The ones I'm now on do not give me a puffy face and I can breathe through my nose again and SMELL! Also, if I keep calm, perhaps I won't even have hypertension. When I come home I'll tell you some of the gruesome and funny details at the hospital in Boston. Typing is very hard for me and I just knocked over the new ash tray as I exuberantly pushed the lever across. As it was full of matches and butts, I must close now to clean up the mess on the rug. Much love, Mother."

To celebrate her escape from the hospital, my parents went to Florida that March for two weeks and stayed with my grandparents in Lake Worth. The respite from taking a mountain of pills didn't last long. She soon went back to Peter Bent Brigham for another two weeks to see how her body would react to a brand new blood pressure pill that had just come on the market.

Over the years I would try to understand why my mother never tried to communicate with her own father. It had been over two decades since she was pushed out of the house when he remarried. He lived in Hartford and we were there all the time. When I asked her about it, she would answer that she had never had a relationship with him like I had with my dad. One time when I was about ten years old I was in a booth in a restaurant and my grandmother, sitting across the table from me, leaned over and whispered, "Sally, what does that man look like sitting right behind me?" I described him to her and of course asked why. She replied, "He has a familiar accent and I thought it might be Albert, your mother's father." That freaked me out and I wondered again why we never met him. He was our other grandfather.

I learned later that he contacted mother before my sister Pam's funeral and asked if he could come to the funeral. She cut him off by saying he had never shown any interest in Pamela when she was alive and she didn't want him at the funeral. My siblings and I have talked about this a lot. Why no attempt at reconciliation? My mother was not a vindictive person. My brother thinks "our grandpa" had made it clear years before that he didn't want mother to stay in touch with her father who had practically kicked her out of her own house. Our grandfather was like a father to my mother and perhaps she didn't want to hurt him by starting a relationship with her father whom she had never been close to anyway. I think there were only eight or nine of us at Pam's funeral so having Albert suddenly show up there would have been very awkward so I understand why she responded the way she did in that instance.

We finally did meet our other grandfather once. I was in high school at the time. His wife Helene had contacted my mother and said Albert would like to see her and her children. He was living in Vermont then, so we drove up to meet him and Helene. We only saw them for a few minutes, my parents, my brother, my sister and I. He had dementia and I don't know if he really knew who we were. Helene was very friendly and we talked politely for a few minutes. I think we met at a park. I know there was no sitting down for a cup of tea or a glass of wine. He was a tall, good looking man and I felt such sadness for what might have been, for us and even more for him. He never saw either of his two children after they were in their twenties until this brief meeting and he probably won't ever see his grandchildren again. He missed out on so much of the joy life brings us. Dorothy, the daughter who moved to Sweden, never came back for a visit and if Frederick, her only child returned, he never contacted any of us. Dorothy died in her fifties, I think of ovarian cancer. She and my mother never kept in regular touch with letters.

When I was in college my parents hosted two couples from Sweden who were friends of Dorothy and they stayed at our house for a few days. Dorothy had written my parents describing her friends and saying she hoped Dad and Mom could show them around the Hartford area. She apologized for her bad English, saying it had become so rusty she had trouble expressing herself. Perhaps that's why she rarely wrote. Her son Frederick, the cousin I never met, was an only child. My brother found out he married someone named Eva and they only had one child, a son named Sven.

My mother's drinking problem did not stop after she became so ill. My father used to go alone annually on a Caribbean cruise for a week every winter. He said he just had to unwind and sit on a boat which relaxed him because of all the stress he was under at work. He always had to reach a certain plateau in sales at the office and then once it was reached, it would be made even higher the next year. My mother became seasick on boats so she never went. He'd bring back snapshots and it certainly didn't look like he was just sitting on the boat reading books. Mother drank heavily when he was gone. Again we never saw her pour a drink. My father locked the liquor cabinet when he went, but it didn't help.

My mother spent a lot of her time alone. My father played golf every week-end and participated in most of the tournaments which were usually Thursday through Sunday. When I was home from college one summer and now more aware of what was going on with adults instead of just worrying about what was going on with me, I asked my brother why it took so long for Dad to play eighteen holes of golf. I had taken some lessons that summer at my father's insistence and my score for nine holes was often the same as his for eighteen holes, and I was never out there for more than four hours. He was gone all day Saturday and all day Sunday. Bill said that he played bridge in the men's lounge for hours after he finished playing golf. I thought that was awful. I'm still angry about it.

This is what I've concluded in my seventy plus years. My dad was an athlete, loved being physically active, especially loved golf. He also was competitive and enjoyed poker and especially bridge. He was very social, loved parties and having lots of friends about. He married someone who was not an athlete, was not competitive and was not a joiner or an organizer of activities. I never doubted their love for each other and maybe if mother had been healthier and able to participate in more activities, her life, at least in my eyes, would have been happier.

I know in my marriage I am the social planner and athletic director of what we do, including our vacations. My mother was not. She did not plan or organize and so she often was left out. Her ongoing health problems were certainly a major factor. She became so ill in her mid-forties, the prime of life, and often did not feel well enough to do much of anything. She did enjoy the business reward outings to the resorts, and loved going to Florida when she could in the winter, but I wish there had been more for her. My dad encouraged her to take bridge lessons which she did, but she was never in a women's bridge group that played on a regular basis. She did play bridge with friends in some of the charity events that were organized to raise money, but she mostly played with her husband and all bridge players know how that can go, not always relaxing.

Part of my pleasure in playing tennis and now bridge on a weekly basis is not only the game, but the friendship that develops between the participants. The conversations are so important. They not only bring pleasure, but a wonderful sense of camaraderie and belonging that is so important when there is a need for solace or solutions at difficult times in life. My mother never had that. I remember when we lived in Cedar Grove my mother told me the other mothers met together for coffee once a week and talked about problems with their children. She thought that was awful, like being disloyal to your family. She didn't appreciate the value of constant, ongoing female companionship.

When Ted was at Harvard Business School in 1960 and we were living in Cambridge, Massachusetts, I came home to Springfield twice a week for about six weeks. I was required to do my Junior League Provisional course within two years of the invitation to join and the two years were up when we left Pensacola so it was now or never. The daughter of my mother's doctor, Sue, was a nurse in Boston and she had the same predicament so we took turns driving the two hours to Springfield twice a week. On one trip home, mother wasn't there and my dad implied something about her blood pressure and that she was in the hospital for observation overnight, but it was nothing serious. Or course I mentioned this to Sue on our drive home and I thought it odd that she didn't ask any questions. I found out later my mother had passed out at home from drinking and was taken to the hospital for observation so I'm sure Sue's father, my mother's doctor, had discussed it with Sue who was a nurse and she probably thought I was making up the lie. So honesty between adults and even adult children did not happen in our family despite my father's talk about the importance of never lying.

I have a lighter story about those trips from Boston to Springfield. I drove our ten year old Ford on Tuesdays and Sue drove her newer Volkswagen, the bug, on Thursdays. On one Tuesday night on our way back to Boston my car literally stopped dead on the Massachusetts Turnpike. I managed to pull over, but no electricity and no power so I couldn't put blinkers on or anything. We both sat there confident the state highway patrol would see our dark car on the side of the road and stop. I don't think either of us was scared which is amazing to me now. After about a half hour in the dark, a trooper did pull up and called for a tow truck. We stayed in the car as we were pulled a couple of miles to a service station. It was around midnight. They did the necessary repairs and told us we were safe to go. I called Ted from the phone at the service station and he will never live this down. This is his reply to my saying the car had just stopped dead and we were in absolute darkness on the highway at midnight until a trooper luckily rescued us,

"Well, is the car okay? Will they be able to fix it?"

Two weeks later, another Tuesday, same car all fixed up, same return trip, same complete loss of all electricity and same wait for the state trooper. The final awful coincidence was the same service station and the same attendants. Sue and I could tell they were coming on to us. They thought we had done this intentionally. They thought we were trying to pick them up! That was very unsettling to both of us. I think what was unsettling to Sue's parents was the thought of us being murdered or raped as we sat in a dark car waiting for a trooper. Dr. and Mrs. Pease said we were only to drive Sue's newer Volkswagen from then on.

Our son, Andrew, was born on October fifth, 1961, two months after we arrived in Detroit. My grandfather came to see us before I was even released from the hospital. He was so excited to have his first great grandchild. My parents came shortly after and my mother stayed on for two weeks and I had never felt as close to her as I did when we were both cradling and caring for my first child and her first grandchild. Ted started playing the song, "Lullaby and Goodnight," on the piano one night and before I could stop him, my mother quietly opened the door to the basement and slipped out for a few minutes. That was the song we always sang for Pamela ever since she was born when we put her to bed and we still couldn't hear it without shedding tears. My mother had lost a lot of weight, but looked very glamorous. After she returned home my father told us how proud he was that she got on the plane, traveled alone and wasn't uneasy about the trip. We all considered her fragile, someone who needed lots of care and love.

The whole family returned for a visit at Christmas and my siblings were introduced to their first nephew. It was a happy, joyous time. I came home for a short visit that next summer with Andy and loved showing him off to my friends and just being with my family. I drove with Andy to Boston to visit Dawn, my college roommate, for two days. She now had two sons. I was five months pregnant and due at the end of December.

My mother was now seeing a psychiatrist and taking one of the new tranquilizers. She didn't feel comfortable with him. He just listened and never offered any advice. She didn't even think he was really listening. He probably wasn't. We found out later he was having an affair with his secretary and soon ran off with her leaving a wife and two children. Mother had changed doctors before he ran away and was now much happier with her new psychiatrist. He not only really listened, she said, but offered advice and counseling that comforted her and gave her direction. She idolized him. She asked him to prescribe the pill for her that makes you allergic to alcohol, causing severe nausea if you drink any alcohol at all. She seemed happy, relaxed and thrilled to see her grandson again, but she was still so thin.

Mother returned to Detroit again for Andy's first birthday on October seventh and our anniversary and her birthday, both on the fifth. My father had some critical conference at work and wasn't able to come. We had a wonderful time celebrating the three occasions. I showed Mom the new crib I bought for the baby, necessary since Andy was still in his crib and would only be thirteen months old when the baby came. Mother slept in the soon to be baby's room in the three-quarter Jenny Lind bed I inherited from my grandparents. I arranged to have a bridge game and lunch at my house with two friends. Mother had taken lots of lessons, enjoyed the game and I thought that would be fun for her. Ted came back to our bedroom before I got up the morning of the bridge party and said something was wrong with my mother. It was the tranquilizers. They affected her like alcohol. She could hardly walk or talk. I cancelled the bridge luncheon and she felt better as the day progressed. Those drugs were in such an early stage then and so much was not known about their side effects or the correct dosage. My mother flew home at the end of the week, again seeming at ease with no apparent nervousness over the trip.

We talked on the phone frequently about the new baby and all the preparations. The baby would be fourteen months younger than Andy who still felt no need to walk because of his amazing agility with his walker. I was due Christmas eve and Mother was planning on flying out as soon as the baby arrived. On December eleventh I was woken up really early when the bedside phone started ringing. It was my father and he was having trouble talking. He said, "Grace died this morning." She was fifty years old. I couldn't go to the funeral because the baby was due in two weeks.

Those nine years with severe hypertension had not only caused my mother to lose so much weight, but had doubled the size of her heart and it was beginning to give out. The tranquilizers also played a major role in her death. The assumption was she had accidentally taken too many in one time frame. There was an autopsy as there always is in an unexpected death. The pathologist's report stated that she had an invasive tumor on her adrenal gland. That is a well known cause of sudden, severe hypertension. There were no MRI's or CAT scans then. The doctors had feared she would not survive exploratory surgery with her acute hypertension.

And they said more than once that her kidneys and adrenal gland appeared to be fine. So another level of sadness added to the story.

My sister, eleven years younger than I, had just turned sixteen days before Mother died. She planned on helping Dad sort and organize Mother's things when she came home for Spring break, but when she got home in March, all Mother's clothes and accessories were gone. We found out later that Dad sold them in a garage sale. Dad had never asked Cynthia or me if we wanted to keep anything of Mother's. All the children's books my mother had saved for the grandchildren were given to the Salvation Army. I know Dad was grieving, but he had a tendency to be headstrong without giving proper thought to his actions. He just wanted to clear things out and never gave a thought to his children's feelings.

My brother was in his first year of medical school at McGill University in Montreal preparing for his finals when Mother died. She was so excited that he wanted to be a doctor and he wanted to from the time he was ten years old. He worked one summer at Wesson Memorial hospital. One patient told his doctor that the intern named Gilbert was his favorite. Bill was still in high school. My brother just told me the reason for his popularity wasn't his "doctoral" personality, but his skill at sharpening needles used for drawing blood. The regular nurses didn't have the time to sharpen theirs, so his needles slid more easily and less painfully into the skin of an older person. Soon after the fifties, disposable needles were mandatory and with only one use they never became dull. Taking the time to sharpen the needles was just one of Bill's many attributes. He showed care and compassion at a really young age. Entering medical school was a dream he shared with our mother.

He returned to McGill after Mother died, but the thrill of becoming a doctor was gone. All those years of preparation and anticipation and it turned out the dream was better than the reality. He didn't like medical school. He finished his classes that semester, but also took a paid teaching assistantship with the biology department at McGill and discovered he loved teaching. This love had crept up on him. During the summers between his four years at Yale he was first a nature instructor and counselor at a camp; then for two summers a trail trip director leading numerous ten day wilderness expeditions around New England; and then a ranger-naturalist at Wind Cave National Park in South Dakota.

After graduation he went on a concert tour of Europe with the Yale Russian Chorus. They were in Berlin when a teenage East Berliner was machine gunned when trying to escape East Germany and left to die while hanging on the barbed wire separating East versus West behind the infamous Check-point Charlie. Neither side dared go rescue the boy as he lay dying in front of hundreds of spectators. After his death the Russian Chorus sang a Requiem Mass at the site in his honor.

Looking at the breadth of his experiences as a young man, it is not surprising that when he left medical school after freshman year, he joined the Peace Corps, hoping with his education they would assign him a teaching job. They sent him to Ethiopia and he was made head of the science department at Haile Selassie School where he taught biology to seniors and ninth graders. He started a music club after school and taught guitar with an emphasis on American folk songs. He became hooked on teaching. I often wonder if he would have quit if our mother hadn't died. She loved the idea of him being a doctor, really of him being a healer and he loved the idea of being able to please her. After Ethiopia he went on to get his doctorate, not in medicine, but in marine ecology. He enjoyed a wonderful career as a college professor which suited him perfectly.

Mother was buried in the graveyard at St. Thomas Church in Whitemarsh, Pennsylvania next to her daughter Pamela. My parents had put up three gravestones when Pamela died and my mother's inscription went on the second one.

My father, Jenny and Molly

10

My father, William Henry Gilbert Jr.

My father was the third generation of only boys in the family. He was born August 26, 1912 in Milo, Maine. His father was the principal of the high school in Milo when he was born. He went on to be principal in two other towns in Maine and one in Massachusetts. When the First World

War broke out the family moved to Old Hickory, Tennessee, a town built overnight by DuPont where his father supervised gun-cotton manufacturing for the war effort while he waited for the new high school to be built. The war ended before the high school was completed and his father decided to leave the educational field and take a job with the Travelers Insurance Company in Hartford, Connecticut.

The home my dad grew up in was a two story house at 91 Linnmoore Street in Hartford. They had the upper floor and rented out the lower one. I'm now amazed writing these memoirs to realize my mother and father never talked about their early school years. My mother didn't even talk about her high school years. The first story I heard about my father's academics was a family tale often repeated. It illustrated that my grandfather was a stern father wanting his boys to excel and if he found them wanting, becoming a man of iron steel with few words. I gather my father brought home a report card at the end of eighth grade with non-stellar grades. My grandfather looked at it without comment and my father thought he was home free. Two days later my father came to breakfast and saw two pamphlets on his plate, one for Loomis and one for Kingswood, two prep schools within driving distance of Hartford. He looked at his father and said,

"What's this for?"

"Choose!!!" was the sharp reply, implying there would be no discussion.

So my father started freshman year as a day student at Loomis. He thrived. I don't think he thrived academically, but he thrived athletically. He told us many times that he had been a three letterman at Loomis. His sports were baseball, football and hockey. Goalie was the position he always played in hockey because he confessed he was a lousy skater. Mother and Dad dated all through high school, but they both also dated other people. Dad was a big man on campus and loved it.

He ended up boarding at Loomis his last two years. In April of senior year he broke two written-in-stone rules – driving a motor vehicle and leaving campus after hours. He was caught riding a motorcycle in Hartford after midnight. He was expelled from Loomis on the spot. He'd already been accepted into the University of Virginia, but they certainly expected him to come with a high school degree. My grandfather contacted Hartford High School where he had graduated many years earlier and talked them into accepting and graduating his son in two months. Perhaps they had no choice, being a public school, but my father's skill in baseball probably helped ease his way in. The season was starting in one week. My father never told me this story. All I ever heard was the critical importance of academic achievement and how he wished he had been more conscientious in school. Little did I know how very non-conscientious he was. In fact, I think he would have been a challenge to any parent. It is interesting that he shared so many tales of his growing up with my brother, who is the real scholar in our family and in many ways the opposite of my father in personality. I am only now hearing about his adventures from my brother.

When my father was a teenager, his parents had a Russian wolfhound which he said was the dumbest dog he had ever known. The dog was afraid to go up or down stars and they lived on the second floor of the two story house they owned. My father's job was to carry that dog up and down the stairs whenever he had to relieve himself. They also had a white collie at some point, very unusual then and now. This collie was related to President Coolidge's white collies.

After my father arrived at University of Virginia, he joined SAE, Sigma Alpha Epsilon, the fraternity his father belonged to at the University of Maine. He loved the freedom of college and he loved the weather in Virginia. The southern graciousness and friendliness, so different from New England, especially appealed to him, but most of all he loved playing poker and he really loved the thrill of gambling when he played poker.

By the spring of his sophomore year it became obvious to my father that his gambling debts had accumulated to such an extent that he would not be able to pay off his debts himself. He had no choice but to call his father. Instead of sending a check, my grandfather came himself. He wanted to know all the details and did feel better when he learned the gambling was only among the students, no Mafia type figures were involved. He wrote enough checks to pay off all the debts and the two of them headed out to dinner before my grandfather started home to Connecticut. I don't know why my father's eye glasses were on the car seat as he was near sighted like me and I assumed he always wore his glasses. But there they were on the seat and he inadvertently sat on them and broke them. All the suppression of anger and frustration over his son's gambling and probably over his expulsion from Loomis which my grandfather had managed to repress, now burst out and he showed a fury seldom seen before, so the story goes. Shortly afterwards, my father was told he was to transfer to the University of Maine.

My mother moved in with my father's parents sometime during his junior year in college. She was estranged from her father, lived at the YWCA for awhile and I don't know exactly what precipitated her moving in with her boyfriend's parents. My grandfather adored Dad's girlfriend Grace. It was certainly an odd arrangement, but it suited everyone's interests. They both still dated other people. That is what I call an odd arrangement.

Over my father's spring break junior year, 1934, he and my mother went to New York City, ostensibly to see a play, but actually to elope. They were married in a civil ceremony at city hall. They came back to Hartford around 3am as though they had just driven home from New York after the play. They planned on telling no one about their marriage for awhile. I never did learn how long they planned to keep it secret. The news leaked out immediately because my mother was a well know amateur actress in the Hartford area and some eager reporter had spotted the legal announcement of their marriage in New York.

My grandparents were very upset, not upset over the marriage, upset because they had married in such an abrupt manner without first informing them. My grandfather was in

California on business and didn't return until June when he laid down the new rules. My father was told that he now had a wife to support and he'd better find a job. He'd have to complete his last year of college at a later date. My brother, on his genealogy quest requested a copy of my father's transcripts at Maine and learned he was on probation first semester junior year and barely keeping a C average second semester, so perhaps he felt he'd just as soon quit and make some money. I didn't know until I was in my twenties that my father had not graduated from college. He never did make up that missing year. This non-graduate fact was something he deliberately kept from his children when we were growing up. He joked with my brother years later that he attended four years of prep school and two colleges and never graduated from any of them.

The year of their elopement was one of the worst years of the worst depression our country had ever seen. My grandfather managed to find him a job at the Travelers Insurance Company, but my father wasn't happy. He thought all his peers and even worse, his bosses, felt he only got the job because of his father and he knew they harbored a lot of resentment toward him. So the desire to find another job, although difficult in 1934 and especially with no college degree, was a necessity to him. He felt confident he would be good in sales and the next year he landed a job with an insurance company in Chicago. Dad started going bald in college and with a balding head and rimless eyeglasses he looked a decade older than his real age. He said this contributed to his success in selling life insurance. He looked experienced. Mother, now pregnant with me, stayed behind in Hartford at her in-laws insistence until they felt I was old enough to travel. My father didn't see me until I was four months old.

My parents lived in Chicago for a couple of years and then moved back to the East when Dad took a job with the Prudential Insurance Company. They rented houses in various New Jersey suburbs close to Newark where my father worked. My brother was born on November thirtieth in 1939 when they lived in a house on Grove Street in Montclair. My father and one of his best friends, Ken Foster, were in Manhattan riding horses when my mother frantically tried to reach him when she went into labor six weeks early with my brother. The only house I ever heard stories about in that era was the one on Grover Street in West Caldwell that they shared with two bachelors, Ken Foster and Bill Chubb. They hired a full time maid named Julia. I'm sure they had some fun stories to relate about their shared residence, but sadly I never heard any.

I did hear about one huge event regarding the three men. A few years after they all left their communal living on Grover Street, the Japanese bombed Pearl Harbor and my father in a fervor of patriotism urged the other two to go with him to the Army Induction Center to see if they could enlist. My father was rejected immediately because of his glasses or his wife or his two children, but Ken and Bill were still bachelors and they enlisted. Ken was made a cook and this is the story my father loved to tell about Ken. The army food was awful and Ken wanted to get some fresh vegetables for his men. They always served canned green peas which are hideous tasting to anyone who is used to fresh or frozen peas. After pulling many strings and doing lots of bargaining back and forth he was sent a shipment of fresh peas. He was like a kid in a candy store, he was so excited over his coup of the vegetables. Then elation turned to disbelief. The soldiers hated the fresh peas. They didn't taste right. Most of them dumped those precious peas right into the garbage can, hardly touched. Ken lost a lot of his zeal for cooking after that. After the Army, he went back to his job with the Prudential Insurance Company and went on to become the chief operating officer of the Prudential. He and his wife, Goodie, remained close friends. The Fosters visited us many times in all our different homes.

Bill Chubb's story is not a happy one. He joined the Army Air Corps as there was no separate Air Force then. He was made a bombardier and had lots of missions over Germany. On one of them his squadron witnessed his plane in a mid-air crash with no parachutes opening from either plane. The Army told his widowed mother that he was missing in action, what they always said when there was no actual body to identify. She lived the next decades praying he would just show up one day. She hoped perhaps a German family had taken him in and nursed him back to health and maybe he suffered from insomnia. She refused to accept the finality of his death.

My father was very active in the community when we lived in Longmeadow. It was probably important to his success as a manager to keep his name out there. He was involved with the American Heart Association and in charge of many of their drives. He was a joiner unlike my mother and always wanted to be active. Golf was his passion and he luckily lived in an era when successful men in their forties and fifties could take off a Thursday and Friday many times a year to enter a golf tournament.

Giving unsolicited philosophical advice was a favorite pastime of my father's, especially in letter format. I'm quoting selectively from one of his lengthy letters in the fall of my freshman year at Vassar. I think it might have been in response to a letter I wrote telling him how much I was enjoying my philosophy classes and perhaps feeling less excited about religion in general.

> *"Spiritual development, Sally, is just as important as intellectual growth. Society is well organized to develop the latter, but does a poor job with the former. The tensions we experience in today's world may very well be the price paid for our negligence in the spiritual area. Never forget that character is the horizontal beam resting on two pillars: Intellect and Spirit. Only the truly great build both pillars to be of equal strength so that their character is perfectly balanced across these two pillars. In college many situations challenge the intellect. This intellect is a vigorous and aggressive thing. It is impatient, vocal, frequently self-centered and invariably vain. Spirit, on the other hand, gets its strength from patience, understanding, hope and grief.*

Spirit comes to only those who invite it. Intellect scorns this gentle grace. It has and always will crash the party. Don't let this happen to you, dear. Remember and never forget, that when you say 'I believe' you concede you don't know. When you believe, don't worry about proof. You have no right or need to expect any. Until man literally returns from the dead, then and only then will he have proven the existence or non-existence of God. Until then, dear, don't worry too much about how much you 'know' and too little about what you 'believe.' Daddy's always thought you had a well developed level character. Keep working on it – it's something we have to earn. We are not born with it."

While I was away from home freshman year an exciting event happened in our backyard. Our lawn was never luscious. Our gardens didn't exist. My father decided to change all this. He had a stockade fence installed around the entire backyard with wide curving beds in front of it designed and planted by a landscape architect. The first year he had the architect put a putting green in one corner of the yard. A putting green does not like to be stuffed in a corner. It likes the free flow of air circling all around. It likes a grounds keeper hovering over it, dispensing daily love and care. It received none of this in our backyard so out the half-dead putting green went the second year. My father bought a prefab storage shed which looked just like a child's playhouse. It had a Dutch door and a paned window with a window box. It was an adorable attention getter. My grandfather brought some flowering perennials from his extensive garden the next year to supplement the bushes planted by the architect, but most of them met a sorry end at the hands of an inexperienced hired helper who plucked them clean in an energetic spring clean-up. However, the final overall landscaping effect was very impressive. That boring backyard was transformed into a beautiful piece of property.

When my mother, in her early forties, was in the hospital in Springfield and Boston for so many weeks with critically high blood pressure, my dad needed a project to keep him busy and to keep his mind from always dwelling on the severity of his wife's health. He decided to finish off a corner of our basement and make a TV room with a couch and comfy chairs. It wasn't a large area, but it was cozy. I don't know how he knew how to build it. His father wasn't at all handy, but he said it was what kept him sane during all those months of worry over my mother.

My father was the one who organized any family trips we took, most of our family activities and all our vacations at the shore. He was the social chairman in our family. I never realized how unusual that was until I was an adult. My three daughters, Julie, Molly and Jenny, and I are definitely the social chairmen in our families. My son's wife, Margaret, comes from a large family and is close to many of her siblings who still live in Chicago so she plans all those family activities and their social events with other couples, but my son Andy is active in planning things with our family. He loves to organize parties with special themes always involving hats, sometimes shirts and lots and lots of props. He says there is no such thing as a real party without hats. He will often order items ahead from the internet, but there's always a last minute dash to the biggest drug store to get prizes or streamers or whatever he needs for the finishing touch to make the event extra special. It reminds me of the pleasure my father also felt when planning an event, although he didn't show the same exuberance and material largesse that Andy does.

When we were in elementary school, my dad more than once put on a ruffled apron and a floppy straw hat with feathers and danced around the living room holding an opened umbrella telling Billy and me that this was how our mother danced when she was in burlesque shows. When we lived in Whitemarsh he loved going to auctions in Philadelphia and bought some interesting things. One purchase was an entire suite of furniture for the master bedroom made out of some bizarre Brazilian wood. I personally didn't care for it, but he said it was very exotic and originally very expensive. He bought a huge desk with a single large drawer on each side. It was an elaborate piece of furniture designed not only to serve two people at the same time, but to look appropriate and gracious in a spacious book lined study. It resided in one corner of our living room on Brittany Road at an oblique angle. Only he used the desk and when he sat down to write the monthly bills, we all stayed out of the living room until the anger and fury over all that money going out subsided. My mother's middle name was Hildegarde and she hated it. The auction find he loved the most was a large silver goblet with the word Hildegarde engraved in huge letters on the side.

When I turned twenty-one on December eighth of my senior year in college, my father sent me a three page typed letter about "coming of age." He loved giving formal presentations on how to approach and manage different stages or crises in life. This letter was also a kind of love letter to me.

> *"On turning twenty-one, we gain certain rights and we lose others. Parents are relieved of all legal responsibility for support or maintenance. You can enter contracts, own property, vote, have medical treatment without parental approval ...and so it goes, but family life can soften the equation a bit. In your home there is no change. I want you to enjoy to the fullest any new rights and to recognize and honor your duties as you always have. The only thing we demand is the same old Truth we have always insisted upon. Sometimes truth hurts, but it is a healthy bruise from which we recover. True pride is probably impossible without it. Real deep character makes a prerequisite of pride. Probably the finest compliment I can pay you is the fact that I recognize that you have known these things for a long time.*
>
> *Your mother and I married young in a depression and having had more than normal medical expenses are quite familiar with an unpleasant four letter word called 'debt.' Debt appears now to be socially acceptable. The idea of use it now and pay for it later is as well known as it is dangerous. For a girl to enter adulthood in debt is not my idea of a*

sound or desirable circumstance. We are therefore forgiving your European trip debt. However from this point forward I expect you to live within your means and to do without when so required.

It's difficult to realize our Sally is now a full grown legal lady. Of course when I look in the mirror and see that telltale bulge at the waist, I realize that Time Marches On. But what Mother and I want you to know is that one of the big reasons we haven't noticed the passing of time, lies in the fact that you have always been a source of pride to us. Parents get their true experience in life from their children. I've always felt that children represented a form of immortality. Religion teaches us that the second life is more satisfying than the first, more important. I quite agree. Children have the awful capacity to create or destroy parental happiness. This is why the job of a parent is so important. If the job is well done, the reward is tremendous. When the job is poorly done, the price is staggering. As with all things, the right to have children is accompanied by the duty to raise them well. Our oldest child has proven a reward to us in every sense of the word, and we love her very, very much.   Love, Dad."

Despite extraordinarily good insurance from the Connecticut General, my mother's years of illness cost my father a huge amount of money. I'm sure my grandfather helped him or we probably would have had to change our manner of living. I can't even comprehend what it would cost now to spend over four months in the hospital.

Golf was my father's passion. He was lucky that his job allowed him to enter most of the golf tournaments at the Longmeadow Country Club. I think he usually scored in the high eighties, but one tournament he and his partner did extraordinarily well in the qualifying round on Thursday and were put in the first division, a very big deal to them. My father had never played in the first division before. They lost on Friday so they went into the Consolation round on Saturday and won. Now they had to play again on Sunday morning. They won again which meant playing another eighteen holes Sunday afternoon. This means they played ninety holes of golf in four days. Neither of them had ever done anything like that before. Now I'll quote a paragraph from a letter written by my mother, which is where I learned about the previous just mentioned details,

> *"When Mrs. Walker, Dad's partner's wife, and I arrived at the club Sunday at 5:30 they looked like a couple of sick chickens or tired ducks. Everyone by now knew that they were so badly chafed they could hardly walk. I had filled the tub Saturday night with baking soda for a 'sitz' bath which Dad said helped. This morning we sprinkled corn starch all over him and he says he feels better, but he is so stiff all over. He won a beautiful hand carved wooden salad bowl trimmed with sterling silver and two servers. His partner won a fancy percolator. Since neither one could hardly walk on Sunday, Mrs. Walker and I went up on stage and chose the prizes. We had eight people at our house Saturday for cocktails and*

then went to the club for dinner. On Sunday after the prizes were awarded we had a delicious buffet supper on the porch of the club after cocktails on the terrace – also eight people. My blood pressure was up a little each night, but I had a wonderful time and it is good to be a butterfly again. I've been a caterpillar in a cage a long time."

My mother died seven years after writing that letter and fifteen days before her second grandchild was born. She was a girl, our first daughter, and we named her Julia Grace Flynn in honor of my mother. Mother is buried in Whitemarsh, Pennsylvania next to her daughter Pamela who died fifteen years earlier.

My father remarried two years later at the age of fifty-two. He was working late in the office one night and flicked off the main light switch as he was leaving when a voice yelled, "Hey, I'm still here." It was Ruth Barrup who had worked in the office for years. She was in charge of the claims department. He apologized and then, hating eating alone, asked her if she'd like to join him for a bite. That was the start of their courtship.

Ruth was in her late forties and had never married. We were all fine with Dad remarrying, but foolishly worried there must be something wrong with someone who had never married. He told us why he was attracted to Ruth. First he said a second marriage is not like the first. You are looking for different things. He could never duplicate the love he felt for our mother, Grace. He liked the fact that Ruth had no baggage, quite frankly, no children, so their attention would be only on his children and grandchildren. He said she was spunky and witty and he enjoyed her company. She had a temper, he said, and he liked that spirit. She had her own house, but she always put her car up on blocks all winter as she was too nervous to drive in the snow and bad weather. That surprised all of us. Completely giving up driving in the winter because of intermittent snow when she grew up in Vermont, did not fit the picture of the independent, liberated woman our father had described. He also said Ruth was one of those women who had become more attractive as they aged.

They were married in a small ceremony with my sister being the maid of honor and my brother the best man. Ruth moved into the house on Brittany road. Ted and I were not encouraged to come to the ceremony because of the expense of baby sitters and airplane tickets. They stayed in Longmeadow four or five years. Ruth loved not having to go to work anymore and she loved the glamour of marrying the boss. She told me one of the men in their office told my father that if he married Ruth and she retired it would seriously screw up the entire claims department and he would regret it. She also told me a couple of years later that another man in the office called her and told her to use her influence to curtail my father's drinking. He said the word out in the office was you better see Bill Gilbert before lunch if it's anything important because after lunch and those multiple martinis he's two sheets to the wind. Ruth urged Dad to drink less and tried to shorten their cocktail hour, but not with much success and in the later years she just learned to live with it.

My father retired early on a medical disability. I think it was described as an emotional breakdown. He said the cumulative years of all that pressure to meet and exceed deadlines did him in emotionally and physically. I'm sure his overuse of alcohol also contributed. He retired at fifty-five and enjoyed a generous disability pension plus fabulous health insurance from the Connecticut General for the next twenty five years of his life. The world was a kinder, more generous place decades ago.

The first year of Dad's retirement Ruth and Dad rented a house in Sarasota on Long Boat Key for three months. I was so excited and asked if we could visit over our children's spring break. We only had Andy and Julie then. He said it just wouldn't work out as the house had all white wall to wall carpeting and he had promised the owner that it would only be the two of them. This owner had never rented before and he was very nervous so my father felt he had to make that promise. I was so disappointed. I couldn't believe my father would agree to rent a house that wouldn't allow him to have his grandchildren visit. I liked Ruth and thought her lively personality would be good for my father, but I knew my mother would never have agreed to such a stipulation. I now realized that my father and step-mother would not be the same kind of grandparents I had growing up, interested in every facet of their grandchildren's lives. It made me really sad.

We were later invited to other visits in Florida. Ruth and Dad ended up buying a condo at Midnight Pass on Siesta Key in Sarasota. The balcony looked over the ocean and the front porch looked over the inland waterway, a fabulous location. Dad was able to lease a dock twenty feet from his door so he bought a motor boat for fishing and cruising. They hired an interior designer to decorate the unit and it looked elegant. The balcony chairs with charming curved lines and a dainty, round seat pillow looked absolutely stunning, but were miserably uncomfortable, a fact so many decorators overlook.

We now had four children and Dad invited us to come over spring break, but only with the two older children, Andy and Julie. The younger ones, Molly and Jenny, were four and two years old and my dad said there just wasn't enough for them to do at that age and it would really limit what we could do. He was probably right, but again I was disappointed and hurt that he wasn't anxious to see all our children. We hired a babysitter for the younger ones and went. He rented another unit in the same building for us at his expense and we all had a really fun time. The kids loved going on the boat and loved being able to run out the door and be on the beach. Same invitation the next year, same restriction, same acceptance, same anger over excluding two children, same guilt for leaving two children behind, but we went.

When I was packing to go on that second Florida trip with the plane tickets all bought, Dad casually mentioned that Ruth wouldn't be there for the first three days of our visit as she was going to be in Longmeadow for the estate sale at our house. This was the first word I'd heard about any estate sale. There was no mention of, "Do any of you children want anything from the house?" My sister who was in school only an hour away wasn't even given the offer of coming home for the sale. We three siblings were stunned. It wasn't as though there were lots of goodies in the house. My parents had eloped so had none of the treasures gained from a large wedding. To be honest I personally couldn't think of anything specific that I wanted, but I expected to be asked. I think my brother was still in graduate school so he certainly could have used some of the furniture. Maybe that was the problem. Dad was afraid Bill would want it all!

My father didn't have a single nostalgic bone in his body, but you'd think Ruth would have been more attuned to the situation. I learned that she, like my father, didn't have a clue about the importance of handing things down to another generation. When she sold her home and furniture after she married my dad, my dad who had two daughters, she gave away a dozen hand made quilts that were made by friends and relatives of her mother's in Vermont to her next door neighbor who had once said they were pretty. She admitted she hardly even knew that neighbor. What an opportunity she missed to please us or certainly to please me. Cynthy was only eighteen, but I know she would have loved a quilt or two. One last gripe, when Ruth arrived in Florida she told me the estate sale was a big success. She said they even got 25 cents for the paper weight Andy had made for her. I remember saying, probably in a shocked, disbelieving voice,

"You sold Andy's paper weight?"

I think she suddenly realized she should have kept her mouth shut. For Ruth's first birthday as their grandmother, Andy searched for a really smooth rock that would be just the right size to put on a desk as a paper weight. Then he hand painted a miniature summer scene with a sail boat and trees and even put Ruth's name on the bottom. I realize you can't keep everything your children make for you. I have cupboards full of handmade goodies from my children that I know I will have to part with if I move to a smaller home, but Ruth only had that one handmade gift created just for her and she parted with it for a quarter.

Speaking of handing down possessions, Ted and I have furniture that has gone on to live one exciting life after another. Our two matching green loveseats that we bought in 1962 for our living room in the first home we owned on Paddington Road in Troy, Michigan, traveled to our second home on Lamplighter Lane in Bloomfield Hills, just a few miles away and kept their honored place in the living room. When we moved to Kansas in 1978 they were placed in our spacious master bedroom, facing each other on either side of a fireplace so they still looked proper and proud. We knew they wouldn't fit in our next house in Oklahoma, so contemplated getting rid of them, but our next door neighbor, Marilyn Thomas, insisted on storing them in her attic until one of our children wanted them which she was sure would happen.

Sure enough, the next year they moved to Plano, Texas with our son Andy who had accepted a job in the claims department of the Connecticut General Insurance Company. (Guess who had the connection to get him an interview for that job?) He didn't last long in that clerical type job and the loveseats met an ignoble death on a rainy day in Texas when Andy deposited them in a dumpster as he drove out of town on his way to Boston. He didn't have a job in Boston and had only been there once on one of our family vacations, but he had fallen in love with the area, was up for adventure and wanted to try living on the East coast where his parents grew up. The loveseats were twenty-one years old and Andy was twenty-three.

Their successors, a cocoa brown couch and orange loveseat were picked to match our favorite oil painting and were bought in Kansas City in 1982. They lived there four years, moved with us to live in Oklahoma City two years and then came to Bloomfield Hills for another ten years. They had always maintained their prime position in our living rooms. Their next stop was East Lansing, Michigan in a tiny basement apartment leased by my daughter Jenny. They almost didn't make it down the stairs in that apartment. That stay was short lived and they were back above ground again in a rented house in Lansing for another year. Their next home was back to East Lansing and for the first time they were not in a living room, but in my daughter Jenny's family room. They enjoyed years of fun in that room with three boys sprawling and jumping on them while they watched TV. Their current place of residence, starting in 2014 at the mature age of thirty six years, is in a fraternity house somewhere on the campus of Michigan State. They were rescued by perceptive fraternity boys who saw them standing at the curb outside my daughter's house, waiting for the trash truck. Now just think what my father missed out on – not knowing "the rest of the story" regarding all of his furniture.

Ruth and Dad were on Siesta Key about five years. What did them in were two things. First, my father agreed to be president of the condo association which meant overseeing the treasurer who had to not only collect the monthly dues, but even harder, collect the assessments. The latter was the thorn. Being right on the ocean there was constant, ongoing deterioration from the salt water and the dues were not sufficient to cover it. The majority of the owners were only there off and on in the winter and rarely at all the other seasons, so it was hard to pin them down for the money they owed. It was a continual struggle and harassing people for money is not enjoyable.

The second negative described by Ruth, but felt by both of them, was it seemed like every time they left their doorway they would run into another owner who would want to chit chat and according to Ruth, "snoop about our business." There were cocktails parties about three nights a week in different units and Ruth often didn't feel like going because she complained you just keep making the same boring small talk with the same people night after night. My more gregarious father enjoyed them more, so he would go and probably talk about his golf game which never bored him. He'd make an excuse for Ruth, the only plausible one being she wasn't feeling well. Then Ruth said, for the next few days, every time she saw someone they would put on a very serious face and ask her about her health.

A friend my dad knew from the Connecticut General, Frank Minninger, raved about Sun City Center, a Del Webb development for seniors less than an hour from Sarasota. They visited it, liked it and bought a typical two bedroom, two bath house with a living room and a family room right on the golf course. A huge porch, extending the entire length of the house, overlooked the sixth green and it was delightful to relax there and watch the golfers.

All the children were now invited to visit, but I only remember being there over spring break with the two younger ones. I know the older ones saw their home in Sun Center, but I think it was on a side trip when they were in Florida over spring break with their peers. I have many photographs of Ted and me and the younger girls with Ruth and Dad cavorting about Cypress Gardens which offered the combo of beautiful gardens and lots of animals. The girls loved riding around in Grandpa's golf cart which all the seniors used as a car to get around the development. When it didn't look too busy on the street my father would let them take turns sitting on his lap and steering the cart.

There were many pools throughout Sun City, but all of them had the same restriction; anyone under eighteen could only use the pool between eleven and one, prime burning time. We rarely used the pool because of that time slot. It was too risky with Irish-English-Swedish skin unused to that tropical sun.

We took an afternoon spin one day on a motorboat owned by my Uncle Hammy who lived on Long Boat Key. Hammy was my father's younger and only sibling. His real name was Hamlin, their mother's maiden name and my middle name. There was a four year difference in their ages. Hammy became a widower in his forties. He had a string of girlfriends over the years and then married a second time to a woman also named Ruth. Betty, his first wife, and he had two children, a boy, Sandy, the age of my brother and a girl, Marianne, a little older than my sister. They were our only cousins. We did have a third cousin, Frederick in Sweden, who we never met.

We used to see my uncle's family at Thanksgiving before my grandfather retired in 1950 and they started going to Florida in early November. After that we rarely saw them. We exchanged Christmas gifts when we were young. My father would buy nice gifts for their two children, but their gifts to us were usually those junky things made by Japan after the war. Inevitably my father would start talking negatively about those gifts almost before we opened them. This upset me because I was very fond of Uncle Hammy and I didn't think my dad should be so critical. He told us his negative cracks were directed at Betty, who he said was a renowned cheapskate.

A brief aside about Betty. First, I was a flower girl in their wedding when I was three years old. I wore a pink and rose colored long gown with satin rosebuds scattered about. I tossed rose petals from my basket as I walked down the aisle. I am told I was very poised. I haven't the slightest recollection of this event, but my mother saved the picture with a long description of the event from the newspaper. We never had an actual photograph of me or anyone else in the wedding.

Betty was attractive with red hair and was known for being very, very neat. I'm surprised she could even cook dinner and bear the moments the pans were dirty and out of the cupboard. Her mother was the millstone around her neck, demanding and unpleasant. Betty covered all her living room furniture in rigid plastic coverings. They lived in a small house in Levittown on Long Island. Betty died young and Hammy said when they had the estate sale after her death many of the neighbors fought over buying their couches which they exclaimed were in such perfect condition it looked like no one had ever sat on them. Now that's a sad story.

On some summer visits to my grandparents, Sandy was also visiting which was fun for my brother. Marianne had two marriages, and became a stepmother to four daughters in her second marriage. She died young and I don't know what caused her death. Sandy was one of the nine ushers in our wedding, conscripted for duty when I panicked that we were short on ushers. Sadly I haven't seen him since our wedding over a half century ago, but we exchange yearly Christmas cards.

My father and Hammy were not close growing up. Hammy was the student my father never was and not really into athletics. You would think he would have been the closest to my grandfather who also was a student and not an athlete, but my father's family was definitely the preferred family in my grandparent's eyes. Even I could see this as a young girl and I think I know the reason why. It was my mother. She was like a daughter to my grandparents. Betty was always busy in turmoil with her mother and made no special attempt to be close to her husband's parents.

When I was pregnant with Molly, Dad said he and Ruth would like to come when I was in the hospital and help take care of Andy and Julie, 7 and 6 years old. They were both in school, although Julie only until noon. I was thrilled. We had never had assistance from any relatives with child care since we never lived within a thousand miles of any relatives and we also didn't have many relatives. I went into labor with Molly almost a week early so I went into the hospital the first night they arrived. I had already written many notes about the house and the children, but I never had a chance to give Ruth a detailed tour of the kitchen. She did not like to cook and maybe that's what did her in. Ted, typical of his era, is not a hands-on guy so he probably wasn't much help. My dad was great with kids and I'm guessing he helped put them to bed and did a lot of the care. When you had a fussy baby he was the one who had that magic touch. He said the secret to his success was gently caressing their tiny feet, holding them tightly and quietly singing a lullaby.

I came home with baby Molly from the hospital four days later and Dad announced he and Ruth were leaving the next morning. I couldn't believe it. I had hardly seen them at all and the real help, from my perspective, was needed now when I would be exhausted from being up half the night nursing the baby. I told him I never had a chance to even visit with them and couldn't they stay just a little longer. He said Ruth wasn't really used to kids and she was exhausted from those four days. Ruth was only fifty-three.

Now I have to brag a minute. When we just had the older two, Ted and I went on a few vacations alone and hired different well recommended babysitters. Inevitably the babysitter would say on our return home that she had never taken care of better behaved children. I would smile smugly to myself, knowing it was because I had been a child psychology major, had taught elementary school for four years, had read all the right books and therefore had the knowledge and confidence to raise such well behaved children. After my fourth child arrived, I stopped patting myself on the back about my child rearing abilities. It was a painful lesson to learn that the type of personality your child is born with is the biggest determinant of the ease and success you will have with producing perfectly behaved children.

Back to Ruth, I felt confident she had not suffered through four days with rambunctious children, she just wasn't used to taking care of children, even perfect ones! She was the oldest of five siblings and did a lot of caretaking growing up, but that didn't appear to be preparation enough. Ruth grew up on a dairy farm in Vermont and the story I loved hearing her tell about her childhood was the round trip from home to elementary school starting with kindergarten. She and her best friend regularly rode their ponies to school and tied them up at a post until school was over and then rode them back home. They went to a one room schoolhouse until fourth grade. She never mentioned ever graduating to horses. When she and Dad retired to Sun City, her pony riding friend from kindergarten was already living there with her husband and another elementary school friend lived just a block away with her husband. So the three pals who went to elementary school together in Vermont, ended up spending their last years together in the same small retirement community in Florida.

We saw Ruth and Dad at least once a year when Dad was still healthy and enjoyed traveling, often over Thanksgiving and always during the summer months. One July they rented a small cottage right on Crooked Lake for two weeks, only fifteen minutes away from our cottage in Harbor Springs in northern Michigan. That was really a perfect arrangement as they could leave when the action became too much for them. I remember the eight of us taking a day trip to Mackinac Island. We did a lot of exploring, eating, walking, riding in horse drawn buggies and having an action filled, exhausting, fun time. We took the ferry back to the main land around six o'clock. I suggested stopping on our way home for pizza. Ruth and Dad said they were tired and were going to just go back to their cottage and relax. Instead of feeling hurt they weren't joining us, I was angry. We four adults should suffer through to the end together. I was really jealous they were able to go back to their quiet cottage and just relax.

My father liked projects, just as I did. Ted hated projects and went to great lengths to avoid them. When we first built our cottage, our semi-psychotic cockapoo would go crazy when we left to go to the beach or anywhere at all. He would frantically scratch on the glass of the doorwalls and even gnaw on the door frames. The basement wasn't finished yet so my dad and I spent an afternoon constructing a gate that would go across the bottom steps so the dog, Dusty, wouldn't be able to come upstairs. I don't know why we didn't just buy a kiddie gate, but we didn't. It looked good when we finished and we both always enjoyed a sense of satisfaction when we created something. I never told him Dusty figured out how to jump over it two weeks after we put it up.

Shopping at JC Penny or Kohl's would never occur to my father. He only bought suits from top men's stores like Brooks Brothers. Same for his selection of dress shirts, which he often had made by his tailor to his specifications. I think his philosophy was the more it cost, the better the quality and he liked quality. I did not inherit that gene. I look at the price tag on a ladies blouse at Saks and think who would ever pay that ridiculous price.

Dad and Ruth were my children's only grandparents and I always hoped they would play an important part in my children's lives as my grandparents had in mine, but it didn't happen. They were very conscientious about sending gifts at Christmas and birthdays and visited us regularly until they were in their late seventies. But my dad showed no interest in watching any of their games or tennis matches when he visited. My sister became a talented tennis player, all by playing and being instructed on the public tennis courts in Longmeadow. She told me neither of her parents ever watched any of her matches and she was involved in lots of tournaments. As my Dad grew older he rarely telephoned and had no interest in the details of our children's lives. They didn't come for any baptisms or graduations. Maybe it's because they lived in Florida and we were always a plane trip away. The furthest my grandparents had ever lived was a six hour car trip the two years we lived in Pennsylvania. And maybe it was because of all the medications my dad was on. I know he didn't feel that well a lot of the time.

The first two years Ruth and Dad were permanent residents in Florida they rented a flat in London for six weeks over the summer. My daughter Julie was touring with friends around Europe after she graduated from college and stopped by to see her grandparents. She asked them to go with her to watch one of the tennis matches at Wimbledon and they said they'd rather stay in the apartment as they could see the tennis much better on TV. Another moment to bond that never happened.

Two summers they rented a cottage in the cool mountains near Ashville. They enjoyed that, but said it wasn't as relaxing as they hoped because all their friends in Sun City expected an invitation to come visit for a few days. The next few years they stayed in a cottage in Camden, Maine owned by my father's aunt, Lydia Godsoe, who was about ten years older than my father. She lived in the manor home on a property of hundreds of acres. My father told me she was the richest woman in Maine, mostly because of all the timber on the land she owned. She had a few extra cottages on her extensive property and invited Ruth and Dad to come and stay free of rent every summer. I think they did for at least three summers. There was a condition, not stated, but expected, and that was to play cards or a game with Lydia most evenings. My father told me he wished it was bridge, but Lydia and Ruth didn't play. They found some fun games and it was enjoyable.

He loved the quiet and the beautiful setting. They certainly weren't bothered by friends visiting from Florida. Lydia didn't drink and they were sure she didn't approve of drinking so Ruth took on the job of bringing all the empty liquor bottles my father had emptied each week when not in Lydia's presence to the town dump. She didn't want Lydia's hired hands who emptied the trash reporting back to Lydia that there must be a lot of partying going on in the Gilbert cottage because of all the liquor that was being consumed. Of course it was all consumed by my father. Ruth rarely drank. It is impressive that my father was able to spend every evening with Lydia and never have a single drink in her presence.

My father and Ruth enjoyed many trips abroad, usually with an organized group on a bus, or coach as the tour leaders prefer to call it. They went to England more than once, but also France, Italy and Germany. Not being adventurous travelers, their trips were usually to Europe. In Germany my father bought a Mercedes Benz to be shipped back to this country. As the crane moved it from ship to shore in New York something ran amok and the car fell into the ocean. I don't know how my father found out, probably the lack of delivery for weeks while they desalinated it or whatever they had to do. He bought that precision made German car so he would never have to fuss with repairs. That jinxed car spent days in the repair shop every few months.

He also bought Andy a pair of leather lederhosen which I saved and gave to Andy's son Brian when he was five. Julie got a wooden music box with tiny figures of children, fir trees, and brightly painted flowers, all carved out of wood. She loved playing it before she went to sleep. It's now in my guest bedroom for Jenny's three boys to enjoy. When Andy and Margaret went to Germany to celebrate their fiftieth birthdays, Andy bought himself a grown-up pair of lederhosen.

Long ocean cruises were a favorite of Dad's and he especially loved the Queen Mary. It was one of the first truly grand ocean cruisers. They went on that ship many times. They sailed through the Panama Canal and found it fascinating. Alaska was another favorite cruise and at least a couple of Caribbean cruises, so life was good.

In the late seventies my sister was working for Pan American Airlines, flying out of London and living in the nearby suburb of Chelsea. Her flat was not special, but she had a small patio in the rear which was lovely. The window over the tub did not close firmly, leaving a gap of about half an inch. She said in the winter it got really cold, but England is a maritime climate so a half inch crack is just something you learn to live with. That was the gist of what her landlord told her. It was hard to find rental flats in a good area so she lived with a cold bathroom.

Cynthy and I decided to plan together an extensive trip basically in a huge circle around London. And we did it without Google, just the library, free travel brochures and hearsay. We asked Dad and Ruth to join us and they agreed as long as Ted did all the driving. We rented a car, pulled out our maps, put Ted behind the wheel and started our ten day adventure.

This was my first touring vacation since my wonderful college whirlwind tour through Europe. It was a fabulous trip. Two events stand out most in my mind. One was the visit to Stonehenge. There were no fences surrounding it then and we could walk right up to the stones and hug them if we wanted. It was an overwhelming sight with such mystery surrounding it that I stood in awe imagining what life was like hundreds and hundreds of years ago. We couldn't believe they built it with such exactitude with no cranes or any mechanical aids to help move those massively heavy stones.

The other special event was staying at Gravetye Manor in Sussex. Ted and I slept in a huge bedroom with a gorgeous fireplace and an ornate four poster bed, with a roof over it, as my granddaughter Grace called the canopy over her bed when she was four years old. It was an elegant century old home with spectacular grounds. A famous English gardener and writer, William Robinson, bought the estate in 1884 and spent his life developing the gardens. He believed that nature should flow into the garden and not be controlled and suppressed in a formal pattern as had been the custom. He revolutionized garden design.

I think I enjoyed the gardens more than anything else in England. Ruth and Dad had a wonderful time. My dad loved that Ted did all the scary driving on the wrong side of the road. He was sixty five years old then and in fairly good health. The other four of us in this traveling group of five did find it annoying that Dad always insisted we eat lunch in a restaurant with a liquor license. That's not a tough requirement for dinner, but for lunch it eliminates many charming spots.

When we first moved to Kansas City I thought we would finally be near a relative as my brother and his family lived in a city nearby, but just as we moved in, he and Mary Ann divorced, precipitated perhaps by Bill causing the family to move again when he accepted a position as a professor at Simpson college in Indianola, Iowa. My parents took Bill under their wing that summer. He was devastated by the divorce and not living with his children. First Dad and Ruth helped him buy furnishings for his apartment. Then, to further take his mind off things, they planned a whirlwind sight seeing trip around the West. They visited a lot of the National Parks, always went out for a delicious dinner and with such a flurry of activities my brother stopped dwelling constantly on what he had lost and gained a small sense of peace.

His two children stayed in Kansas with Mary Ann and they lived less than an hour away from us. So my brother drove down from Iowa on week-ends, picked up his kids and they all stayed at our house. Luckily our house was large so it worked out well. Bill's daughter Melodie is the same age as our youngest daughter Jenny. Billy, the adorable toddler who wore his Superman cape at every opportunity, was loved by everyone. We had some wonderful Thanksgivings with my parents and sister also coming. I loved having our family all together. Thankfully the divorce was short lived. They soon remarried and have now retired to Nova Scotia. They built a house on land owned by Mary Ann's parents, close to the cottage in which she had spent many of her summers growing up.

After we moved to Kansas, my sister Cynthia became engaged to James Marlow. She had joined Pan American airlines as a flight attendant right after graduating from Wellesley in 1969, the same class as Hillary Clinton. After being in London for a few years she moved to the San Francisco area. Her fiancé was Canadian and a Cornell graduate who always planned on working in this country. He lived in Rochester, New York so it was definitely a long distance romance, made a little easier because my sister could fly for free.

Neither one was originally from the town they were living in, so where to have the wedding? His parents were in Vancouver and Cynthy's were in Florida. I now lived in the middle of the country and in a town convenient to a major city. My sister thought, why not Kansas City? All their friends from both coasts could fly in and those few in the middle could drive. She didn't like what they now call a destination wedding because she wanted all her friends and family at her wedding. I was agreeable. It was decided the wedding would be in Kansas City. We belonged to a small tennis and swim club with a lovely dining room and dance floor and it was available April fourth, just a few months away. We attended an Episcopal church and lined it up for April fourth. Now it was just the hundreds of other details to plan.

My father loved big events and loved giving his opinion. Cynthia and James were paying for the wedding themselves so cost was a concern. My dad said for sure we needed five limousines to take the bride and all the attendants to the church as nobody would have a car since they were all coming by plane. Now that would be a major expense, so I quietly reduced that to one limousine, large enough for the bride, my father and the maid and matron of honor. We were best friends with our neighbors next door, Butch and Marilyn Thomas, who were coming to the wedding and they said they would use their two cars to chauffeur guests to and from the church and reception. My brother would also have his car. I chose the florist, but Cynthia somehow did all the rest of the planning long distance. We picked out her gown and the bridesmaid's gowns together in Kansas City. Cynthy asked me to be her matron of honor, her best friend Linda, who lived in California, to be her maid of honor and JoAnne, James' sister who lived in Vancouver, to be her third attendant.

Our house had an enormous walk-out basement with a twenty foot bar and a huge dance floor. We decided it would be more fun and economical to have the rehearsal dinner at our house. We would start upstairs for the cocktail hour and then go to the lower level for dinner. Our plan was to set up tables and chairs on the dance floor, and also use an adjacent living area with a fireplace and all our former porch furniture to seat even more guests. Cynthy wanted to include everyone who flew in Friday night. Turned out that was most of the guests. We had fifty-four people at the rehearsal dinner.

I have always planned ahead my entire life. I hate being under stress. My papers in school were always written at least two days before being due. I have all the food organized five hours before a dinner party. I lay out my clothes ready for the suitcase two days before we're leaving on a vacation. I am an organizational guru. I somehow failed to realize that setting up tables and chairs and putting on tablecloths and laying out silverware and napkins and glasses for fifty-four people would be very, very time consuming. I had not allowed sufficient time and we were all running around in a frenzy. I was the matron of honor so I had to go to the rehearsal and then as soon as we left the church, fifty-four people would be either waiting for us at the house or on their way and, HELP. everything wasn't perfect! I must have originally thought that since it was catered it wouldn't involve all the work that I always expended preparing for dinner parties. It might not have come off perfectly in my eyes, but the dinner happened and everyone looked happy and well fed. The guests were from all walks of life and all parts of the country and they melded at that rehearsal dinner. By the time of the wedding the next day you would think they had all known each other for years.

For the wedding my father bought an all silk dinner jacket in a muted pattern of black and taupe. It was stunning. He told Cynthy he was too uneasy and too nervous on his feet to walk her down the aisle which was a huge disappointment to her. He was only sixty-nine. She walked down the aisle alone with a big smile on her face and I don't think it was shocking to the guests as they all felt after the festivities of the night before that they now knew Dad really well and he must have a legitimate reason.

The Thomas' next door and Ted and my brother ferried guests from their hotels to the church for over an hour. Since there were few cars and many people, some arrived at the church forty minutes before the ceremony. All the guests were in their seats and ready before the stated hour for the wedding to begin.

Ten minutes went by and the florist's helper walked in and sheepishly placed the flowers I had ordered weeks before on the altar. Good thing I wasn't there to shoot visual arrows at her. I wasn't there because we were still at my house where Cynthy, dressed in her wedding gown and I in my matron of honor gown and Linda in her maid of honor matching gown and my father in his elegant silk dinner jacket were all waiting for that one limousine. I finally called the service and the owner protested that she had never been given the final confirmation for the rental and she was so sorry, but she had no extra limos. My father couldn't resist commenting that if we had ordered the five limousines he had recommended, this certainly would not have happened. He had a point, but what to do! Our two cars were at the church, my brother and his car was at the church, the Thomas' two cars were at the church. We couldn't reach anyone. Cell phones weren't invented yet.

I called a taxi. The guy arrived fairly quickly and was sitting in his cab reading the newspaper when the four of us rushed out the front door. I'm holding up a huge bed sheet to wrap around Cynthy which billowed out like a sail as I ran. Linda and I squeezed in next to the white mass of Cynthy, the gown and the sheet and my father got in the front seat next to the driver and off we went. The cab driver was speechless throughout our embarkment. My father asked him if he'd ever had a bride dressed in her wedding gown as a passenger before. He just nodded negatively, still muted by the spectacle of it all. Meanwhile back at the church the suspense grew and with no cell phones to quickly and quietly uncover the problem, that suspense kept growing.

We finally arrived at the church twenty minutes late. Linda and I met up with JoAnne, the third bridesmaid and gathered ourselves together to start the procession. My father walked down the aisle to take his seat next to Ruth, at which time my brother said there was an audible sigh of relief heard throughout. My father turned around before he sat down and said,

"My daughter hasn't been on time for anything in her entire life so we didn't think we should break tradition right before her wedding."

Many laughs, many smiles and we attendants started down the aisle.

My brother Bill, me, Cynthy and Dad.

The wedding ceremony went off without a hitch and the reception was fabulous. It was like a family party. There were ten children, my four, my brother's three and the Thomas' four. Betty Decker, our helper in Whitemarsh and good friend ever since, flew in from Connecticut. Sadly, Bob had died of a brain tumor when he was in his forties. Towards the very end of a wonderful evening of dinner and dancing, the bride and groom left amidst confetti and yells of good wishes from everyone. Very soon the band stopped playing and everyone started leaving.

Ted and I collected our children and drove the three minutes to our house. The phone rang ten minutes later. It was Linda, the maid of honor from California and my sister's best friend. She had just exited from the women's locker room where she had been collecting and organizing all Cynthy's bridal clothing, make-up, shoes and such and when she opened the door to the main room which had been full of people twenty minutes before, there was nobody there. The room was completely empty. She said luckily she still had my phone number. I was aghast. First, the late delivery of the flowers, second the lack of delivery of the limousine and now this. I was guilty of three screw-ups. I had completely forgotten about Linda. I felt terrible. What a shock for her to enter an empty room and realize she's been deserted and in a strange town at that. She was just diligently doing her maid of honor duties which maybe I, the matron of honor, should have been doing. I couldn't apologize enough and raced back to the club to retrieve her. Many would say, "What disasters you had at your wedding." Not my sister, she said it was the most fun wedding she had ever been to and the taxi ride was just hilarious. Attitude counts for a lot!

My father did not enjoy good health as he got older. Looking back now that I am older and afflicted with a few ailments myself, I realize I was not very sympathetic. I falsely attributed many of his health problems to his drinking. I now realize the drinking was probably not the cause of his many afflictions. I'm sure it didn't help and he probably continued drinking heavily because of the multitude of those health problems. Ruth and I often discussed his drinking problem. She had tried in the beginning to urge him to drink less with no success so she finally became resigned to it. She did tell me that when Dad was told he could not drink any alcohol at all for six weeks because of some test or sudden health problem, he would stop cold. She said this happened three or four times, but he always started up again.

I knew the problems with his heart were not because of his drinking, but because of his arteries. He ended up having to have quadruple bypass heart surgery. He came through it well, with his biggest complaint being his sore leg where they took the artery out to use in the bypasses. I'm told they don't do that anymore. He'd also been treated for prostate cancer for years and they started treating it very aggressively in his late seventies with female hormones. He really slowed down then. He stopped playing golf and even stopped playing bridge because he had trouble remembering the cards. He liked reading, enjoyed a variety of television programs and especially loved sitting on his porch reading or watching the golfers. So life was relatively good for him in Sun City.

My father's seventy-fifth birthday was August 26, 1987 and we three children wanted to plan something special. My sister had the best idea. She and James had moved from Palos Verdes Estates in Los Angeles to San Francisco when James took a new job with Xerox. They hadn't been able to sell their house in Los Angeles so Xerox agreed to pay the rent on a house they found in Woodside, just outside San Francisco. It wasn't really a house, it was an estate. It was so grand that they never wanted to invite any of the Xerox people over as they were sure they would be overwhelmed and worse, jealous of the grandeur they were enjoying while their house in southern California sat unbought.

The main house was huge and beautifully appointed. There was a Japanese tea house on the grounds that looked just like the pictures we have all seen of Japanese tea houses. The large pool had a formal adjoining pool house along one entire side. It had changing rooms and a bathroom. The owners had left all the chairs and lounges to relax in around the pool plus floats and toys to use inside the pool. The grounds were a hilly two acres with pathways bordered by shrubs, stone walls and a stone staircase in the middle of one section. There was a redwood grove with a hot tub in the middle. The views from the grounds and the pool were beautiful. It was one spectacular rental.

Cynthy described it to me in detail and we concluded that spectacular as it was, there weren't enough bedrooms for all of us plus there was no handy cook standing by to plan, prepare, cook and clean up all the meals fifteen people would require. We decided to spend a couple of days there and then retreat to a gorgeous resort just thirty minutes away right on the ocean called Asimilar.

My brother's family, Mary Ann, Melodie and Billy, did a sight-seeing drive from Iowa in a huge station wagon hauling a trailer. Our family was less ambitious and just flew directly to California. While at Cynthy's we spent hours enjoying that private pool. My father didn't go in swimming, but he enjoyed sitting by the pool and watching all the kids cavort about. James and Cynthy's daughter, Ashley, was only four years old so all the kids wanted to play with her in the pool.

Our next stop, Asilimar, was perfect for a family reunion. We didn't have to cook or clean up and we were located right next to a gorgeous, sandy beach on the Monterey Peninsular. The resort provided us with a private room for opening all Dad's presents which we decorated with balloons and pictures the kids had drawn. For the birthday dinner, we ate outside at a picnic table large enough to fit all fifteen of us around it. The cooks at Asilimar baked a delicious birthday cake. They put Ruth's and Mary Ann's names on it too as their birthdays were within days of my father's. I asked my father that night in honest curiosity,

"Dad, how does it feel to be seventy-five years old, three quarters of a century! Do you feel a lot older or is it really no different than being another year older?"

"Sally, the oldest I ever felt was when you turned fifty!"

The day of the birthday bash we hired a professional photographer to take pictures of all of us together and each family separately which are now very special keepsakes.

Cynthia, my father, Ruth, Bill and me.

When we left that lovely resort we took a side trip on our way back to the Marlow's house to see some famous and beautiful gardens at an estate called Filoli in Woodside. They were similar to the spectacular gardens in England, perfection in every garden bed. The house was magnificent inside and out and that alone was worth the visit. The formal gardens are on over sixteen acres and the estate has a total of 625 acres.

We spent another full day enjoying all the wonders of San Francisco. It was a memorable vacation for all of us and sadly my brother, sister and I have not yet been able to get our three families all together at one time. The cousins aren't even that familiar with each other's names. I haven't met most of my brother's grandchildren.

Dad and Ruth decided to go on a cruise that wouldn't require a long overnight plane trip before boarding the ship so it would be less strenuous for my father. They chose a Smithsonian Study tour and Seminar cruise up the coast of Maine, including the Bay of Fundy. They invited Ted and me to go with them as their treat. Unfortunately Ted could not go with us as he had just accepted a new job as Vice President of Operations at Renaissance Center in Detroit. The owner of his current company, Samuelson Development, was in the process of dissolving the company and moving to Colorado. So we were thrilled about Ted's new job, but unfortunately he was to start the day the ship left dock.

I flew out to Logan Airport in Boston alone, met up with Dad and Ruth and we boarded the ship, the Nantucket Clipper, in nearby Quincy. It was a small ship with only forty-four passengers. We left August 23, 1992 for the ten day cruise. The first night on board we received a formal invitation to sit at the Captain's table along with two other birthday celebrants. My father's eightieth birthday was August twenty-sixth. I had packed all the presents from our family and the three of us had a private gift opening celebration in their cabin with a bottle of champagne.

I learned there were 3000 islands off the coast of Maine. We saw forts, lighthouses, bays, eagles, osprey, seals, whales, museums, Acadia National Park, Bar Harbor and more. My favorite part was visiting Campobello Island, Franklin Roosevelt's summer home all during his youth. The furnished house and well maintained grounds are all open to tourists. The most amazing part was the Bay of Fundy which has a twenty-eight foot difference in its water level at the dock between high and low tide. Dad would go on some of the excursions off the ship if he felt up to the walking. He used a cane now. The doctor had given Ruth a list of Dad's pills and afflictions should anything remiss happen on the trip. It fills an entire type written page. I still have it.

The worst part was his unpleasant demeanor, so unlike the affable, outgoing father I grew up with. Ruth and I started putting our coats over the fourth chair at our table because we learned he was rude to anyone who joined us. Dad was now on female hormones to slow the advance of his prostate cancer. I found out years later that most of the men with prostate cancer who were given female hormones during that era became belligerent and mean-spirited just like my father. The irony is that one would assume female hormones would do just the opposite. Perhaps the doctors made that mistaken assumption too. They don't prescribe them for prostate cancer anymore. It was a tragedy because we were cheated out of the father we knew the last few years of his life.

"Make It a Girl, Gracie"

Two weeks after Dad returned to Florida from our cruise he had a stroke. This was more serious than the minor strokes he had suffered in the past. Those would tire him out and cause slurred speech, but he'd recover in a couple of days. This time he was unconscious, but his eyes were wide open and unfocused. Cynthy went down to be with Ruth and see Dad in the hospital the first week. I flew down the second week. I talked to him about things we had done together and about the activities of my children, but did not get any reaction at all. It was eerie that his eyes were open, but they only stared at the ceiling and other than blinking, he did not move at all. At the end of the week the doctors told Ruth they would recommend removing the feeding tube. He had not gained consciousness and they didn't feel there was any hope for recovery. We talked all evening and Ruth finally decided she would tell them to remove the feeding tube the next morning. The phone rang very early that morning, waking us both up. My dad had just died.

Sun City Center doesn't have funerals as we know them, perhaps because they are such a constant event. The funeral or memorial service is not a separate event where mourners dress appropriately for the service and sometimes have a lunch or dinner afterwards put on by the deceased's family. Ruth and Dad belonged to a large church right in the center of the village of Sun City which I believe is basically Methodist, but they only promote it as Protestant. The custom is that after the regular Sunday morning service, the name of the deceased person is read by the minister, who then asks if there is anyone who would like to give a eulogy.

My brother had prepared some very moving remarks, which he read to a modest number of parishioners who remained after the regular service. The minister offered a prayer and then asked the relatives of the deceased to form a line so the attendees could greet them personally. This memorial service was on the third day after my father's death. This gave our family time to fly to Florida. Our lineup included my husband Ted, our two eldest children, Andy and Julie, my sister Cynthia, her husband James and her daughter Ashley, and my brother Bill. We all went back to Ruth and Dad's house afterwards. Ruth told their friends going through the line to please stop by the house afterwards and about six of them did, so we all had a chance to share favorite stories about my father. He died on September 29, the same day my sister Pamela died. His ashes are buried in the cemetery of St Thomas Church in Whitemarsh, Pennsylvania, next to his wife, Grace and his daughter, Pamela.

Ruth remained single for another few years and then started seeing George Bauman who was a former colleague of my father's from the Connecticut General. He was my father's age and Ruth was three years younger. George was a widower and lived in a huge four story complex for senior citizens at Sun City. After a courtship of a few months he told Ruth that once it started getting dark at night he couldn't drive, so they'd have to break it off or get married. Ruth chose marriage. The ceremony was in October and Ruth moved into his apartment on the fourth floor which was spacious with a panoramic view of the grounds. Ted and I were very excited for her and wanted to come to the wedding ceremony. She insisted it was just a small private service, no drama and it was silly to come. She was quite firm so we didn't go. That winter Ted and I flew down for a long week-end and met George, saw the apartment and the lovely complex. Ruth loved not having to cook anymore and George seemed easy going and kind and I was thrilled for her after what she had been through those last few years with my father. Ruth looked fabulous, didn't take a single pill and walked briskly at least a mile every day.

George had planned a dinner party for ten friends to celebrate their first anniversary. A few days before the party, Ruth told George after dinner that she didn't feel well at all and hoped she wasn't coming down with the flu. George probably encouraged her to see the doctor who was very accessible, but knowing Ruth's stubbornness, I'm sure she said she'd wait and see how she felt in the morning. There was no morning. She had a heart attack and they couldn't revive her. She died on September twenty-ninth, the same day of the month my father and my sister had died.

Cynthia, James, Bill, Ted and I flew down immediately. We met George for dinner at a restaurant the night we arrived. He told us about the dinner he had planned weeks before to celebrate their first anniversary. He said the dinner was tomorrow night and now it will be a memorial dinner for Ruth. We assumed as he relayed the details that we would be included. But he wrapped it up by saying there really wasn't any more room at the table for five extra people so he would see us on Sunday at the service. I couldn't believe it. I wanted to see Ruth's friends who I had met over a twenty year period. I probably knew those friends better than George.

The next morning after church and the typical cursory funeral which wasn't a funeral at all in my eyes, I greeted many of Ruth's friends as they went through the line with a nod or shake of the hand. I could feel a coolness toward us and I'm sure George told them we were too tired to come to the dinner or something like that. I'm confident he did not relay what he told us, that there was no more room at the table! We had been Ruth's relatives by marriage for over twenty-five years. George also did not invite anyone back to his apartment. I think he was sad Ruth died, but also ticked off at the unfairness of it all. His first wife had been in a wheelchair for the last five years of her life. They had no children. It had been a hard five years for him. Ruth was three years younger and enjoyed perfect health when he married her. She told me when he proposed he said they should enjoy at least five years of marriage together. I'm sure he felt cheated, perhaps thinking only a year together was hardly worth the bother.

A final story of the three friends of Ruth's who went to elementary school with her in Woodstock, Vermont and spent their last years together in Sun City, Florida. One friend was diagnosed with colon cancer five years before Ruth's death and decided not to treat it aggressively with chemo or radiation. She would do anything that would keep her life more pleasant, but that was it. The other friend had a stroke two years before Ruth's death and like Ruth was gone in minutes. So the gal with cancer survived them all. Ruth's ashes are buried next to my father's and she shares with him the last of the three tombstones that my parents erected forty-five years ago when their daughter Pamela died.

11

My Grandmother, Sally Hamlin Gilbert

In many ways I had two mothers, a full time mother and a part-time mother. My grandmother was only forty-two when I was born. She went with my mother to the hospital when she was in labor and brought me home to her home where my mother was living at the time. My mother and grandmother were very different in personality and a wonderful balance

"Make It a Girl, Gracie"

for me. My mother never wavered in her love and praise of me. When I was at that awkward age of twelve or thirteen with thick glasses, ugly braces and hair that I thought never went right, she would tell me I had beautiful eyebrows that reminded her of Elizabeth Taylor. I had a mirror so it was obvious to me I looked nothing like Elizabeth Taylor, but I knew my mother's love would always surround and encourage me no matter what. My grandmother embodied strength and confidence. With her, I knew I could always count on support and help in any project or non-athletic activity in which I was involved. She had so many interests, so many abilities and so many friends. I wanted to be like that, but I also wanted to be pretty and pleasing like my mother.

My grandmother was born in Milo, Maine in 1892. Her parents were only sixteen and nineteen when they married. When she was born, her mother, Caroline Sophia Godsoe, was eighteen and her father, Percy Manton Hamlin, twenty-one. She was their only child. The first Hamlin ancestor came to America in 1634 to Kittery, Maine. The Godsoe line has a Captain John Godsoe of the Revolutionary War. My grandmother joined the Daughters of the American Revolution through her maternal grandmother, Annie Augusta Warren Hamlin.

Percy, my great grandfather, was the only child of Annie and Orin Hamlin. Annie's sister, Abigail Peaks, died very young of what was then called "galloping consumption." We call it tuberculosis. She left three young children. Her husband, Willard Peaks, played the violin and traveled performing from town to town so was in no position to raise them.

So Annie raised Abby and Willard's three children to adulthood, making Percy's three cousins more like three siblings.

Orin died when the children were teenagers so it seemed logical that when Percy and Caroline married, they would move in with his mother into the large family home in Milo. Percy worked in a spool factory and with the skills he developed there he started making furniture as a hobby, using strips of different colored wood which he must have glued together to make a flat surface. We called it the zebra furniture when we were little. My grandmother inherited this furniture and I now have all six pieces. Percy died on the operating table in 1916, but Caroline lived until 1943. I called her Nanny. She was sixty-one when I, her first great grandchild, was born, the same age I was when Brian and Grace Flynn, my first grandchildren, were born.

After she became a widow, Caroline served as a housekeeper for Dr. Simmons whose wife was an invalid. The Simons lived in St. Louis where he had a very successful medical practice. He was also on the United States chess team for several years and possessed a fabulous chess set made by J. Jaques and Son, Ltd in London. They were known as Staunton Chessmen and were lead weighted, felt bottomed and hand carved of two different woods, black ebony and blond mahogany. When Dr. Simmon's wife died, he moved to his club, disposed of all his furniture and gave Caroline his chess set. My father inherited this treasured set and we played with it growing up. The chess pieces had this wonderful smell of wood, a little like cedar, and were heavy and impressive to hold in your hand. Their beauty didn't improve my chess game. My brother became our family's best player and inherited this beautiful set of chessmen.

After Dr. Simmon took up residence in his club, Caroline moved back to Maine and soon married a Dr. Fulton from the town of Blaine who also owned a chain of drugstores. He lived for about twelve years after their marriage. After she was widowed for the second time, Caroline often stayed with my grandparents in their Ridge Road house and that's when I really got to know her. While my grandmother was like a second mother in many respects, Caroline or Nanny seemed like a grandmother to me. She was very quiet and read a lot. She also liked to read stories to me. She died at sixty-nine when I was in third grade.

My grandmother looked like a grandmother even though she was in her forties until I turned eight years old. She wore a lace up girdle with what looked like shoe-

My father, me, grandmother and nanny.

laces that had to be pulled together and tied. The only other one I'd ever seen was on Scarlett O'Hara in *Gone With The Wind*, but my grandmother did not pull hers to achieve an eighteen inch waist. She also wore black shoes with laces. She hated her hair, which she lamented was wispy, mousy brown and thin.

She loved to sew and whenever I was around she would ask me to help her thread the needle on her sewing machine. When I was little she loved making my clothes. I had panties and bonnets that matched most of my outfits. She made a prom dress for me in high school that I loved. I've already described my mother basically failing the sewing portion of home economics in high school and vowing to never pick up a sewing needle again. Mother would keep a pile of mending in a big wicker basket and when my grandmother visited, which was often, out that basket came. This was the era of even mending or darning the holes in the heels of socks.

During the Second World War my grandmother spent every summer canning. My grandfather grew lots of vegetables then along with his flowers. "Victory Gardens" were promoted as the patriotic thing to do. In the basement there was shelf after shelf laden with glass jars full of vegetables. After the war my grandmother read a frightening article about fatal food poisoning that could occur if the canning wasn't done perfectly. The article scared her and she threw out those dozens and dozens of glass jars that took her countless hours to fill. She also made trays of soap during the war, another act considered patriotic because of the shortage at home.

She loved arranging flowers and got a lot of practice with the profusion of flowers my grandfather grew. I remember one summer when I was visiting, my grandmother was rushing about in a hurry to get to a meeting of the

Daughters of the War of 1812. She was a member and she was also doing all the flower arrangements for the tables. When we lived in Upper Montclair for one year with no lawn, let alone no flowers, my school was having a contest among the fifth and sixth graders of flower arranging. My mother and grandmother, knowing how unhappy I was in my new school, didn't want me to feel left out so my grandmother drove the four hours to New Jersey with the back seat of her car laden with flowers.

Unfortunately, I had never arranged flowers in a vase before in my life. I couldn't very well practice with the only ones I was to use in the contest. I should have practiced. It became a humiliating experience. I know that back seat was heaped with different flowers, but the only ones I recall were the tulips. I still can't arrange them unless I have a vase with a top that squeezes them together. Tulips naturally want to bend and droop over and that's what mine did. I remember pathetically tying a string around them in an unsuccessful attempt to hold them up. Even my mother couldn't come up with a word of praise when she saw that sad looking bunch of drooping tulips. The girl in the desk next to me had a shallow banana shaped dish and a tiny, metal frog to hold flowers. She put three iris in that frog and they sat at rigid attention while she then plopped a couple of leafy things at their feet. It was stunning. I still remember there were two white iris and one purple. It won first prize.

I spent many weeks at my grandparent's house in the summer over the years. Sometimes my mother was there and sometimes she wasn't. My fondest memories of shopping as a young girl are with my grandmother. There were two big department stores in Hartford, Foxes and Brown Thomsons, right next to each other. We preferred Foxes and always parked in the lot behind the store. Often Lucy Ringrose, who lived one house away from my grandparents and was my age, went with us. My grandmother took us to lunch after we had shopped for awhile in the Foxes dining room which had waitresses and what I remember best, cut crystal, amber colored, stemmed water glasses! Now I'm sure they weren't cut crystal, but Lucy and I thought they were elegant.

One shopping expedition my brother and my mother accompanied us. We were shopping for a blazer for my brother who was probably eight or nine years old. The salesman brought out a plaid jacket that we all liked, but my grandmother said the lapels didn't match. The stripes went one way on the left lapel and ran the other way on the right. My grandmother haughtily asked him to bring out another copy of the blazer as the seamstress on this one had certainly made a grievous error. The salesmen argued that they were all like this and it was commonplace with young boy's clothing. Those were probably the last words he uttered. He was lambasted with a dialogue on proper sewing techniques and sloppy, inferior work and not at a low decibel level. I looked down at the floor and prayed this moment would pass. My mother looked equally uncomfortable. She was not adversarial and if saying nothing and just not buying the coat which mother would have done was considered wimpy, I was all for wimpy over being embarrassed.

My cousin Sandy, Uncle Hammy's son, was just six months younger than my brother. Sometimes he would also be at my grandparent's house the same time we were, both with absent mothers. The antics of little boys did not overwhelm my grandmother and she expected and demanded a certain level of obedience. One day the boys and she had not agreed on some rule and as they were climbing the stairs to their bedrooms for a time out decreed by my grandmother, Sandy said to my brother, "I hate our Grandma, don't you?" I don't recall my brother's response, but I gather it was in the affirmative. Many grandmothers, and I'm one, would have been devastated by a comment like this, not mine, she thought it was hilarious and often told that story.

A special treat, and one we looked forward to with great anticipation, was going to Hammonasset State Park for a day's outing at the seashore. It was closed to everyone except the military during the Second World War so I didn't go until I finished fourth grade. It was about an hour's drive and we always went well equipped with beach towels, blankets, shovels, pails, blown up rafts, huge beach balls, a picnic lunch in a wicker basket, a huge thermos of lemonade and always, a beach umbrella. We lugged what every story book has picnickers carrying. Hammonasset had two miles of shoreline on the Long Island Sound so the waves were not high. The boardwalk went on for blocks. We would plan these day outings about three or four days ahead and

I would pray each night it wouldn't rain. At least once or twice each summer it would start pouring on our designated beach day and all plans had to be cancelled. I remember rationalizing my disappointment by telling myself that the rain would be good for the farmers and how happy they must be.

There were no sun block lotions in the drug stores those days and little acknowledgement about the dangers of burning. In fact, getting a tan, which often was preceded by a burn, was considered giving yourself a healthy glow. We did have one beach rule, never to be broken. After we ate we had to stay out of the water for one long hour. The explanation given to us was that if we went into cold water right after eating we would get cramps and might drown. I think the adults believed there was a little bit of truth in this. It certainly gave them an hour of relative relaxation. Today, it's been completely debunked. We were also warned about the undertow in very somber tones. It would suck us under and drag us out to sea so we must be very careful to never go too far out into the water. I know that concern has validity to this day.

My grandparents always had dogs when my father grew up, but did not after they had grandchildren. So our dog was always especially welcome at their home. The collie we bought in 1947, Baron, loved going to my grandparent's house. I always looked forward to seeing Lucy who lived one house away, my brother wanted to see the Hills' kids next door and Baron could hardly wait to see Duchess, a German Shepherd mix, who lived the other side of Lucy's house. We would all tumble out of the car after arriving from New Jersey or Pennsylvania, throw our bags in the same rooms we always slept in, hug our grandparents and rush out to see our buddies. Baron would race over to call upon Duchess.

Once a summer at least, and thankfully not too much more, my grandmother would cook a pot of kidneys for Baron. According to her, this was the ultimate gastronomic treat for a dog. Baron did gulp them down with great gusto, but the smell in the house was as offensive as a skunk's spray, maybe worse. This smell didn't offend my grandmother because these kidneys were a special treat for our loyal and wonderful dog and we would just have to suffer through the obnoxious smell. One of my grandfather's golfing buddies exclaimed once that if he was to be reincarnated, he wanted to come back as my grandmother's dog.

Instead of a dog, my grandmother had a parakeet. His name was Benny and he was a prolific singer which really pleased her. One day another parakeet unexpectedly joined the household and I will quote from my grandmother's letter of July 7, 1955.

"We have an addition to our bird population. I don't know as Benny is particularly thrilled, but he does try to be friendly and chirps away with never an answer from the visitor. How we came to have the extra one is as follows. I opened the back door and there was what I thought was Benny standing on the stepping stones. I couldn't see how it was possible for Benny to escape, but there he was as far as I could tell. He

almost let me walk up to him and pick him up, however, he decided to make things difficult and flew about two feet. I had nothing to throw over him to catch him, but being an ingenious Yankee I quickly removed my only removable piece of clothing, namely my underpants, and managed to catch him. He lay perfectly still in my hands and I realized it wasn't Benny. Gramps got the extra cage from the basement and we installed him in his new quarters. His feet are in terrible condition, toe nails about two inches long, and we plan to take good care of him and see if he is a singer. If he proves to be one I think Mother and Cynthy might want him."

The next letter I received about the birds was ten months later and my grandmother never explained in the letter how she located the owner of the bird on the back stoop. I probably was told, but I don't remember.

"Well I suppose Timmy and his owner were happy to be back together, but I still think he was a very fortunate bird to have had such tender care all during his absence. Our beautiful, adorable Benny was found dead in the bottom of his cage one morning. Apparently he had been killed by something or he died of fright. We think it must have been a rat as we saw one later. How the rat got into the house we do not know. We miss Benny so badly and he was so pretty to look at and his singing was lovely. The radio has helped some, for Benny sang practically all the time, so now we keep the fm station

on, but sweet as the music is, his songs were sweeter and they were sung just for us."

At the end of my junior year in college I must have written my grandmother a letter complaining about school and never seeing Ted and just feeling out of sorts. This is her response,

"I think you were sort of low when you wrote last, but I hope you have had lots of things since then to make your spirits soar high as the Empire State building. I well remember in my high school days one morning when a pal of mine was leaving to be married and he walked me to school. We were not sweethearts in any sense of the word, but we enjoyed the same sport and books. He enjoyed music and was a wonderful companion. He had been engaged for a long time, but that did not make it any easier to break our friendship when the actual time for his marriage came along. I realized it had to be a clean break for no single girl continues to share the confidence of a married man. Well, I was very sad that morning, but I ploughed through the day and have never seen or heard from him but once since so you see even in Grandma's day we had our problems with the studies and the men we thought so very important in our lives at the time. Moral, don't neglect the studies."

I loved Thanksgiving and Christmas at my grandparent's house. My grandmother brought out all her silverware and her serving dishes and platters and we would inspect the accumulation to see if we needed to polish anything. My parents, who had eloped, had none of these special silver pieces or sterling silverware. We put extra leaves in the table and I was in charge of making the place cards. Some years my Uncle Hammy, Aunt Betty and their children, Sandy and Marianne, would also be visiting which made it even more fun.

After dinner, my grandmother sat down at the baby grand piano in the living room and my father pulled out his trumpet and often placed a derby hat over the end to muffle and soften the sound. He blew his trumpet, my grandmother played the piano and sang and the rest of us joined in. My grandmother had an operatic voice and had sung professionally at weddings and other events in her youth. I preferred my mother's softer, more melodic voice, but was impressed at the volume and intensity of my grandmother's voice.

In July of 1944, after I had finished third grade, I was staying with my grandparents for a few weeks. Mr. Ringrose had bought three tickets to take Lucy and me to the Ringling Brothers and Barnum and Bailey Circus. It was in town for a week. I was excited about going although I remembered the stories my parents told about my first time at the circus when I was four. My adoring grandfather had taken me and was so disappointed because I didn't seem to enjoy it at all. I kept saying over and over,

"But why do they make the elephants do that? The horses must be scared. Why do they have to do that?"

Despite hearing that story a few times, now that I was older, I was anticipating having a really fun time. I woke up the morning of our circus adventure and saw pimples on my tummy and arms and they really itched. I ran to see my grandmother who was already up and making breakfast and she knew immediately what it was – chicken pox. She said I was certainly contagious and absolutely couldn't go despite my protestations that they didn't itch that much and I could wear a long sleeved shirt. My parents knew I was going to the circus that day, but my grandma said we would call them that night and tell them about the chicken pox as it was just too expensive to call in the daytime.

I stayed in my pajamas and my brother, my grandmother and I decided to spend the day on the screened porch as it was so hot even my brother didn't want to go out and play. Nobody I knew had air-conditioning in their house. We turned on the radio as we usually did when we sat on the porch. It was mid-afternoon when the radio program was broken into by an announcer saying there were reports of a fire at the circus. He was very emotional as he talked and said it was feared many people were trapped inside as some of the exits were blocked. I sat in disbelief listening. One of my best friends and her father were inside. They talked about nothing else on that station for the rest of that afternoon and evening and the whole next week. It was a live, running account of an unfolding disaster, a glimpse of what CNN, with the addition of pictures, would become in fifty years.

Fairly soon after that first announcement, we got a call from Ken Ringrose. He and Lucy had been sitting mid-height in one section and Ken noticed some smoke on the other side of the arena. He immediately stood up, grabbed Lucy and headed for the exit. He was in his car before the true horror of the disaster unfolded. We listened that entire day and evening. For the next few days I would come downstairs in my pajamas and as soon as I finished breakfast, I'd head for the porch and turn on the radio. I still remember the tone of the announcer's voice as he read off the names of the victims, hour by hour, as each new body was identified. We were told there were some bodies too badly burned to immediately be identified, but dental records would confirm who they were. Days later there was only one unidentified body. Her picture was put in the newspaper. She did not look burned at all and her face was clearly recognizable. She was a young, blond girl about seven or eight years old, wearing a white dress. She became known as Little Miss 1565, named after the number assigned to her body at the city's makeshift morgue.

My parents in New Jersey also heard about the fire and knew I was going that afternoon. For two agonizing hours they were unable to get through to us because all the telephone lines to the Hartford area were in use and they just kept getting a busy signal over and over. Finally they or my grandmother got through and we all exclaimed how lucky we were that I had the good fortune to come down with the chicken pox.

I own a fascinating book about the Hartford circus fire, but I can't find it so I'm quoting information from Wikipedia. The huge canvas tent this circus performed under could seat 9,000. As was regularly done with those tents to make them water proof, the canvas was coated with 1,800 pounds of paraffin dissolved in 6,000 gallons of gasoline. The day of the fire was a Thursday and the estimated 7,000 attendees were primarily women and children.

The fire began as a small flame, first noticed after the lions finished their act and the Wallendas were just starting to perform. The circus bandleader noticed the flame and immediately told the band to start playing, "The Stars and Stripes Forever," which traditionally signals distress to all circus personnel. The Ringmaster urged the audience not to panic and leave in an orderly fashion, but the power failed almost immediately and most people didn't hear him. Dozens burned to death or died shortly after from their severe burns. The panic and chaos and rush to the few exits resulted in even more being trampled to death. Most of the dead were found in piles, some three bodies deep, at the most congested exits. The estimate was that 168 people were killed and over 700 treated for injuries. The only animals in the tent at that time were the lions and they were quickly herded through the big chutes which led directly from their performing cages to several cage wagons so they escaped unharmed. Sadly, these huge chutes effectively and tragically blocked two of the exits from the tent.

The radio announcer also told the story of one boy in his Boy Scout uniform cutting through the tent with his handy Boy Scout knife, allowing many people to escape this way. The tent collapsed in just eight minutes, trapping hundreds of spectators beneath it. Involuntary manslaughter charges were filed the next day against five employees of Ringling Brothers. The circus accepted full financial responsibility and by 1954 had paid out over five million to the 600 families who had filed claims. The five men did not go to jail, despite being given prison sentences. They were pardoned after a few weeks.

Little Miss 1565 was identified at one point as Eleanor Cook, but there were too many discrepancies, one being that Eleanor was a brunette, not a blonde and secondly, her mother claimed the body was absolutely not her daughter. Two of the policemen involved in solving the mystery, which was never solved, decorated her grave every holiday and after they died a local flower company continued the tradition. As a child about the same age as Little Miss 1565, I was especially fascinated by the intrigue and mystery surrounding her identity. The discussion went on daily for weeks after the fire. Who could she be, why hasn't anyone claimed her. I was mesmerized by the horror of being dead and unknown.

I also came down with another childhood disease at my grandparent's house the summer before sixth grade – the measles. Unlike the chicken pox I felt really miserable with the measles. I stayed in my bedroom and mostly in bed with the shades drawn for about a week because the light hurt my eyes. I was allowed to have a radio in my room. During the day there wasn't much on except the soap operas and I got hooked in two days. I became glued to each one of them and they ran in tidy succession to each other. The name of one program I listened to was called something like, "Is there life after thirty-five for Helen Trent?" I might have the title wrong, but it definitely explored the hypothesis that any excitement in your life was pretty much over by the mature age of thirty-five. What I remember is agreeing with the title - thirty-five was old and you'd better have fun before you reached that milestone.

My other activity as I lay in bed hour after hour was drawing floor plans for houses. I thought I did a really good job, with many interesting room layouts, so interesting that I saved all the plans. I even thought maybe I would become an architect. I ran across these plans somewhere when I was in my thirties. I was aghast, remembering my cocky feeling of a job well done. I only had one bathroom even in the five bedroom houses and often these plentiful bedrooms didn't even have closets. I tossed out the plans with nary a comment to anyone.

My grandparent's house had a big attic with a regular staircase leading to it with a door at the bottom. It was very hot up there in the summer. Just opening the door to those attic stairs felt like the blast of heat you feel when you open an oven door. Out of curiosity I would go up there with my grandmother when she was searching for something. One time I ran across her high school yearbook and of course brought it downstairs to read in detail. There was a descriptive write-up of every graduate and I only remember part of my grandmothers and it went something like this,

"Sally is like an aristocrat with high principles to which she has the courage to adhere."

Then as I read on I found the page where classmates vote on different characteristics of their classmates and my grandmother was voted "Biggest flirt." Of course I ran to find my grandmother when I read this and her reply was,

"Oh Sally, in those days if you even looked at a boy they called you a flirt."

That reminds me of one of the times I was complaining about not having the bosom I wanted and my grandmother said she had the same situation growing up. I found this hard to believe as she appeared ample all over to my eyes. She said when she was a teenager she would stuff pieces of lace in her bra to help fill it out. And she was a teenage bride at age nineteen.

When I wrote my grandmother about my trip to Canada and skiing in the Laurentian Mountains with a group of college kids, she talked about winter in Milo, Maine.

"When I was a little girl in Milo in the month of March we always used to go coasting for then a crust would have

formed on the top of the snow and we would go-like-the-wind. Up to that time we snowshoed and that was my speed. Skiing was not the sport it is today and I am sure I could never have mastered it anyway.

Both my grandparents played bridge and often played with other couples, especially in the winter when they started going to Florida for six months after my grandfather retired. My grandmother also played with her women friends, many of whom did not golf, like her. She had another group of female friends in Hartford that often lunched together or went to events like flower shows, guest lecturers, club meetings, many different activities. She would say she was going out with "the girls." My clique of friends in high school always referred to our group as "the ladies." My grandmother thought this was hilarious. The "girls" were past middle age and the "ladies" were under twenty!

My grandmother had one special friend, Mildred. I must have met her, but I don't recall anything about her looks. In one corner of the front hallway of my grandparent's home, they had built in a table just large enough to hold a telephone with a shelf underneath to hold the fat phone book. Next to this was a triangular bench, squeezed into the corner, giving a back rest to anyone using the telephone. Good thing there was a backrest as my grandmother could easily be over an hour talking to Mildred. We all tittered over her name and even my grandmother admitted her parents had made an unfortunate choice.

In the fall of 1953 my grandparents redecorated their house, new paint, new upholstered furniture, new drapes, a real overhaul. This time my grandmother did not do the re-upholstering herself or sew the curtains herself or start painting the furniture, all favored activities in the past. She was now in her sixties and I recall also being less enthused as I got older over sewing and wall papering and painting and all those projects I tackled with gusto year after year when I was younger.

The timing of their redecorating was fortuitous for me as I was just entering college. I was offered all kinds of furniture for my dorm room as they redid different areas, and ended up with a maroon and pink striped loveseat, a couch that I can't remember in any detail and a saggy green wing back chair. I learned from rereading her letters that my grandparents delivered the furniture in person and I have no idea how as they then owned a Lincoln Zephyr sedan which doesn't lend itself to furniture delivery.

Whenever they visited me at college a huge tin of homemade cookies or brownies came too. Both my mother and grandmother also frequently mailed a box of cookies to Dawn and me. The food at Vassar was hurting and I probably complained a lot. Unlike today in college, there was no way to easily supplement what the kitchen offered. We always complained about being hungry. In rereading my grandmother's letters to me in college I came across this line.

> *"When I was entertaining college boys and your daddy and Uncle Hamlin brought their friends home, they were always hollow to their toes, so I guess that's the rule."*

My grandmother had so many expressions and I'm hoping more will come to my mind. One I do remember, "That just sticks in my craw," she used frequently when upset over someone's actions or words. A couple of oddities to me were two snacks she loved mid-afternoon. One was pulled apart pieces of white bread that she soaked in milk and ate like a bowl of cereal. The other was leafy lettuce out of my grandfather's garden which she sprinkled generously with sugar and ate with a fork. She enjoyed baking cakes and I loved the job of measuring out the sugar and flour, cracking the eggs and especially licking the beaters.

I am going to quote from a letter my grandmother wrote me in January, 1954, my freshman year at college. Parts of it remind me of the type of letters I often received from her son, my father.

> *"Dear Sally, I expect that at least a few of the much dreaded mid-year exams are over with by now and for your sake I am glad. All my life I worried about exams, singing in church, singing in concerts etc. etc. and I do hope that you will be able to take a more rational view point in all your undertakings. I feel that "worry-wart" is only another name for pessimist and you just must not become one. It takes half the joy out of life to be continually expecting unpleasant things to happen*

at every turn. The good Lord did not intend life to be that way and you must never lose sight of that fact. When you were a little girl and we would want to get you dressed in a hurry you would calmly say, 'Me do' and 'Me did.' Poise and a well balanced mind have always been two of your biggest asserts and if you ever get pessimistic just count on your fingers the happy outcomes of so many things you have accomplished and you won't be worried about or afraid of new perplexing situations and their outcomes, especially exams.

Gramps and I are glad that you are enjoying the oranges. Just hope your friends don't help themselves too often.

We both are reading the book that you sent. I am in the middle of "The Sound and the Fury." The style certainly is very different and I will report on it later. At present I am a little confused as to why it was written. What did you think of it?

We have a rat in our car. He is concealed someplace and comes out at night to mess the floor and pull out the packing around the break and gas pedals. We are trying to trap him, but he's a clever devil. Of course we have to be careful what methods we use for if he dies we will have to rip the upholstery apart until we locate the source of the terrible odor. Well here's hoping we catch him tonight.

Friday am: We have not caught the miserable rat, but last night we resorted to poison, cleaned the car this morning and saw no trace of him. It has not been wonderful riding around all week expecting him to pop out any minute

We had a fun time at the Parkers last night. We ate on the patio and played Samba in the evening. There were six of us so we had a jolly time.

I truly do think it is shocking that some of your friends do not believe in a God. What has brought about this state of mind? Surely their earlier education could not have given them such ideas. Our religion and faith in God and His infinite goodness is most essential to our well being if we are to live normal active lives. Most learned men of all times have believed in God and prayed for his guidance when momentous decisions had to be made by them. In the life of everyone there are times when the cares and burdens seem to overpower and it is then that I have found solace and comfort in my belief and faith in God. Yes, Sally, I do believe there is a God and in my opinion there are but few people who do not.

At the Four Arts Theater Grandpa and I saw the comedy "The Importance of being Earnest" by Oscar Wilde. It is a satire on society and beautifully done by a group of English actors. Tomorrow we see "Bonzo goes to College," the story of a chimpanzee, which proves that our programs are varied.

Goodnight now and we both send our love.   Devotedly, Grandma."

I mentioned in an earlier chapter that I went to Europe for a six week whirlwind tour with five friends in the summer of 1956, the summer before my senior year in college. The boat bringing us home landed in Montreal and my parents and grandparents came to meet me with the plan being to stay in Montreal for the week-end and sightsee. On the trip there from Hartford my grandmother suffered a stroke a few hours short of Montreal. She was admitted into the nearby hospital and their advice was to get her home to see her own physician as soon as possible. My dad met me at the dock, relayed the bad news and I drove one of the cars and he the other as we literally raced back home.

The stroke affected her right side, both the leg and arm. She was soon able to navigate with a walker and a brace on her leg, but had difficulty writing as her hand and arm tired easily. My grandfather hired a woman to help with dressing her, doing the laundry and some cooking. She was probably ten years younger than my grandmother, ate her meals with my grandparents and they all watched television together so it was like having a cousin coming in to help out.

My grandmother had always been so active and now it was a chore to move about and painful to write letters. It dramatically affected both their lives. They went to Florida for six months in the winter, but now instead of driving, they took the train and paid extra for a drawing room. A driver was hired to take the car to Florida and they decided to leave it there permanently. Instead of renting a house they stayed that first year after the stroke at the Gulf Stream Hotel in Lake Worth. My grandfather arranged for a nurse to come in every day from one to five pm to give him some respite from being a care taker.

In a letter my grandmother wrote in March, 1957, right after my engagement was announced, she talked about the plans for the wedding and the beauty of a candle lit service and how busy mother and I would be that summer making all the plans. Then she described their new way of life in Florida, living in a hotel.

> *"The shuffle courts are right under our windows and at times the players are very noisy. When you sleep is very much guided by the doings of the guests in hotel living, we find. Here everyone retires early and then begins the day really early which is contrary to the habits of the Gilberts. We are sad we didn't get to know Ted well, but did know his mother and father. His father was an officer in the Travelers like your grandpa and was a wonderful man. His mother was very beautiful and charming. She used to wear gardenias always and everyone loved and admired them both. Gramp and I belonged to a group with them that played and danced. We had such fun together!"*

On my twenty-first birthday I received a telegram at school. I should frame it as I don't think that mode of communication exists any longer. In a telegram all the letters are capitalized and there is no punctuation.

> *"MISS SALLY GILBERT   456 MAIN VASSAR*
> *ON THIS MOMENTOUS DAY OUR THOUGHTS*
> *ARE OF YOU WE KNOW FROM PAST 21 YEARS*

*YOU ARE SUPERBLY EQUIPPED TO MEET FUTURE
WITH CONFIDENCE SUCCESS HAPPINESS YET WE
RELUCTANTLY ACKNOWLEDGE THE TRANSITION
OF OUR FIRST GRANDCHILD TO WOMANHOOD
LOVE BEST WISHES FROM GRANDMA AND GRANDPA"*

After that winter in the hotel they decided to go back to renting a house and just hiring someone to come in daily. My grandmother gained more strength in her leg and in her last letter to me in March of 1960 she said they had definitely decided to put the house on Ridge Road on the market which made her terribly sad. She was still using a walker, but hoped by summer she might graduate to a cane.

Three days after I received that letter, I got a call from my mother. Ted was now at Harvard Business School, I was teaching kindergarten in Norwood and we were living in an apartment in Cambridge. Mother said my grandmother had suffered another stroke and this one was fatal. She never regained consciousness. They were bringing her body back home via the train and the funeral would be in a week. I was in a state of disbelief. I just couldn't believe she was dead. My grandmother was only sixty-eight. She had been an integral part of my entire life.

The funeral was delayed over a week due to the difficulties of bringing a deceased body across state lines. After going through all this red tape, my father told us he wanted to be cremated when he died. The funeral was held in Hartford and someone in the family had decided on an open casket.

I didn't know this and walked into this large room with sad, melodramatic music playing, and there was my grandmother lying there with her hair fixed all wrong and way too much makeup on her face. I burst into tears over the reality of her death and the way the undertakers made her look, nothing like my beloved grandmother had ever looked. I decided that I would never allow my children to have an open casket at my funeral. The awful sadness I felt at her sudden and unexpected death made me realize how lucky I had been to have had the love of such a wonderful grandmother for the first twenty-five years of my life.

12

My Grandfather, William Henry Gilbert

My grandfather was born in Brooklyn, New York in 1886. His mother, Emily Louisa Miller, was born in 1853 and married late, at age thirty-two, to Henry Stille Gilbert, a man twenty-six years older than her. He was a widower with a son her same age. Henry was born in 1827, and went to medical school at New York University. His practice and his home was at 311 Cumberland Road in Brooklyn, New York. He and Emily had two sons just a year apart. My grandfather was born exactly nine months after their marriage and his brother, Lou, thirteen months later. Henry Gilbert died in 1897 at the age of seventy when his sons were only eleven and ten years old. Henry's father, Raphael Gilbert, was raised Episcopalian as was the entire family, but left that faith and became a circuit-riding Methodist preacher. Raphael's home base was Sugarloaf, a village near Chester, New York. His mentor was the famous circuit-rider Francis Asbury who emigrated from England in 1771. Henry was the second son of Raphael and his wife Betsy.

Emily was left well off financially after Henry's death. She moved with her two boys, after her own mother died in 1900, to the family home in Glastonbury, Connecticut where she had been raised. Her sister Julia, who never married, inherited the house from their parents. This huge house had been in their family for over a hundred years. After her boys left home, Emily made New York City her base and did what was fashionably called "traveling with the seasons." She went from Augustine, Florida to Sea Island, Georgia to Groton, Connecticut, and then on to Bar Harbor, Maine. She returned to NYC for the winter to enjoy its theater and opera life. She retained her box at the Metropolitan Opera until she was elderly and decided to return again to live in the family home in Glastonbury. She lived there until her death in 1943 at age ninety. Her son Lou and then one of Lou's sons were the next occupants.

I want to share a few details about this home at 1155 Main Street in Glastonbury. It was erected in 1802 by Elijah Miller, my grandfather's great grandfather on land bought by the family in 1715. For a brief period it was an Inn and a stopping off point for stage coaches. In 1884 Elijah Miller Junior and Louisa Gildersleeve, my grandfather's grandparents, celebrated their golden wedding anniversary with a gala party at their home that was written up in great detail in the newspaper. I am quoting,

> *"The bride's father, Sylvester Gildersleeve, at the age of eighty-nine is still alive and hale and hearty, sound in body and mind and enjoying life with the best of us. The guests must have numbered one hundred and fifty. The solid worth and number of the presents were silent witnesses to the estimation which the Colonel and his wife are held by their friends. The ball was opened about 10pm. The upstairs has swinging wood partitions which are raised to convert the entire front of the upstairs into a ballroom. It made the young girls turn green with envy to see Louisa lead off with the old style grace and coquetry. The colonel asked the prompter after the first round if they couldn't play a little faster. Don't you tell, but I had to kiss the bride twice, she looked so charming. A gentleman remarked that he couldn't see for the life of him how they could have been married for fifty years for he didn't believe the bride even looked fifty years old. Between one and two am the party began to break up and some one expressed to the Colonel the hope that this crowd would not tire him out, and he says 'I would just love to thresh off one more flooring.'*

> *Through God's mercy their lives have been spared these many years, still we can but think that the parties themselves have had a little something to do with it. Always happy, ever ready to greet and serve their friends, hospitable to a fault. What a life. May God bless and keep them free from sorrow, trouble and pain for many years until in His wise provenance He sees fit to call them to their just reward.   Portland, Dec 25, 1884.*

Now that is an example of an article you will not read in a newspaper today. Emily's ancestors on both her mother's and father's side emigrated to this country from England in the early 1600's. In my grandfather's spacious study on Ridge Road in Wethersfield, which we called the library, the walls were lined with framed documents signed by our ancestors, primarily in the 1700's with some from the 1800's. Most noticeable is the exquisite handwriting. I have copies of some, but my brother, the genealogy keeper in our family, has the originals. I think it's interesting to see what these early settlers did so I'll just mention briefly two of the earliest ones. On Emily's mother's side, the first relative to come was Richard Gildersleeve who emigrated from Suffield England in the 1630's. He helped organize the New England Federation. He was a magistrate, commissioner, constable and town attorney from 1664 to 1677. Emily's father's line goes back to William Miller. He helped found the town of Northampton, Massachusetts in 1654. He was a tanner by trade. He married Patience who was the first woman physician in Northampton. I told my grandchildren that this set of their relatives goes back twelve generations in this country.

My grandfather graduated from Hartford High School in 1904. This school is the second oldest secondary school in the nation. His freshman year he attended Trinity College in Hartford as a day student. Then he transferred to Stanford University in Palo Alto, California in the fall of 1905 as a sophomore. Stanford had free admission then through 1920. Today, in 2015, it's about $60,000 a year. One of the many questions I wished I'd asked my grandfather was why he had no interest in the dozens of excellent colleges in the East and wanted to go so far away to school.

His mother had been on a cruise around the horn of South America that winter. The Panama Canal would not be completed for another decade. Her cruise ended in Mexico where she was staying with friends for a couple of weeks. It was the middle of April, 1906. My grandfather was in bed at 5:18 am on April 18th when the first tremor of the infamous earthquake struck San Francisco. Californians refer to it as the San Francisco Fire of 1906 because the fire caused the most devastation. Over 3,000 lives in total were taken directly or indirectly, with 498 deaths in San Francisco.

It took my great grandmother, Emily, three weeks to locate her son. When she finally found him, she told him he was to leave Stanford and California and "come back home to civilization." There actually was no Stanford left - it was decimated by the fire. He transferred to the University of Maine for his last three years of college. It was three years instead of two because he couldn't get any official credit from Stanford for his fall semester and two-thirds of his spring semester because of the fire. There were no records available for him to show the University of Maine that he even attended the school. All student records were incinerated in the fire. The school completely shut down, no exams were held or final credit given to anyone for that second semester. When transferring to the University of Maine he could only use his transcripts from his one year at Trinity, so he needed three years at the University of Maine to graduate.

My grandfather joined a fraternity right away, Sigma Alpha Epsilon. My father and uncle who also went to the University of Maine joined this same fraternity. He became very active in the drama department and being only five foot seven inches tall often played the female roles as proper girls did not act on the stage then. He was not only short, but overweight with a small size seven and a half shoe.

At his fiftieth reunion in 1960 there was still a picture hanging on the wall outside the college's theater of him dressed in the role of Ophelia. He received several offers when still in college to go professional, but told my father that because of his build he could only be a character actor and there was no money in that.

When he graduated in 1909, his mother took him on a grand tour of Europe for the whole summer. His brother Lou could not join them as he had decided not to attend college and by then was working full time. Upon my grandfather's return, he took a position as a principal of the high school in Limestone, Maine. The following year, 1910, he changed towns and became the principal of the high school in Milo,

Maine where he met my grandmother, Sally Alwilda Hamlin. (She hated the name Alwilda just as much as my mother hated her middle name, Hildegarde.)

My grandmother had just graduated that June, three months before my Grandfather started his job as principal. She was interested in teaching music at the high school which is probably how they met. To my knowledge she never did teach music. They were married twelve months later in August of 1911. She was nineteen and he was twenty-five. My father, William Henry Gilbert Junior, was born on August 26, 1912, in Milo, one year after their marriage.

After three years in Milo my grandfather accepted a job as principal of a high school in Millinocket, Maine. This was known as the company town for Great Northern Paper. After just a year he again changed jobs and became the principal in Gilbertville, Massachusetts. He told my brother that he got this job even though he told them he would not sign their pledge, as he did smoke and drink and had no intention of stopping either. His second son, Hamlin, was born in 1916 when they lived in Gilbertville.

During three of those summers he went to Columbia University in New York to study for his Masters Degree in Education. He received his degree in 1917. I remember him saying once, when I was studying to be a teacher, that John Dewey taught one of his classes and was the most boring teacher he had ever had. I don't know why my grandfather kept changing schools. He was ambitious so I'm assuming the progression of towns meant a rise in his income or a rise in the affluence of his students' families or a rise in the prestige of each town's school system and maybe all three.

When the First World War started he applied for the principal's job at a high school soon to be constructed in Old Hickory, Tennessee, fourteen miles east of Nashville. My brother thinks there might have been a huge increase in salary and that's what tempted him to leave Maine. Perhaps he wanted to live in a different part of the country. I know he was an adventurer, unafraid of unfamiliar places, since he'd traveled across the country to attend Stanford. Distance was much greater than with no airplanes and long distance telephone calls being prohibitively expensive. When I was growing up, we only called long distance after 7pm because it was much cheaper and then we tried to talk for only three minutes. After that three minute window, the rate went way up. The cheapest time to call was after midnight.

The construction of the high school in Old Hickory began in 1917, right after the United States entered the First World War. The town had received a contract from the government early that year, for DuPont to construct the world's largest smokeless powder plant to produce guncotton and also to build a town for the workers who would run the plant. My grandfather took a supervisory position at the plant while waiting for the high school to be built. He probably also helped advise architects designing the new high school regarding labs, library, the gym and such. He certainly would have had a role in recruiting and hiring the teachers and perhaps the rest of the staff.

Old Hickory was called a tent city. The town hardly existed before the DuPont contract. The housing consisted of hastily constructed wooden buildings with sidewalks, also made of wood and dirt streets constantly throwing up dust. It was not gracious southern living, but it grew and grew. The DuPont engineers built, in less than a year, an entire city for 30,000 workers with almost 4,000 buildings and over seven miles of railroad. The week before the school was to open in September,1918, the new school building burnt to the ground. My grandparents, who now had a two and a six year old, decided to stay on for another year of rebuilding. Then the Armistice came two months after the fire on November 11, 1918. To put it dramatically, Paris time, the war ended the eleventh hour of the eleventh day of the eleventh month. My father remembers my grandfather saying,

"The town just folded up like an umbrella and everybody left."

I wish I had heard more details about this sojourn into Tennessee when my grandparents were still alive. I would love to know exactly why my grandfather took this job and what my grandmother thought. She had lived in Maine her entire life except for a short time in Massachusetts. She moved to an unfamiliar state in a different part of the country in her early twenties with two young children and no relatives within a thousand miles. I also moved in my twenties to an unfamiliar state in a different part of the country, had two young children within two years and no relatives within a thousand miles. It wasn't easy, but the distance seemed shorter for me, forty years later, with easy access to the telephone and the airplane. How I wish I could talk to her now about those years.

Here's a quick historical update about Old Hickory. It remained a ghost town from late 1919 until 1923 when DuPont converted the plant into producing rayon instead of gun cotton. This was followed by cellophane film, then yarn, then Dacron, next Corfam, leading to Typar and currently it's Sontara spunlaced materials and Crystar PET resin. Today there is a country club, a large golf course and city parks in Old Hickory. Many of the larger homes built for management by DuPont are now on the National Register of Historic Places.

Perhaps supervising all those men in the guncotton plant changed my grandfather's perspective on the enjoyment of a career in education. They left Tennessee right after the armistice and moved to Hartford, Connecticut where he took a job in 1920 at the Travelers Insurance Company. His career as an educator was over.

Hartford was considered the "Insurance Capital of the World." Everyone seemed to work for the insurance industry the way everyone in Detroit once seemed to work for the automobile industry. After the Civil War, Hartford was one of the wealthiest cities in the country. My grandfather joined the group department of the Travelers. The concept of group insurance was revolutionary at the time. Now, companies could buy life insurance for their workers as a group at a much more reasonable rate and these employees would not be required to apply individually, undergo a physical exam or pay the full cost of the coverage. The first policy was written by the Equitable Life Assurance Society in 1911 which covered 125 employees of the Pantasate Leather Company. Eight years later in 1919, twenty-nine insurance companies were writing group insurance policies. My grandfather had timed it perfectly. He entered a burgeoning field right at the beginning. He had an extremely successful career, culminating with him being made an officer of the Travelers.

He traveled all over the country promoting and selling group policies. There were no commercial airlines and President Eisenhower had not yet built the country's wide highway system so trains were the only logical mode of travel. They weren't cheap and they weren't fast so my grandfather would be gone months at a time. I only heard him discuss selling these policies once when he was talking about Henry Ford. He said Ford was the most bigoted, ignorant man he had ever met.

Soon after the family moved to Hartford, they bought a two-family home at 91 Linnmoore Street. These two-family houses were very popular in Hartford and many still exist today. They lived on the upper floor and rented out the lower one. I wish I'd heard stories about their tenants. My father grew up in this house and my mother lived there for many months before their marriage and even longer after they were married. She was active in amateur theatricals, always playing the leading lady with pages of lines to learn and my grandfather, being a former thespian, enjoyed helping her practice her lines.

I was born in the Hartford Hospital and came home to this house. I mentioned in another chapter that there had been no girls born in my grandfather's family for three generations and he desperately wanted a granddaughter. As my mother was being wheeled down the hall to the labor room, my grandfather cried out,

" Make it a girl, Gracie."

I broke the run of three generations with only boys and was revered by my grandfather for doing so. I was told by my father that my grandfather had a reputation as a father and as a businessman for being stern, demanding and intolerant of those who didn't live up to his tough standards. I broke him down. I called him Panpom and my mother said he almost cried when at the age of four I started saying Grampa, despite his pleas of,

"No, no, I'm, Panpom. Call me Panpom, Sally."

My grandfather brought me to his thirtieth reunion at the University of Maine. I was three years old. They owned a bulldog then named Violet who went to Maine with us. We also stopped at a very rustic cabin my grandparents owned and vacationed at when their sons were young. It had a refrigerator that used ice to cool food and a stove that used wood to cook food. It was primitive and tiny. I visited it once again years later, just before they sold it. I only remember Violet from snapshots. She died young, they assumed, from licking grass under a tree that had been sprayed with poison.

I spent most of my first year of life in Chicago, but came home that next summer with my mother to stay with my grandparents for a long visit. I have a snapshot of me with my great grandmother, Emily Louisa Miller, at the house my grandpa had just built at 624 Ridge Road in Wethersfield, Connecticut. Many family stories were told about Emily, my grandfather's mother.

My grandpa, mother, great grandma Emily, father and Grandma, holding me.

Emily was very outspoken, bright and headstrong and these are the two stories told about her over and over. She was advised by her doctor, because of her high blood pressure, to give up the generous glass of brandy she drank every evening. She loved repeating that she never even considered giving up her brandy and she "buried three doctors," all of whom had given her that same advice. The other story is that in the summer of 1929, when she had been a widow for thirty-two years, she told her stockbroker to sell all her stocks as the market had "become ridiculous." And he did. In October, a few months later, the market crashed and the country went into the "Great Depression," not alleviated until the start of the Second World War.

Emily died at age ninety in June of 1943 when I had just finished second grade. I visited her a few times at her home in Glastonbury. She lived in the family homestead, called the Elijah Miller home, built by her grandfather in 1802. I loved the really tall ceilings and the windows that went all the way to the floor. The house had dark hardwood floors with Oriental rugs in every room. I was always told to kiss her when we left and I hated feeling the prickly whiskers she had on her chin.

When Emily died, there was a large, impressive funeral for this matriarch who had lived such an interesting life. My grandfather's brother, Lou, got very drunk at the funeral. My grandfather was furious and decided to never have anything to do socially with Lou again! And he didn't. However I do know from my grandmother's letters to me that she had lunch on occasion with Lou's wife, Ruth. I don't remember even meeting my great uncle who lived twenty minutes away from my grandparents. Lou also had two sons, just like his brother. My father and my brother reached out to Lou's family after my grandfather died and my brother has made a point of contacting Lou's children and their children. My brother Bill has compiled over five volumes of our family's history and I am pressuring him to put all of that fascinating material into a book.

When I was little, my grandfather loved to tell me long, involved stories about the drugstore he was going to open in Maine when he retired. I was intrigued and thrilled over the thought of having a drugstore in the family. This was the era of the romantic drugstore. It was THE place, and often the only place, to go for ice cream sodas and ice cream cones. There was usually a wonderful, long counter where you sat on stools that you could swivel around and look at all the customers while you ate your ice cream. When I couldn't fall asleep at night, I planned all the things I would ask my grandfather to sell in that drugstore and all the things I would buy.

My grandfather retired in early1950 at age 64 on a disability due to high blood pressure and a mild stroke. I was in ninth grade then and our family was living with my grandparents in Wethersfield that entire year. I still believed the story about the drugstore. I asked him in full sincerity where exactly in Maine he would open his drugstore. First he was amazed I remembered that story after so many years and then he was even more amazed that I thought he had been serious. At first my feeling was an initial wave of huge disappointment over the no-drugstore news, followed by a bigger wave of, "How could I have been so naïve."

After he retired he stopped playing golf, on orders of his doctor, and planned on spending his time gardening. As anyone who has done both knows, gardening is much more strenuous than golf. He soon figured that out and decided he might as well take up golf again, but only on the weekends. Monday through Friday was devoted to tending to and enlarging his garden at the home they had built on over an acre of land in Wethersfield. Their house at 624 Ridge Road felt like my second home when I grew up. My grandfather used to say nothing would make him happier than if I would buy his house when I married. The back yard was huge and sloped down hill with a fabulous view of the valley below. He created a magnificent arboretum on that acre and a half.

Every day in the spring and summer he worked in the garden. He never quit for lunch which amazed me as a child. In the basement there was a garden work room that opened directly to the outside. All his annuals were raised from seed in flats which were then put out in the yard under panels of glass tipped at an angle. He created an English formal rose garden with a boxwood hedge in a quadrangle shape with four entrances into the rose garden. I remember him holding a can of kerosene in one hand and going to each of his rose bushes and tapping the branches with his other hand so the Japanese beetles would fall into the can.

My grandfather's rose garden in the winter.

There were over two dozen peonies of all colors circling the base of the driveway in front of the garage. At the bottom of the hill was a white picket fence with an arbor in the middle with benches and grape vines growing over the arbor. My friend Lucy and I loved to stand on the benches and try to pluck the grapes directly off the vines with our teeth. One garden bed was reserved only for annuals and usually zinnias won out and every year the vibrant colors changed. Around one side of the porch, which was two stories up because of the incline of the hill, he always planted hollyhocks and they grew over six feet tall. On the other side of the porch there was a trellis with a spectacular honeysuckle vine with bright yellow flowers. The perennial gardens had sweet peas, purple and pink asters, tall iris and other plants mixed in. They sold the house before I became a gardener and how I wish I could go back in time and visit it now.

I don't know how he managed to garden for eight hours straight, day after day, in his sixties. As a young girl I thought it would be awful to miss lunch and just work in the garden all day. Now in my late seventies I can't garden for more than two hours without a sore back. I am amazed at his stamina and healthy joints. This detailed description of his garden is not due to my superior memory, but aided by an essay I had written at MacDuffie in 1950 and just pulled out of the basement, entitled, "My Grandfather's Garden."

When we lived with my grandparents, I was in ninth grade and taking Algebra I and Latin I. Those were my two worst subjects in terms of my interest and my abilities. My grandfather was my tutor. He didn't even have to look at the book and flip behind or ahead a few chapters to refresh his memory. He remembered both subjects as if he was currently teaching them. I was impressed then and I'm flabbergasted now. When I taught fifth grade just out of college, I had to skip ahead in their math book to review the sections on equations. I remembered less than my grandfather who had been out of school for decades.

My grandfather was not a gracious recipient of gifts. No matter what my father bought him he always made a negative comment with remarks like,

"What will I ever need this for?" or
"You should have saved your money," or
"This book got terrible reviews."

We all knew this would happen and always waited in anticipation to see if perhaps this year he would like his gifts. His grandchildren were the exception. He always thanked us warmly for any present we ever gave him.

My grandmother died suddenly in March of 1960. She had needed a walker since her stroke in 1956 so their activities had been limited in the past few years. My grandfather decided he would like to travel and instead of Florida, he wanted to go to Portugal and Spain, where it is also warm in the winter. He knew some Spanish, but decided to take lessons in the Portuguese language. He also had to apply for his passport. That became a crisis. The court house in Brooklyn that held his original birth certificate had burned to the ground decades earlier. He did not have a copy of his birth certificate with the required official seal on it. No passport would be issued until he could prove he was born in this country. The only option open to him was to get certified letters from three people who had known him since birth. He luckily found them, they wrote the letters and he got his passport.

He didn't sign up for a group tour, but made all his arrangements through a travel agency. He only planned the beginning of the trip, wanting the flexibility to change his plans as he saw fit. The mode of transportation he chose was first class on a ship landing in Lisbon. When he boarded the ship he needed to take oxygen twice a day and had a sore on his right leg. Luckily he became good friends on board with a doctor who was on the staff at a hospital in London with connections to the hospital in Lisbon. This Lisbon hospital redressed his leg sore daily for a week until it healed. He left October seventh and planned on staying through April, traveling all over Portugal and Spain. After a week in Lisbon he went to Estoril, Portugal and was disappointed. The weather was partly to blame, no sun with constant drizzle. The only stationary he could find to buy was extra thin onion paper that looked and acted like toilet paper. He had to write lightly in pencil or it ripped. My father later had his secretary retype his letters for all of us to keep. I will quote from a letter written to my parents the third day he was in Lisbon,

"This morning after the hospital visit, I took a taxi with a driver who spoke a little English and drove thru the various

parts of Lisbon. Without question, it is the most beautiful city I have seen. Of course, there isn't a level street, and it is like San Francisco except the hills are not so steep. Only the very, very rich live in private homes along the Tagus River. This is really a city of apartment houses from the shabby to the elegant.

The women are all very short. When you see a tall one it is a foreigner. The men are slightly taller. Both have very black hair and darker complexions – seldom a pretty girl. Tomorrow afternoon I plan to go to Sintra which is considered especially beautiful. It is about twenty miles from here by electric train. It has a well known museum which was a former King's residence and on the grounds there is a famous collection of trees from Northern firs to tropical palms. This is also where the poet Lord Byron lived and wrote."

He continued to travel around to different areas, usually by train, and loved sitting on the beach when it was sunny, but admitted sight seeing was becoming too exhausting. He complained that flies were everywhere, bedrooms, dining room, just a constant drone because there were no screens anywhere. He said the servants, of which there were so many they fell over each other, were supposed to spray regularly, but if they did spray, the flies didn't know it. His letters were not the happy letters of a contented tourist and his last letter from Portugal was written on November 9, 1960, just a month after his arrival.

"Dear Grace and Bill,   I am coming home. I have not had a good time and for the first time in my life have

been homesick. My health, likewise, has not been good, and when I compare the next six months over here with what I could have in Florida, I just said to hell with it and luckily got a cancelled stateroom on the Vulvania, Italian line, sailing tomorrow. My decision was made in five minutes. I anticipate a tedious, tiresome voyage home, but so what! I will visit you in Longmeadow before heading for Florida."

My grandfather, upon returning to Florida, was heralded as one of those rare widowers who was interesting and fun with a quick wit and therefore in hot demand as an escort by all the wealthy widows. He called them Tizzie, and my letters from him start with Tizzie II, in January of 1961, so I don't know what happened to Tizzie I. My grandfather is now seventy-four. I am quoting,

"Dear Sally, As you probably surmised from my letter to the folks I am having a hectic social life although I must admit I enjoy it. To bring you up to date, Tizzie II left for Miami about three weeks ago where she is to spend the winter. I met Ruth Carson on John Richard's boat on December 18 and after the departure of the late lamented Tizzie II, she has become Tizzie III. She is a wealthy widow firmly established in the Palm Beach social set, member of the Everglades Club etc. So I am on the Palm Beach merry-go-round. Dinners formal and informal, cocktail parties, even luncheons and what not, practically every day and evening. But with my

usual luck (?) she leaves January 18 for a round the world cruise on the Kingsholm and will not be back until about April 15. I have my eye on a good candidate for Tizzie IV. She is also a Palm Beach widow who winters here only and lives in Norwalk, Connecticut. Of course I may not make the grade, but I can at least try.

I play golf regularly three times a week with my old partners. My leg is much better and every sunny day I let it soak in the sun and salt water. Last Sunday we were on the Richard's boat and caught ten pompano ranging from 3 to 5 pounds. They made a beautiful rack of fish and were admired by all who saw them. I caught 3, the largest number by any one person. Monday night Tizzie III (Ruth) had the whole party to her house and our fish was part of the dinner and it was most delicious. I am going to a dinner party at the Breakers tonight, another farewell party for Ruth. It's lucky I brought my tuxedo as most of these send off parties are formal. It is certainly going to require about two weeks rest when the hullaboo is over. Love to you and Ted, Grandpa."

His next letter was a month later. He was leaving in a half hour for Fort Lauderdale to have lunch with my parents. The day before he wrote the letter, my parents had visited him and they all went on that well traveled Richard's boat again, and I quote,

"We did the usual sail on the inland waterway. In the evening we took Norma Brown, our former next door

neighbor, to dinner at the Brazilian Court Hotel in Palm Beach. She is leaving the end of this month on a freighter for the Orient. She plans to roam around Asia, Africa and Europe for about eight months. Claims she can live cheaper there than in Florida.

Tizzie III now wants me to join her, her daughter and son-in-law at Baden Baden, Germany, to take the cure there for five weeks and then go to Sweden, Norway, Holland and Belgium, returning to New York about September first. Your parents as well as your Uncle Hamlin think I should go and Ruth writes that her daughter and son-in-law really want me to join them. So I may try Europe again. Must close to go meet your parents."

My last letter ever from my grandfather was written three months later on May 7, 1961. We were still living in Cambridge, Massachusetts and Ted was about to graduate from Harvard Business School in three weeks and I was very pregnant. He said his trip to Europe and Baden Baden was cancelled due to Ruth Carson's sudden illness and that he was relieved. It was expensive and his zest for travel was over. To quote further,

"I am delighted to hear of Ted's offer from the Ford Co. and I judge he has accepted. I always liked Detroit and its suburbs and think you will also. I'm glad to learn from your dressmaking and sewing activities that my first great grandchild is on the way. I shall be in Detroit or wherever you are when the happy event occurs. I leave Florida May

15th and should be back at Ridge Road around the 18th. I hope I can sell the house this summer. I'll probably have to reduce it. Your stay in Boston is approaching its end and I know you will be sorry. Much love, Grandpa."

When Ted and I moved to Detroit in August of 1961, I was enormously pregnant, but my grandfather wanted to come right away for a visit to see our rental house, inspect the baby's room and just hang out with me. I had taught school the past four years, but now was going to be a stay-at-home mom. We took a tour of the Rouge plant, we went to the zoo twice, we checked out the country's first mall at Northland and I've forgotten what else. It was a lovely time together.

He said he'd be back as soon as the baby was born. True to his word, the minute I entered New Grace hospital in Detroit on October seventh, he made his airline reservation. He arrived when Andy was three days old and of course came to the hospital to peer at him through the glass window looking into the nursery as all visitors had to do then, even the Daddies. I was to come home in two days and both Ted and Grandpa came to the hospital to bring Andy and me back home.

We had insurance from Harvard University when I got pregnant and insurance when Ted took the job with Ford, BUT, I had a preexisting condition, pregnancy, and Ford's policy, like every insurance company until Obamacare, was not obligated to cover any condition I had prior to enrolling in the Ford plan. We knew this, but were naïve in thinking the hospital would just send us a bill. We discovered we could not leave the hospital until our bill was paid, or rather, Andy and I couldn't leave. Ted had not yet transferred money from our savings to his checkbook so Grandpa, with his checkbook in his pocket, came to the rescue! We did pay him back the next day. In 1961 the bill for four nights in the hospital was around $1,500.

. The Ridge Road house sold that summer which was a sad day for me. It was my anchor growing up. It was on the market longer than anyone anticipated because as the realtor said,

"Those gardens are intimidating to prospective buyers. They all say they're too beautiful to tear out and too much work to keep up."

Unlike my father, my Grandfather dispersed much of his furniture among his grandchildren. I was given all of the Percy Hamlin striped furniture, six pieces in all and my brother got all the mahogany marble topped pieces which had been Elijah Miller's, Grandpa's grandfather. I also was given the Jenny Lind three-quarter bed, the bed I slept in when I stayed with my grandparents. It then became my oldest daughter Julie's bed growing up. I also got my great, great grandmother's spinning wheel. These pieces of furniture have lived in seven different houses in three different states and will go on to be enjoyed by my children or I will come back and haunt them!

After his house sold in 1962, my grandfather lived with my parents, not being sure yet where he wanted to live in the summer. Once November came, one month after Andy's birth, he was ready to head back to Florida. All his bags were packed for his airplane flight the next morning, November seventh, to Palm Beach. That night he was in his pajamas playing solo bridge on the bed, dealing different hands to decide what would be the best bid to make. At some point he either had a stroke or sudden cardiac arrest. My sister Cynthy, went in to wake him up the next morning to get ready for his flight and saw he was no longer breathing. He only lived a year and a half longer than my grandmother. He was seventy five years old. I wish he had lived to ninety five, but he died the way most of us hope to go, just not waking up in the morning with a calendar full of upcoming activities.

Having spent so much time in Florida the past few years, he had lost touch with many of his friends in the Hartford area, so my father planned a small funeral at our church, St. Andrew's, in Longmeadow. He was buried next to my grandmother in Rose Hill Memorial Park in Rocky Hill, Connecticut. Andy was only four weeks old and I was nursing so my family didn't think it wise for me to make the trip to Massachusetts for the funeral.

One year and one month later my mother died, three weeks before I had my second child and again I couldn't travel to the funeral. I lost three of the people dearest to me in just three years. I know how fortunate I was to have had such caring and loving grandparents. It was like a double fortress of adults protecting and caring for me as I grew up. I am still amazed that my grandmother was only forty-two when I was born and my grandfather, only forty-eight. I was sixty-one and Ted sixty-three when our first grandchildren were born. These first grandchildren are my son's twins, Brian and Grace, and this past May, 2015, they graduated from high school. They have been followed by seven grandsons ranging in ages from four to seventeen. My three daughters all had boys. Julie has Alex, James and Matthew and Jenny has Jack, Henry and Charlie. Molly has one boy, Danny. Grace is my only granddaughter. I know these memoirs will describe a very different world from the one in which they are growing up, but it's my hope that they, as well as my four children, will find them interesting and fun to read.

Epilogue

Although this memoir is about growing up, ending when I married at twenty-one, I do mention my children and grandchildren in the chapters about my parents and grandparents, so I decided to include a picture of my family who are the most important part of my life.

The above picture is the last one taken of our entire family. We were at my seventy-fifth birthday celebration at the Grand Hotel on Mackinac Island in Michigan. We now number nineteen. In this photo our youngest grandson, Danny, is missing as he was born a year later.

It is difficult now as the grandchildren get older to corral all of them together at any one time as camp and sports activities compete with family gatherings. I am celebrating my eightieth birthday this December and at that event we might make an attempt to capture all of us in another photograph. I like to think we ten adults look about the same, but the grandchildren – WOW, have they grown!

I have loved writing these memoirs of my childhood, twenty-one years of being Sally Hamlin Gilbert. I wish my parents and grandparents had written memoirs of their childhoods. I'm hoping this book will motivate my children and my grandchildren to capture some of their memories on paper in the years ahead for their children to enjoy.

Made in the USA
Middletown, DE
17 January 2016